READING AND EXPRESSIVE WRITING WITH TRAUMATISED CHILDREN, YOUNG REFUGEES AND ASYLUM SEEKERS

Writing for Therapy or Personal Development Series
Edited by Gillie Bolton

Writing for Therapy or Personal Development, a foundation library to a rapidly developing field, covers the theory and practice of key areas. Clearly exemplified, engaging and accessible, the series is appropriate for therapeutic, healthcare, or creative writing practitioners and facilitators, and for individual writers or courses.

other books in the series

The Writer's Key
Introducing Creative Solutions for Life
Gillie Bolton
ISBN 978 1 84905 475 1
eISBN 978 0 85700 854 1

Poetry and Story Therapy
The Healing Power of Creative Expression
Geri Giebel Chavis
ISBN 978 1 84905 832 2
eISBN 978 0 85700 311 9

Therapeutic Journal Writing
An Introduction for Professionals
Kate Thompson
Foreword by Kathleen Adams
ISBN 978 1 84310 690 6
eISBN 978 0 85700 493 2

of related interest

Expressive and Creative Arts Methods for Trauma Survivors
Edited by Lois Carey
ISBN 978 1 84310 386 8
eISBN 978 1 84642 499 1

Life Story Therapy with Traumatized Children
A Model for Practice
Richard Rose
Foreword by Bruce D. Perry M.D.
ISBN 978 1 84905 272 6
eISBN 978 0 85700 574 8

Empowering Children through Art and Expression
Culturally Sensitive Ways of Healing Trauma and Grief
Bruce St Thomas and Paul Johnson
ISBN 978 1 84310 789 7
eISBN 978 1 84642 624 7

READING AND EXPRESSIVE WRITING WITH TRAUMATISED CHILDREN, YOUNG REFUGEES AND ASYLUM SEEKERS

Unpack My Heart with Words

Marion Baraitser

Foreword by Sheila Melzak

Jessica Kingsley *Publishers*
London and Philadelphia

First published in 2014
by Jessica Kingsley Publishers
73 Collier Street
London N1 9BE, UK
and
400 Market Street, Suite 400
Philadelphia, PA 19106, USA

www.jkp.com

Library of Congress Cataloging in Publication Data
Baraitser, Marion.
  Reading and expressive writing with traumatised children, young refugees and asylum seekers : unpack
my heart with words / Marion Baraitser.
    pages cm. -- (Writing for therapy or personal development)
  Includes bibliographical references and index.
  ISBN 978-1-84905-384-6 (alk. paper)
  1. Bibliotherapy for children. 2. Narrative therapy. 3. Creative writing--Therapeutic use. 4. Psychic
trauma in children--Treatment. 5. Refugee children--Mental health services. I. Title.
  RJ505.B5B37 2015
  616.89'16500835--dc23
                            2014015128

British Library Cataloguing in Publication Data
A CIP catalogue record for this book is available from the British Library

ISBN 978 1 84905 384 6
eISBN 978 0 85700 747 6

Printed and bound in Great Britain by Bell & Bain Ltd, Glasgow

To the courage and toughness of the young refugees and asylum seekers at the Baobab Centre, who voiced for themselves, and for us, these fragments of their traumatic experiences.

To the memory of my father, Professor Dr Max Feldman, who, on returning from serving as a South African medic behind the lines in Africa during World War 2, came to the UK to train at Maudsley Hospital as a psychiatrist, and returned to his native country to help in the initiation and practice of psychiatry.

CONTENTS

Part 3 Derring-do: Entering the Symbolic World

Part 4 Social Dynamics

Part 5 Brain Works: Putting the Mind to It

Part 6 Mapping the Research: The Efficacy of Writing on Trauma: An Evaluation

Foreword

It has been a pleasure to prepare this foreword to Marion Baraitser's book about her energetic, imaginative, hopeful work and thoughts about the intrinsic therapeutic value of writing for young asylum seekers and refugees. Marion has written in this book about her work at the Baobab Centre, where she has been developing this model of working while in the role of Writer in Residence. Her book explores the ways in which the combined activities of thinking with others about written stories, exploring feelings, ideas and memories that emerge and then writing on the themes explored can help young people to process both destructive and nourishing experiences, and those aspects of experiences that are either forgotten or are present as repeated intrusive thoughts and flashbacks after child and adolescent specific human rights abuses. Such difficult to process and painful experiences lead to various problems including stuck and regressed development. The book describes some ways in which to reduce this stuck-ness and to move forward psychologically through the development of verbal and written language that increase understanding and insight.

My first meetings with Marion Baraitser coincided with a time some years ago when, at various international multidisciplinary conferences about disadvantaged children, I spoke with several specialists working in the fields of neuropsychology, neurobiology, neurology and psychiatry and asked each of them the same question: 'How might a young person's brain and nervous system heal after experiences of sequential traumatisation?' I was interested in questions about the limitations and possibilities of the plasticity of the nervous system. Each of the specialists I spoke with separately told me that rehabilitation in this context was likely to be achieved by a flexible model of psychotherapy which included work on the development of insight about various aspects of the body and the mind. Relevant accounts of these ideas include those of Van der Kolk (1996), Hüther (2014) and Diamond (2013).

These authors and specialists talked about the particular efficacy of dance and music, and of work in the open air such as gardening and farming in order to supplement and complement verbal and non-verbal psychotherapies. While some young people are able to communicate their experiences both verbally and non-verbally, for others their memories and feelings are initially unthinkable and unspeakable. These feelings are linked with helplessness, terror, rage, shame and guilt after abuse, where they routinely and paradoxically feel responsible for the actions of the perpetrator. After experiences of sequential violation and abuse verbalising and processing feelings and memories takes a long time as do finding ways to take care of your self and coming to manage your own feelings and memories.

A key neurological idea is that rehabilitation is achieved not by the repair of neural pathways but by the growth of new neural pathways. All experts emphasized that reflection and writing at certain times during the therapeutic process were especially effective in improving executive functions and abilities for reflection and regulation. In the early phases of therapeutic work young people are profoundly affected by the long-term consequences of child and adolescent specific human rights abuses. At the Baobab Centre we have always held a flexible and holistic perspective where clinicians, teachers, social workers and artists work together. An experienced writer and teacher enabling young people to write about significant memories, would fit well with our team. It was in this context that Marion Baraitser joined the Baobab Centre.

Marion's work at the Baobab Centre is part of our essentially psychosocial approach where we work using many different models with the aim of recovery and social reintegration in a context that sustains health, dignity and self-respect (Karp 2005). We aim both to give each young person opportunities to build a space with one trusted listener in order to explore their most private experiences and also to help young people to participate in the community of exile through time spent in the transitional space of the Baobab Community. Marion's work gives young people a way to access and to come to understand and process repressed, painful and complex memories, feelings and experiences, and facilitate cultural change.

The process of exploring experiences in displacement, through reading stories, poems and novels or even parts of novels, and subsequently writing down these experiences, helps to develop what child psychotherapists call the observing ego, that is our capacities as humans to reflect on our own actions, thoughts and feelings. This process facilitates emotional regulation and is effective because observations and ideas are shared with an attentive and involved reader and listener. Both the events and the feelings and emotions connected to these events are explored. This is essential so that the kind of mind-sets that attempt to avoid thinking and feeling after traumatic experiences are challenged and in fact overlaid with rich and multi-layered experiences. Relevant here are Ravi Kohli's (Kohli 2005) ideas about thick and thin stories. Inevitably after a series of overwhelming experiences young people can consciously only bear thin partial versions of their stories.

The kind of work described in Marion's book contributes to the development of thick and rich narratives which sustain young people's identities and over time enable them to share their complicated, contradictory and true experiences with their legal representatives and with the authorities. Young asylum seekers are often refused asylum after interviews that take place soon after they arrive when they are unable to share detail of their full and complex narratives.

The elements of the process of Marion Baraitser's work can be distinguished by observing her ways of working as a facilitator. Her first session at Baobab was with a group of older adolescents, of mixed genders and coming from different countries in Africa and Asia. Some could read and write but not all. All had experienced organised violence and as a result had had to leave their countries as unaccompanied minors. I sat silently in the room, as someone the young people knew well, present, listening but not speaking. Marion, a very experienced and talented teacher and group facilitator, immediately had the very diverse group of young refugees absorbed by the combination of her energy and the content. She was quickly able to connect with their experiences. Having thought a great deal about material that would be suitable she read some stories by Sholem Aleichem who wrote about Jewish rural village life and relationships in the early 20th century. Marion was able to link the themes in the stories with the young people's experiences of village life and encourage them to share humorous memories. She then enthusiastically encouraged the group to write about their own personal humorous experiences, from the past or the present and was able to create an atmosphere through her empathy with the group where each member of the group wrote a story and then the majority were confident enough to read their stories to each other. The growth in self-confidence was palpable.

In another memorable session with a group of young men from different African countries Marion brought into the room some African objects. I recall a pestle and mortar, a broom, and some beads. The young men shared previously repressed memories of their mothers' domestic work, some talking with affection and joy and others becoming distressed thinking about separation and loss. Marion had to contain the various emotions in the room by talking about the comments, feelings and important fragments of their narratives before she firmly encouraged them to write down their memories and share these with the group. This model also worked with a group of pre-adolescent children who wrote in diverse ways about their ideas of home. Marion regularly works during our holiday projects with clinicians and young people, some of whom generally avoid groups and others who attend regularly. For these sessions she carefully chose suitable material for the particular group and themes that we were working on. We have had holiday projects on 'feelings', on 'masks' and on 'losing and finding'. She has also worked with individuals and very small groups as she describes in the body of the book. Each piece of work aims to build different aspects of resilience. In our context a sense of belonging, the capacity for reflection, for agency and skills in problem solving, creativity and caring for the world are key resiliencies.

The young people attending the Baobab Centre learn through a variety of interventions to develop a language for their own vulnerabilities, to change and develop. They also reconnect with past resiliencies and with the possibility of choice and little acts of resistance even in situations where they feel helpless and trapped. Marion Baraitser's book highlights the complexity of this work and its effectiveness. I hope that its publication will lead to others learning the skills to work in such an energetic, careful and creative way with young refugees and asylum seekers in various contexts.

Sheila Melzak
Consultant Child and Adolescent Psychotherapist
Executive and Clinical Director of Baobab Centre

ACKNOWLEDGEMENTS

My thanks to Sheila Melzak for opening the Baobab Centre to the relatively new field in the UK of therapeutic reading/writing for the health and well-being of traumatised young asylum seekers and trafficked and traumatised children. To dedicated colleagues at the Baobab Centre – psychotherapists, art therapists, interpreters and counsellors – my gratitude for teaching me about asylum seekers and how to be with them. Thanks also to Laila Sumpton's independent survey of my work for her MA, which was a welcome confirmation and support when I was in Dante's dark wood of uncertainty.

My thanks to Gillie Bolton who has been my guide through the making of this book, to Lisa Clark for her advice as an editor, to Lapidus colleagues for support on the relationship of writing to health and to the informative work over the years of fellow writers at the National Association of Writers in Education (NAWE).

I am grateful to the friends, writers and supporters of my small press, Loki Books, for allowing me to publish their stories of victimhood as Holocaust survivors and as Jewish women who write for peace. Thanks also to Exiled Writers Ink, Five Leaves Publications, Oberon Books and Jewish Quarterly for their support in publishing my own writing on survival.

To the many students, who over 17 years attended my literature sessions at Birkbeck, University of London, creative writing sessions at City Lit and Morley College and London Metropolitan University script writing course, my gratitude for setting me on the path to this book. And to the directors, actors, audiences and readers of my plays over the years, thank you for 'bearing witness' with your creative listening.

To my stalwart husband, Michael, for his support, advice, patience and love especially during those times when I was quite ready to give it all up and go touring. To my daughters, Paula, Lisa, Vanessa and Alexandra, so vigilant and dedicated in their own sterling work, for their love, support and knowing bird's-eye views of their mother and her commitments.

And last but not least, to my granddaughters, Nina, Sasha and Libby, and grandsons, Sam, Joel, Max, Saul, Ivan and Ben, who, large as life, teach me something new each day, my gratitude.

All the young refugees and asylum seekers included in this book have given permission for their stories to be shared. To prevent identification, the names of individuals, their details and their countries have been changed.

Introduction

That I, the son of the dear murdered,
Prompted to my revenge by heaven and hell,
Must, like a whore, unpack
my heart with words...

WILLIAM SHAKESPEARE, *Hamlet*, Act 2, Sc. 2, l. 588

CHILD VICTIMS OF VIOLENCE NEED TO 'TELL' THEIR TRAUMA

'Unpack my heart with words' is young Hamlet's cry of fury and despair at the moment he learns of the secret murder of his father and his realisation that he is powerless to take action. Many of the young victims of child- and adolescent-specific human rights abuses who are seeking asylum, the subject of this book, may have witnessed their fathers, mothers or other family members being violated, held in captivity or murdered, or may have been forced to take life themselves, the memories of which have left them feeling overwhelmed and helpless. Unlike Hamlet, they find they cannot 'unpack their heart with words'.

This is because they relive in their bodies and in the unconscious parts of their minds the moments of terror that they cannot yet describe in words. As Judith Herman writes, they 'disconnect' or dissociate from the social domain of language and memory, in order to survive (Herman 1997). Yet unless suffering is transformed into words there will be 'nothing', according to the great Russian novelist Mikhail Shishkin in *The Light and the Dark* (Shishkin 2013). The scientist Dr James Pennebaker, who spent a lifetime investigating the necessity of expressive writing for mitigating trauma, concludes that 'writing organises trauma' (Pennebaker 1990, p.185). This is the subject of this book.

Here is Amina, one of the survivors we shall follow through this book, who found her voice by being encouraged to write a poem that 'tells' her anger, helplessness and terror after suffering abuse, allowing her to take the next step towards the recovery of her selfhood. It is a voice not often heard by adults – children are the most powerless of victims, as they are so dependent upon their abusers, and their chance for justice or being heard is so remote. If the poem moves you as much as it did me, you are my reader.

The Mood
… She wants to seem normal.
For a minute or two she feels courageous,
but alone, at dark, the big fat
monster looms above her, nags her,
shakes her awake, forces itself in her head/mind, screams at her,
and finally she listens to that big fat monster, she believes
every word it says. Now she's scared
how she sees everything like before.
She's once again that little scared
gal alone asking the big fat monster
why? why? why? Me!

Once she had found refuge and while she was seeking asylum, Amina's voice was heard within a supportive community offering safe relationships and a variety of therapies over time, including reading and expressive writing, to encourage her to undertake 'the difficult task of exploring the theme of survival, the costs of survival, the compromises of survival and the paradoxes of survival', facing the reality that 'to survive is not always "good" and it is not always about helplessness but about active choices that challenge previously held moral values' (Melzak 2010).

This book is about how troubled young asylum seekers and refugees have the chance to use one of the therapies open to them that uses appropriate texts to help them to transform their war trauma into words and to re-narrate their stories so they may bridge their inner and outer worlds and their past with the here-and-now. The process uses thinking, feeling and imagining to access and help to release stored problematic memories by reading, talking and writing about them, reconnecting their feelings, language and thought. This gives them a greater sense of clarity and control over their suffering. Inner moments occur – a kind of 'knowing', which is about psychological change. These moments are the beating heart of this book, for in telling them, the young people re-tell themselves.

Defining a 'child' and a 'child soldier'

'Children' by the UN's definition are 18 years and under, but some countries set the age at 16 or 17, so there is a vagueness in defining a child in the law. It is also difficult to prove the age of a child on which asylum depends – there is controversy over telling age from dental proof (which has been dropped). This presents problems when traumatised young asylum seekers, who are desperately in need, face a hostile Border Agency for legal permission to stay as refugees, and then as asylum seekers.

There are also difficulties about the legal definition of a 'child soldier'. They can be defined as 'children associated with armed forces and groups', or as 'men of fighting age and boys'. The age of a child soldier is defined by the Geneva Convention of 1989 on the Rights of the Child as being under the age of 15. The Convention tried to raise the age to 18 but failed, and although countries can sign an additional agreement that raises the age to 18, those under this age are still recruited for training as child soldiers. However, their role constantly shifts as they move from being fighter, to cook, messenger or spy, or being used for sexual purposes, so their definition as child soldiers is complex. Some children choose to become fighters because it gives them access to a gun, food and women. People are now being found guilty of recruiting child soldiers under the age of 15, though child witnesses do not trust the courts, and their evidence is treated as tainted, though they are entitled to certain reparations (Kuper 2013). Abducted young girls are raped and abused and have no redress.

A background of mass terror

The traumatic consequences of organised violence, war and the abuse and exploitation of children has become a world-wide phenomenon that involves whole populations, including children and young people, who are silenced by terror. Judith Herman, psychiatrist and director of training at the Victims of Violence Program, Cambridge, USA, whose life work has been with victims of violence, reminds us that the 'study of psychological trauma is an inherently political enterprise [calling] attention to the experience of oppressed people' (Herman 1997, p.237). Global human rights are necessary to protect traumatised young asylum seekers, but it is only recently that 'crimes against women and children have been accorded (at least in theory) the same gravity as other war crimes' (Herman 1997, p.238).

UNICEF estimates 30 million children have been injured or killed in conflict, and that there are 300,000 child soldiers in 30 different countries (UNICEF 2005). The world is flooded with small arms that children can hold. According to the UN Refugee Agency UK, there were 15.4 million refugees worldwide at the end of 2012 (www.unhcr.org.uk).

Human rights abuses experienced by child victims caught in conflicts are on four levels:

1. experiences of traumatic violence and loss in their home countries;

2. neglect of developmental needs including basic needs for food and drink;

3. physical and sexual abuses on the journey into exile;

4. for some young people, their ongoing contact with family members in their home countries, including sending proportions of their meagre subsistence to offer support to family members.

(Melzak in Kuper 2013)

Conditions facing young asylum seekers in the global north

Many of the young asylum seekers and refugees who reach the shores of the UK and other countries of the global north as victims of war violence have lived under conditions in which they have lost their human rights to freedom. Many of them have been left to rely on their own resources and to fend for themselves, are vulnerable and often been trafficked and exploited. This compels them to act like adults when they are still only children. They may have been held back in their normal development and education by war. They have been separated from what they know, abandoned and betrayed and have witnessed those close to them being tortured or destroyed, which leaves them with a burden of shame and guilt that can be triggered at any time or causes them to go into a state of denial. They have lost everything they know.

These young people arrive on the shores of the global north destitute, alone, homeless, often in poor health and unable to speak the language or trust anyone. They bear with them the psychological and physical effects of their past traumas (see Chapter 1). They are uncared for, as they are orphaned or their families have arranged for them to leave because of persecution and their lives are under threat, they have escaped war or they have been kidnapped. They are in dire need of protection and the promise of a better life.

When speaking to the social worker at the Baobab Centre, Jodie Bourke, I learned that local authorities have a duty to safeguard and promote the welfare of *all* children in need under Section 17 of the Children Act 1989. Unaccompanied asylum-seeking children fall into this group, as they have no parents or carers in the UK to support them and often no financial means. Some come to the attention of local authorities when they are contacted by immigration officers at a local port of entry, where they are placed in hostile detention centres, anxious and demoralised to the point where they may self-harm or threaten suicide, not knowing what is to become of them (Kohli and Mather 2003). The children may be found on the streets, in which case the Home Office must refer the child – as an unaccompanied minor who claims asylum – to a local authority's children's social care team, though this may be done by the police, another professional or a member of the public. If under 18 years of age, the unaccompanied young asylum seeker is referred by a solicitor to social services for a needs assessment by a social worker – a continual process with other professionals involved – and a care plan is agreed. Section 20 of the Children Act 1989 contains a duty to provide accommodation when the child has no parent responsible for them or if they are lost or abandoned.

Because the asylum-seeking children often have no identification or proof of their age, which is crucial to their asylum application, the initial part of the assessment concerns establishing their age to determine the kind of support for which they are eligible, and leads to many disputes. Age-disputed young people are referred to a welfare solicitor and social services for re-assessment, involving other professionals and a court decision, but as the age of an asylum seeker is difficult to ascertain and is often disputed by the courts, the young people are kept waiting for lengthy times before their asylum claim is, if ever, ratified, although social services has a duty to support them during this period.

Once their position has been accepted by the courts, a care plan is put in place and they are given financial help with education and training and continued accommodation or supported housing. Within these circumstances there are long waiting times, documents are lost, there is little face-to-face contact with those concerned, their medical assessments are often poor, appeal processes are complex, there is no interim assistance while an application is being processed and there is a lack of awareness of the young people's circumstances. The young people feel isolated, food is expensive, the housing they are given is poor and unsafe, they are often threatened with violence and they are given little support by house managers (Coram Children's Legal Centre 2013).

The young people also face a hostile press. Paul Kenyon, documentary writer, points to the 'non-stop campaign against asylum seekers and the wilful misreporting of the issue' (Kenyon 2010). He says that distinctions between asylum seekers and economic migrants are 'fudged or overlooked…the language is inflammatory, there seems to be a lazy hostility towards them' (Kenyon 2010). Those who have this attitude imply that illegal immigrants cost a billion pounds each year and that criminal gangs are helping them (Kenyon 2010). Dr Catherine Lido found that negative tabloid media coverage creates the use of negative stereotyping (Lido 2006). Arun Kundnani reports (2003) that in a study at the Cardiff School of Journalism, those seeking refuge in Britain were called 'asylum cheats' and 'illegal' by the local press. The numbers claiming asylum were unsourced and exaggerated, the men who sought asylum were seen as 'threatening' and the women were marginalised. Individual asylum seekers are hardly quoted in the press while reports rely on comments from politicians and the police (Kundnani 2003).

Rachel Tribe and Nimisha Patel are psychologists working with refugees and asylum seekers, which they do in the context of hostile media coverage that conflates 'terrorism' with 'asylum'. This goes hand in hand with punitive government policies and public fear and resentment of those seeking asylum in the UK. They report that:

> people have often assumed that refugees are a 'challenging' group with whom it is not possible to undertake psychological work because cultural differences are seen as insurmountable and working with interpreters as too difficult, and they have a poor understanding of the legal system. (Tribe and Patel 2011, p.150)

It is interesting to read the personal account of a refugee who is himself a psychologist. He comments on the 'victim discourse' that developed around counsellors and psychologists. Refugees are often seen as 'passive victims' in the face of racism. In reality, refugees are mostly survivors with a tenacity that is hidden or underestimated from those who are not part of their communities. Because the National Health Service (NHS) regards refugee communities as a burden, it is the voluntary refugee services that undertake 'innovative, accessible and culturally appropriate services with little and insecure funding [that] carry the weight of the responsibility of supporting refugee people' (Yesilyurt 2011, p.151).

The young refugees are 'lost in translation'

Displaced, hurt young people are living in translation – they are not only reading but also talking and writing in a language that may be foreign to them, one that they must try and enter in order to survive within it. Eva Hoffman's *Lost in Translation* tells about her feelings as an outsider and a misfit when she came from Poland to live in the USA as a refugee, unable to speak English. She felt alone and isolated – 'lost in translation' – until she started to read American literature, which made her feel at home – part of her new society – by 'reading' its values and ideals from its literature (Hoffman 2000). Debbie Hicks's report on reading groups, which she calls 'creative bibliotherapy', notes that most are composed largely of white, middle-class people who are comfortable with speaking and reading English (Hicks 2006). The young survivors I work with, using reading and writing, working through literature, come from many cultures where women have little status, to whom the English language is foreign and bears overtones of colonialism and who are not used to books at all, as their cultures are largely oral. Yet English is the language in which they must think and find themselves anew, and one of the indirect functions of the developmental use of books therapeutically is to achieve this goal. Refugees mostly want to learn English – one of the symbols of success and of belonging. It also helps them to provide structured activity as a counterpoint to their psychological difficulties. The will to learn English can be seen as a therapeutic endeavour in itself (Kohli and Mather 2003).

They have defeated identities

On arrival in the global north, the young people come from a situation in which their families, and they themselves, may have been politically defeated, which could leave them with a profound sense of self-doubt or shame or guilt. Their political histories may put them in conflict with the culture of the global north where they find themselves living. As this is also their place of safety, they feel conflicted about being here. The facilitator needs to be aware of the 'ethnicity, degree of acculturation, family and peer socio-economic status, gender development, and religious and spiritual affiliation of each individual' (Malchiodi 2005, p.169). Amina tells me of her father's tribal position of power as a traditional healer and her own atheism. Nomif teaches me about his culture's Italian colonial traces and his country's civil war in which his father disappeared. Asoum, who wants to study international relations, tells me of the political regime controlled by one powerful family. Asola, only 12 years of age when I first meet her, tells me with pride of her family's status of kingship, which yet ignores the position of women as possible rulers.

LITERATURE AS A CREATIVE INTERVENTION FOR HEALTH FOR TRAUMATISED CHILDREN

Interventions encouraging resilience to cope with the traumatised young people's plight have become necessary, both to them and to the societies in which they find themselves. 'The search for simple and reducible models of intervention has now become an international cross-cultural project, as part of a growing effort to mount an international response to outbreaks of war and mass violence' (Herman 1997, p.241).

REDRESS finds that expressive writing is a crucial part of a traumatised young person's reparations process, because the 'disclosure or translation of traumatic experience into words as a testimony can have psychological benefits' (REDRESS 2001, p.30).

Expressive writing from the reading and discussion of books as a health intervention may be preferred to the 'talking cure' – or considered as a valuable addition to it – because writing encourages independence and self-reliance through re-narrating painful memories, which allows people to listen to themselves (McLoughlin 2004). The facilitator's sessions are brought into play only when a hurt young person is able to receive them, when they feel safe in a nurturing relationship and when they have been taken through the process of mourning, so they are more ready to reconnect with others. Then 'writing can be a way of uncovering the unacknowledged or recovering the repressed', which allows them to speak about things that are too painful or too shameful to be addressed directly, even in the safe space of the therapeutic relationship (Thompson in Bolton, Field and Thompson 2006, p.27).

Therapeutic writing is 'of great value within medicine, healthcare, many branches of psychotherapy…race relations, care of asylum seekers and victims of torture… Yet it still needs to be established as a complementary therapy in the UK' (Bolton *et al.* 2004). Bolton writes that 'considering its power, it is not being used enough: it needs to be offered within mainstream provision…and included within training… It is under-researched, and under-reported, especially in British clinical practice. Accounts of experience, which others can learn from, are invaluable' (Bolton *et al.* 2004, p.229). This book serves to redress this need.

Literature's potential in trauma intervention comes through pleasure in making, doing and inventing, play, imagination and enhancement of self-worth through self-expression. 'To contain traumatic material within an object, image or story provides a sense of control over terrifying and obtrusive memories' (Malchiodi 2005). In this way it provides an intervention for those who find themselves unable to talk face-to-face with someone about their trauma because of social circumstances or personal inhibition. The use of expressive writing from reading and talking about texts is a therapeutic intervention that crosses boundaries between psychology and the creative arts. 'The writing paradigm has attracted researchers with interests in cognition, social processes, clinical disorders, and health and personality psychology, as well as those primarily interested in mind-body issues' (Pennebaker 1990).

Okonkwo and Jane Eyre: characters and their stories as therapeutic mediators

I bring into a session with the young people Chinua Achebe's *Things Fall Apart* (2001), not only because he is an exceptional writer, but also because it is in this novel that he tells the troubled young refugees' stories from their perspective. As Nelson Mandela wrote, on reading Achebe's work in prison: 'There was a writer named Chinua Achebe in whose company the prison walls fell down' (quoted in Gordimer 2013). Achebe writes about a flawed African hero, caught on the thorns of colonialism. Achebe knew and valued both his Igbo culture and the Christian values his parents adopted, a position held by many young refugees. He allows the listening hurt and displaced young people to feel and know both cultures as potentially valuable. Achebe fought for Nigeria's secession from colonial rule, which led to devastating civil war – a situation the young refugees recognise. The writer's own courage, the characters and their stories in his work and the very Igbo sayings in the text all encourage in the young people a sense of recognition of their own selfhood. This is the aim of the therapeutic intervention using books.

If the young people are ready and able to deal with the language level, I also bring Jane Eyre's story of survival in a cold northern country. Jane Eyre was as maltreated and hurt as the young people sitting in the session with me who, through her story, imbibe her courage, self-determination and strength of will as a way of thinking about possible life solutions. By drawing from the best and most appropriate literature of both cultures, the young people reach a developmental dialogue about themselves.

Nossrat Peseschkian is a Persian therapist who works therapeutically with adults using oriental fiction in his psychotherapeutic work. He believes that stories 'with their playful character and their closeness to fantasy, intuitions and irrationality' can be used as mediators in therapy (Peseschkian 1979 in Shechtman 2009, p.200). Stories can be used as a basis for identification and at the same time as a form of protection for the story-teller. By associating with the stories, the story-teller asks about himself, his conflicts and his desires. Then, 'by suggesting a change of position, which at first has more the character of a game', the person comes to see his 'own-sided concepts in relation to others, to reinterpret them and to extend them' (Peseschkian 1986). This can be applied to working with hurt children.

Writing the self for recovery

Creativity is an element for recovery. 'Self is a linguistic creation. It's hard to have a self without words. Every self has a story. It exists in relation to other selves and other stories in a continuum' (Parks 2011, p.65). Books are used to tell life stories that overlap with that of the individual reader in order to re-build that life in words.

Dr James Pennebaker's experiments test the effectiveness of writing as a supplement or even a substitute for psychological and medical treatments. He writes: 'Translating important psychological events into words is uniquely human... Psychologists specialising in language, cognition, social processes and psychotherapy can work together in better understanding of this phenomenon' (Pennebaker 1997, p.165). Writing that asks people to confront deep, personal issues has been found to promote physical health, subjective well-being and adaptive behaviour (Pennebaker 1997, p.162). Cathy Malchiodi reminds us that verbal communications of thoughts and feelings is a central part of therapy in most situations: 'books can enhance trauma intervention when used appropriately and sensitively' (Malchiodi 2008, p.168).

When disturbed young people have read a strong text aloud together, talked about it with a practised facilitator in a roomful of trusted community members, discussing characters and subjects that concern their own lives, *and then written about it*, it can transform their ideas of themselves and of their future lives. They are better able to externalise selfhood so they can exist in the world while feeling that their internal being has connected to the outside world through books in some profound way – a form of 'being-in-development', a process of growing and changing the many selves they can uncover by this process. The facilitator brings energy, optimism, warmth, responsiveness and even inspiration, or at least motivation or affirmation, to each session.

Here is Amina on the value of writing in helping her to heal:

Writing is helping me to put down memories, different perspectives, to try to find the line... Talking doesn't do this. When I write I am having a relationship with my journal. Writing is like having a conversation with yourself. I tend to be more honest...pick up on things that lie deeper. I love myself, in writing... I am lucky to be here... I am lucky to be alive... You must keep going and finding yourself, at the same time staying true to yourself...even though you cannot forget where you started from.

To encourage the young people in this, we mounted an exhibition of the work from the therapeutic reading/writing sessions over three years, entitled *We're not Here: We're not There*. In the introduction I wrote that the act of writing is complex – it takes the mind off itself and into itself in new ways. It involves concentration on detail, the relevance of theme, the nature of character and the finding of a voice. The achieved work in the exhibition was each young asylum seeker's personal encounter with the challenging act of writing and the reading of a stimulating text, which took place in different groups or in one-to-one sessions, often in English as a second language, as a form of therapeutic resilience. We worked from suitable texts chosen from all over the world, dealing with many cultures and beliefs, which we discussed and wrote about. 'The work is a process, a long process' (Baraitser 2009).

Literature as a bridge from the 'helpless self' to the 'coping self'

Therapeutic writing, reading and dialoguing from appropriate books with disturbed young people may be used as an adjunct to psychotherapy as a way of promoting psychosocial well-being, and as a form of protection and containment if this is practised at a time when an individual is able to respond to it. It enhances the psychotherapeutic process by giving it a new emphasis, as writing is *with* and *by* rather than *about* and *to* the client (Wright and Chung 2001).

Creative writing as an intervention with traumatised children is a skill that is 'the application of specific literature within a therapeutic context' (Malchiodi 2008, p.12). It helps children to understand [their] traumatic experiences and learn adaptive coping skills and new perspectives. Like other creative activities, a book can help a child to remember early emotional connections. 'Stories link past, present and future in a way that tells us where we have been, where we are, where we are going' (Taylor 1996). Being encouraged to listen to the stories of others and to tell their own helps the young asylum seekers to re-establish their sense of the past in relation to the here-and-now and to the future.

A traumatised child's sense of self and identity has become fragmented and split into different aspects. They experience one part of themselves as degraded and helpless, and the other part as heroic.

The therapeutic interventions aim to unite them through processes of mirroring and displacement.

Building trust through using the arts

Camila Batmanghelidjh of Kids Company and Place2Be – charities for traumatised inner-city children – emphasises that the greatest damage for abandoned children is that they have lost trust:

> The self begins to hide in order not to suffer further assault on its integrity… Somewhere behind the intellectual discourses and explanations of violence, exaggerated power and denial, is the littleness that once risked trusting, and took years to do it again. (Batmanghelidjh 2006, p.53)

It is this 'littleness' I try to access through discussing stories and characters in books and the young people's own stories in developing a relationship that allows trust and hope to grow again. Carl Rogers found that 'human beings become increasingly trustworthy once they feel at a deep level that their subjective experience is both respected and progressively understood' (Rogers in Thorne 1992 in Bolton 2011, p.265).

Camila Batmanghelidjh feels that her training at Regent's College and the Tavistock Clinic, although brilliant, seemed insular: '*There is a need to return to care giving as a vocational and spiritually creative task*' (Batmanghelidjh 2006, p.106; emphasis added). She suggests using the skills of facilitators trained in the arts who can 'explore emotional issues through symbolic expressions' (Batmanghelidjh 2006, p.33).

'Being there': a collaborative working relationship

Perhaps the forming of a relationship with each person undertaking writing and reading sessions is the gradual unfolding of a kind of intimacy in which the facilitator's role is therapeutic. The work becomes that of the 'listener' – being there for them and taking the shattered young people seriously, helping them towards new goals. Many of the young people missed crucial developmental experiences, so writing sessions help them to regain a foothold in a place where they feel safe – a place where they are seen as good and capable. In health terms, these processes encourage resilience (though some young people may be more resilient than others and more able to ask others for help or to help themselves). The facilitator strengthens and stabilises their self-experience through the use of literature, introducing new perspectives and new challenges to their awareness (Lemma 2010).

Books to enlighten not cure: an adjunct to psychotherapy

Trauma can be defined as an experience of terror and helplessness rather than an illness. It is easy to describe trauma and post-traumatic stress disorder (PTSD) as medical syndromes to be diagnosed, treated and cured rather than as 'painful and distressing aspects of experience' (Blackwell 2005, p.19). Interventions, including counselling, psychotherapy and the use of reading and writing therapeutically, exist to further a constructive relationship.

Because therapy is lengthy and expensive to maintain, the briefer and more cost-effective approaches like Cognitive Behaviour Therapy (CBT) have become a dominant paradigm practised in the NHS. These tend to label, diagnose and 'treat' individuals and are not appropriate for the needs of traumatised children. Self-help books for psychological healing based on the Books on Prescription scheme for libraries and GP surgeries have been put into place across England by the Reading Agency. These are seldom accessed by traumatised refugees and young asylum seekers.

Including psychoanalytic concepts

Freud has written that some of his greatest insights were borne of his knowledge of literature and philosophy (quoted in Yalom 1998). His writings on the 'talking cure' allude to classic literature, such as Shakespeare's *Hamlet* and Euripides's *Oedipus*, as works that illuminated his uncovering of the psyche, which allowed him to avoid referring directly to his actual cases (see Freud 1953–1974). The reading/writing therapeutic intervention with the young refugee asylum seekers uses literature as the talking point around which trauma may be indirectly approached, with the facilitator using psychoanalytic *concepts* of identity, mirroring and catharsis. James Pardeck, who developed therapeutic techniques using books for health over many years at the School of Social Work, Southwest Missouri State University, USA, describes how the process works in three stages based on psychoanalytic concepts: it begins with 'identification and projection' when clients, with a facilitator's guidance, come to recognise themselves in the life and problems of a character in a book; then follows 'abreaction and catharsis' when the client responds 'with passion' to elements of the story; and finally 'insight and integration' is achieved when the client becomes aware of the problem and the need for a solution (Pardeck and Pardeck 1984a). We shall see the processes by which literature is experienced and integrated also 'involve unconscious and preconscious materials including dreams, daydreams, and fantasies...that include condensation, displacement and symbolism' (Rubin 1978, p.36; see Chapters 12–14 in this volume).

Literature makes others feel 'alive in the mind of another'

The psychoanalyst Stephen Grosz warns us that he does not provide a final explanation or cure for those who come to him, but rather that the 'encounters' he has with clients are to allow a person to feel 'alive in the mind of another' (Grosz in Linklater 2013).

When we read an engaging text aloud, in a sense we become the author. As Anthony Kerrigan points out: 'When a man recites William Shakespeare, he *is* William Shakespeare' (Kerrigan 1998, p.11). The Nigerian writer Ben Okri holds childhood memories of civil war in Nigeria, of his schooling in Lagos 400 miles from his family and of how, on reaching England, he lived rough, by his wits, homeless and miserable. He went to London because of Dickens and Shakespeare, but he also loved African writers such as Chinua Achebe and Wole Soyinka. 'Literature doesn't have a country. Shakespeare is an African writer...Dickens's characters are Nigerians' (Okri and Emeagwali 1992). As the young people read aloud in the company of a facilitator and a like-minded group, they *become* the writer, they are taken out of themselves and, if the writer is worth his or her salt, that encompasses a whole new set of dimensions that can change the way they regard life and their place in it.

Books for children who have been hurt, rather than adults

The intervention of using books for insight and change in the past has applied more to adults than to children. Ever since returning shell-shocked soldiers from World War 2 were helped by physicians and librarians to use reading and expressive writing as health interventions, the subject has made a gradual impression as a useful, effective and inexpensive intervention for *adults* to cope with psychological problems in our increasingly fragmented and divided society. Aileen Hynes and Mary Hynes-Berry in America in the 1960s described what was then defined as biblio/poetry therapy as 'a finding of the self through words in a…spiritual, personal process' (Hynes and Hynes-Berry 1994, pp.10–11), but they were referring to adults.

English PEN's creative writing workshops provide a safe space for adult asylum seekers and refugees in which 'creative writing is therapeutic, but creative writing is not delivered as therapy. The workshops help refugees define themselves and manage their trauma by defining it' (Sumpton 2012). The organisation Freedom from Torture assists, protects and promotes the rights of torture victims in the UK; Write to Life is its creative writing project to help adult survivors of torture explore and share in group sessions their experiences of torture and life in exile. If they wish, they are encouraged to develop their expressive writing, which builds a sense of their individual abilities, and the group is further motivated by publishing their writing to promote awareness of their plight.

However, in using literature to help troubled *children and teenagers*, therapeutic reading and writing is about the relationship between a facilitator, a text and the disturbed young people who have gone through the stages of 'hanging out', 'hanging on' and are now 'moving on'.

Books as weapons of construction

Albert Camus's *The First Man* (Camus 1994) is the account (based on Camus's early years) of a highly intelligent boy growing up in poverty in Algeria. This text is but one of my weapons of construction. The boy's upbringing is under the whip of his grandmother (his father died at the battle of the Marne when the boy was a year old, and his mother is mute). The story resonates with the group of young asylum seekers. The hero knows he must learn to rely on himself to survive, but he comes to understand that this must be done without the violence his grandmother practises. But he finds himself retaliating to a schoolmate's attack:

> He wanted to be glad, and he was glad, somewhere in the vanity of his ego, and yet, when he looked back at Munoz as he was leaving the green field, a bleak sadness suddenly seized his heart at the sight of the crestfallen face of the boy he had struck. And then he knew that war is no good, because vanquishing a man is as bitter as being vanquished. (Camus 1994, p.121)

By confirming the futility of senseless violence for the young victims of war, this great writer's setting of his life against violence informs, gives insight and comforts the traumatised young asylum seekers.

These texts that I gather in my skirt, come in translation into English from many languages, but all of them contain a sense of courage, perseverance and hope, greatness of soul and basic ethics – whatever the society, culture or class from which they are written. They are 'literary', that is, they are books that give important insights into human experience, in which the language is heightened and figurative and that is recognised by humanity in general as valuable writing (see Chapters 6–8 in this volume).

THE IMPORTANCE OF WORKING IN GROUPS

Reading together in groups, which the Reading Agency's director of research Debbie Hicks defines as 'creative bibliotherapy', uses the therapeutic power of reading together to promote well-being and to make people feel better (Hicks 2006). It has been endorsed by the Department of Health, the Royal College of General Practitioners and the National Institute for Health and Clinical Excellence (NICE). Jane Davis is director of The Reader Organisation, which, established in 2008 and based in Liverpool, is a national charity that encourages great books to be read aloud to groups all over the UK. She writes: 'Reading is a force for social good that can build community and enhance lives [using] the power of reading to inspire change and wellbeing' (The Reader Organisation 2009, p.133).

Reading is the key element with which therapeutic reading/ dialoguing/writing sessions begin. Applying it to young asylum seekers is not always easy, as there is no tradition in place to encourage this endeavour. A way round this is to rely on the oral tradition of story-telling, applying the idea of enacting a 'read' story with group participation, in addition to discussion and application of events and characters to the individuals within the group.

HOW LANGUAGE AND MEMORY WORK IN TRAUMA: THE BODY–MIND LINK

We need to know how 'the body remembers' trauma. We also need to know how memory is stored, as using literature therapeutically helps to release deeper traumatic memories so they are manageable by communicating them through language (Malchiodi 2005; see also Part 6 in this volume).

Winnicott wrote that the separation of emotion and thoughts from physical sensations begins in the first weeks of birth, and that separation from the mother allows the baby to start experiencing feelings as different from body sensations (Winnicott 1960 in Howlett in Bolton *et al.* 2004, p.87).

In traumatised young people, difficulty in expressing feelings may remain linked to physical symptoms, and writing can play a key part in encouraging the recognition and expression of them, helping to allay their body trauma. Trauma reactions are psychological and physiological, and because using books as an intervention for health works in language and thoughts, we need to understand not only how language works in the brain but also how the brain processes trauma, where reasoning, communication and language reside, as well as how the brain copes with the capacity for language and consciousness.

Researchers such as Professor Adele Diamond show that though trauma 'knocks out' the workings of the pre-frontal cortex where damaging memories are stored, creative writing after trauma, with the need for concentration and discrimination, helps to restart effectively these areas of brain function. She shows that writing and reading are the links between body and mind, the brain and memory (Diamond 2011a). Writing is the key creative intervention in which the brain and its working neurobiology make it particularly suitable for unblocking 'frozen' memories, reordering feelings and finding a way forward with this renewed grasp of the traumatised young people's own stories.

Others, such as Dr James Pennebaker, have proven that traumatised young people who write expressively get better sooner than those who do not (Pennebaker 1990). The findings of these scientists are encouraging, as they underpin the evidence in the workings of the brain in the responses, insights and transformations that facilitators and therapists encounter (Herman 1997).

EVALUATIONS

I include the results of quantitative and qualitative research to help to assess the effectiveness and value of therapeutic writing with traumatised young people, undertaken by both scientists interested in how expressive writing promotes health and well-being and those working in the humanities who use therapeutic writing to record and debate how and why it works for different purposes.

Four characters in search of a writer

There are four young people who weave in and out of this text on our journey, who will guide you, dear reader, on the way. The literature I use in sessions with them is mainly fiction or poetry: it comes from many countries, gives insight into human experience and uses language in a heightened way, which allows what Alain Badiou calls 'the event' that ruptures the nature of being, allowing the invisible truth to become evident (Badiou 2005). Some were traumatised young asylum seekers and others were trafficked, but the infrastructure of civil war was different for each of them.

Let me introduce them to you:

- Amina is 18 years old and arrived here from her village in Africa as a young girl, abused and rejected by her family, then trafficked on her journey to England.

- Nomif is 26 years old and fled his country when his father 'disappeared' for being on the losing side in a civil war that split his country. He was forced to turn back despite a horrendous, hazardous journey to the UK, but undeterred, he came again, and survived months under terrifying conditions of detention, and also imprisonment, finally gaining asylum.

- Asoum came from a background of organised violence in which he lost his father and brother in their support of the opposition side. Asoum's family expected him to do well enough to study in Paris, but the ruling government wanted young people to work, not study, His mother, not wanting to lose her second son, sent Asoum into exile as a young teenager, even though he had a severe disability.

- Asola is an intelligent young girl descended from the ruling tribe in her country, forced to flee organised violence with her mother, then further traumatised by her experiences in detention, and is coping with a difficult family situation.

With their permission, I recorded our encounters (changing names and countries of origin). Their journeys towards selfhood – their stories – draw together the threads of this book.

Having entered the young asylum seekers' world both before and after their arrival in the global north, and having detailed their rights to be here in relation to the conditions that exist for them in actuality, I could begin my first steps on a long journey to find and develop ways to allow them to tell their stories to me in a safe place, in order to heal themselves.

PART 1

Terror and the Telling

*Entering the Young Asylum
Seeker's World*

CHAPTER 1

War Trauma, Abuse and the Interrupted Narrative

The exceptional moments of 'peculiar horror and physical collapse'... It is only by putting it into words that I make it whole. This wholeness means that it has lost its power to hurt me.

VIRGINIA WOOLF, *Moments of Being* (1978)

When they reach 'another country' young asylum seekers must face the present first, the future next, and the past last of all. Yet it is from the past and their harsh memories that they need to find a way of freeing themselves. Because memory can 'split off' what is painful to remember, or cut off feelings, thoughts and meaning within the memories of terror, the traumatised young person becomes fragmented. They need to discover how to construct a symbolic universe, giving 'meaning' to their past through expression in the language of individual consciousness.

LEARNING ABOUT THE PAST LIVES OF TRAUMATISED YOUNG ASYLUM SEEKERS

I discovered the terrain I was about to enter by raiding journals, articles, newspapers, the internet and refugee associations for information. I read personal accounts such as Dave Eggers's story of his fury and helplessness at being orphaned and solely in charge of his eight-year-old brother when Eggers was barely out of his teens himself. He describes his 'telling of the world of suffering as means of flushing or at least diluting of pain aspect' (Eggers 2000). In *What is the What* he 'voices' young Valentino Achak Deng, a Sudanese traumatised young asylum seeker, taking us through the young boy's dangerous and exhausting journey after a forced separation from his family in his country's war against extremists (Eggers 2008). Deng finds himself alone and running for his life across hundreds of miles of terrifying terrain, with a host of other lost and abandoned children, crossing rivers, starving and attacked by militia and wild animals. 'When I first came to this country, I would tell silent stories', says the young boy, 'I would tell them [of those], who died after eating elephant meat, nearly raw, or about Ahjok and Awach Ugieth, twin sisters who were carried off by Arab horsemen and, if they are still alive today, have by now borne children by those men or whomever they sold them to' (Eggers 2008, p.29). I read Ishmael Beah's *A Long Way Gone* that gives a graphic personal account of the trauma and abuse experienced by a child soldier. His parents and brothers were killed and he joined a band of boys foraging to survive in the surrounding countryside, until they stumbled on the army base. Terrified, they were given guns and drugged and told to kill (Beah 2008). In a news report, Beah stated:

> If you didn't do what you were told you were badly beaten or even killed… You lose your mind because you are already fighting and traumatised by the things you are seeing. You cannot even feel your own skin. That's how much you are removed from yourself. (Beah in Poole 2013)

I asked myself if, and how, reading and writing their stories could reach or change such horror.

THEIR PRESENT LIVES IN 'ANOTHER COUNTRY'

As victims of violence and abuse, the young people's personal and social narratives have been interrupted by terror, a deliberate strategy that destroys all they have known – religious buildings, houses, schools and food crops. When they reach 'another country', they do not know where they belong (Eisenbruch 1988). They feel disconnected and confused about their identity. They can only face the present first, the future next and the past last of all (Kohli and Mather 2003, p.201). The trauma remains with them. '[This trauma] does not get better by itself. It burrows deeper under the child's coping mechanisms' (Terr 1990, p.238). To help to prevent this, they need to find the words to tell their stories.

If you ask young traumatised asylum seekers and refugees what they perceive as their greatest need, they will most likely answer: an education, a job to be 'someone' in the future and to have enough English to be understood. They also need to belong to a community, to have practical support and guidance from adults and to be treated kindly. They have lost a perception of the world as meaningful or comprehensible – they find themselves in a world that seems all-powerful, in which they are without a sense of autonomy. 'Their will and boundaries are overwhelmed' (Janoff-Bulman 1985).

They are also lonely – they most likely have few friends and are often without family, and feel they are without a mentor. At first, they may find themselves sharing a room with people who are much older than they are, who may take drugs or drink, or use forms of racial or sexual abuse. They may wait, sometimes years, for permission to stay (many are repatriated). They are confused by a new society and some may not even be able to express themselves to carers unless they have an interpreter (see 'Recognising hidden abuse' later in this chapter). They have to deal with psychological and physical health problems. They struggle with moral and ethical challenges related to injustice and human rights abuses.

For many of these young people, the trauma is cumulative. Many struggle with psychological stress, and when this is overwhelming, the individual's personality may break down, so they feel out of control and regress in their functioning skills such as being able to think clearly and to concentrate. As their defences collapse, new ones form – defences that may inhibit access to ordinary life – they regress and become stuck in their development and some may return to the 'magical thinking' of childhood. They are further confused and traumatised by problems of immigration and the inhumane asylum process they are subjected to after terrifying journeys that often involve walking for hundreds of miles or being packed into lorries for long intervals with little food or water and, for some, even holding on to the underside of lorries. They often bear within themselves unspeakable memories of extreme violence. They may have feelings of 'going mad' or of being inadequate or bad, flooded with shame, guilt and anxiety and paradoxically as victims carrying the responsibility for the actions of the perpetrators (Melzak 1992). They may be in a state of frozen watchfulness. They need to be supported through the process of mourning their losses and of acknowledging the feelings connected with this – rage, love, anxiety, ambivalence, shame, guilt – in order to come to terms with what has happened to them.

To counteract all this, they are surprisingly resourceful (Masten 2001), and though a minority are deeply troubled and need therapeutic interventions, the majority are not as 'psychologically dishevelled' (Kohli 2001). They need to relearn what Amartya Sen calls the 'valuable states of being' (Sen 1993). Welfare professionals find the young people want to succeed and to settle (Richman 1998). The intervention of therapeutic writing is one of several processes that can help to achieve this.

SOLVING THEIR PROBLEMS: PRACTICAL SOLUTIONS

Providing a safe place

The young people experience the world as threatening because they have been forced to trust those who were untrustworthy. A place of safety must be provided where they can eventually learn to trust their own judgement (Sutton 2013). They need to re-establish a sense of a protective home (Papadopoulos 2002). They need a safe community in which they can slowly begin to piece themselves together again. As part of this community work, literature as a form of therapy is brought into play as a bridge between the traumatised young people's inner and outer lives as a way of connecting their memories of what they endured in the past with the reality of their present lives.

Finding the words to tell their story to a listening carer

The psychoanalyst Stephen Grosz talks about the therapeutic telling of a story, which comes into play when we are disconnected from ourselves and in denial of loss. He quotes Karen Blixen: 'All sorrows can be borne if you put them in a story, or tell a story about them' (Grosz in Henley 2013, p.10). Grosz adds that not everyone can achieve this: 'The most important stories sometimes can't be talked about directly. People don't have the words...[or] they have a story they cannot tell [because] the past is alive in the present...[and] the future is an idea alive in our mind now' (Grosz in Henley 2013, p.11). I have found this to be true of many of the traumatised young asylum seekers who may need to voice their stories *indirectly*, that is, through other people's stories that mirror their own in some way that is important to them. This may allow them to confront their past that is still with them in the present, so that they may face the future.

Finding the lost narrative

The writer Jeanette Winterson's adoption as a young girl by a mentally unstable person left her abused and deeply wounded. In her autobiography *Why Be Happy when You Could Be Normal?* she writes that 'the wound is symbolic and cannot be reduced to any single interpretation. But wounding seems to be a clue or a key to being human' (Winterson 2012, p.42). She struggled with the wounded self given to her by her adoptive mother, discovering that she could not ditch this self for another – the wound had formed her. Her wounded childhood self coped by reading books and discovering hope from them. Her adoptive mother burned her books, so Jeanette had to keep them in mind to soothe and inform and make herself with words, poems and stories:

> I had been damaged and a very important part of me had been destroyed – that was my reality, the facts of my life; but on the other side of the facts was who I could be, how I could feel, and as long as I had words for that, images for that, stories for that, then I wasn't lost. (Winterson 2012, p.221)

This is the journey on which the therapeutic intervention of literature hopes to take the young asylum seekers and refugees.

Dealing with memories of terror using words

Terrorised young people may experience intense feeling but at first have no memory of the event because they dissociate from their memories of the terror, or they may remember the event without feeling anything, so they are in a constant state of high alert or irritability but do not know why.

Their memories return suddenly, unexpectedly as flashbacks or nightmares, vivid and emotional, triggered by small reminders that are frozen and *wordless* images. Their actions may change too – the play of children who have experienced trauma is obsessive, literal and humourless (Terr 1990) – an example of Freud's 'repetition compulsion' linked to the death instinct, which can also be seen as a way of attempting to integrate the trauma that is stored in the active memory but that needs to be changed (Herman 1997).

At first, severe trauma often leads to a loss of voice or 'speechless terror' that is both a psychological and physical response so that the sufferers are unable to identify, regulate or express themselves. The traumatised young people are disempowered and grieving. The security, trust and optimism on which their self-narrative depends has been undercut. Even when they are able to 'speak', the words they use cannot capture traumatic events.

Yet, in time, the act of mourning needs to be given a meaningful account to preserve a sense of continuity and to control feelings. The young survivors have been denied the grieving process not only communally and culturally, but also psychologically. Their distress is exacerbated because the deaths they are mourning were a violation of the natural order – caused by political punishment or murder, using victimisation and humiliation (Van der Kolk 1994).

They need to reconstruct personal meaning in a coherent self-narrative that allows them 're-learn' the self and the world. They make sense of the horrific world they have witnessed by finding some 'life lesson' in their loss. They must construct a symbolic universe to cope with it. This can be done by giving meaning through expression 'in the language of individual consciousness, or through our working model' of self and of the world (Neimeyer, Prigerson and Davies 2002, p.248). Using guided imagery and literal and symbolic narration for recall makes them feel less helpless (Malchiodi 2008). This is the task I set out to perform: it included researching the theory of these ideas, finding appropriate books for age groups ranging from children to teenagers and young adults, and discovering new ways of applying the study of psychology and literature to reading and writing for therapeutic self-expression of shattered young people.

Recognising hidden abuse

In her novel *Mrs Dalloway* (published in 1925), Virginia Woolf described her inner psychological instability and distress by projecting it onto the character of the shell-shocked and suicidal World War 1 soldier Septimus Smith. This desperate and overwhelming state of being, now known as PTSD, was not recognised or understood by her society at that time, which included a remote and indifferent psychiatrist attempting to 'treat' her hallucinations and suicidal feelings. Prophetically, she understood that 'the public and private worlds are inseparably connected…the tyrannies and servilities of one are the tyrannies and servilities of the other' (Woolf 1938, p.142). She may well be hinting here at her own sexual abuse by her older cousin, when she was a young girl. We are still reluctant to recognise or understand the depth of psychological suffering that comes from the relationship between community and interpersonal violence and abuse. Woolf was able to articulate her experiences veiled in her novel though it did not prevent her suicide, but can traumatised young asylum seekers find a way to articulate in stories their sense of horror at what they have experienced? This was a question that needed answering in terms of finding, practising and debating a system that could achieve this aim.

Those who specialise in the treatment of trauma victims of organised violence and of rape, which includes finding suitable treatments for children and adolescents, speak of the experience the children undergo as 'atrocities' – those destructive forces overwhelming and overpowering children that are caused by human beings. Such traumatic events 'overwhelm the ordinary systems of care that give people a sense of control, connection and meaning' (Herman 1997, pp.32–33).

In situations of organised violence and war, children are abused by adults they do not know. They are sold and trafficked for sexual slavery and domestic work. Familial child abuse is defined as an adult–child relationship:

> where the adult to which the child is attached fails to be sensitive to the child's needs, is unavailable, physically or emotionally, is more inconsistent, neglectful, or punitive than the child can manage at his [or her] age... The adult in both these kinds of abuse often requests secrecy and threatens to severely punish a child who betrays secret abuse. If these events are kept secret... the child feels to blame. If an attempt is not made to address and process these experiences, these feelings connected with trauma or abuse are likely to be repeated through the generations. In situations where processing is prevented, the young people are left feeling out of control, incompetent, insignificant and unable to think clearly or to concentrate. (Melzak 1992)

Realising the abuse, speechless terror, helplessness and humiliation the young asylum seekers have experienced, in relation to what they want and need, it became clear to me that in order to practise any kind of therapeutic intervention, my first task was to establish a safe relationship of trust.

CHAPTER 2

Linking External and Internal Worlds

Forming a Relationship

Traumatised young people need someone to believe in them, and they need to form emotional attachments to people, places, culture and politics to try and replace lost parents, relatives, friends, and their selfhood. A relationship with a caring person gives them a chance to interpret their experiences, and this can include the use of fictional stories similar to their own with which they can identify and through which they can express themselves.

A SECURE RELATIONSHIP WITH PRIMARY FIGURES TO COUNTER PARENTAL LOSS

Anna Freud wrote of how children who experienced war conditions could survive these experiences that place them at such enormous odds if they had a safe substitute parental figure, but if this person was absent, they develop serious emotional problems. This is because they are forced too early into independence, are frozen at a period of their development or have regressed (Freud and Burlingham 1943).

Children and young people cannot easily permit themselves to acknowledge what has happened to their parents, whose adult power and authority has been taken away, often in front of their own eyes. Children's coping mechanisms are linked to their parents' coping mechanisms. They have had their idealised fantasy of the power of their parents to protect and care for them in the present and the future shattered. They have lost their childhood innocence, which creates problems in their subsequent development for identification and mourning. Adolescents may witness parents supporting the regime, or defying it, so they may deliberately forge a different relationship with the regime of their parents, denying their history and community. They may feel overwhelmed by the sense of adult corruption as they slowly become aware of this, and may try to hold on to culture and traditions or reject their past. Some may strike a balance between the two possibilities (Melzak 1995). Survival in exile and being estranged from parents, familiar people and their own culture is especially difficult for children who themselves have undergone torture and other child-specific human rights abuses, as they cannot differentiate between feeling bad and being bad. Not all young refugees break down psychologically, but for some of those who do, it happens only after many months of being in exile or when they are adults (Melzak 1992).

Because of these personal losses, traumatised young people need to form emotional attachments to people, places, culture and politics (Marris 1974). Mary Fabri, at the Marjorie Kovler Centre for the Treatment of Survivors of Torture, writes that the young people need to create a secure internal unconscious 'working model' or models, based on their experiences with primary figures, to help them to interpret their experiences. For this they need to build confidence in an available protective, supportive figure to help them reconstruct meaning in the wake of loss (Fabri 2001).

One young survivor sums this up:

> [You]…made me realise that this is my life and no matter what happens I am the only one that can move it forward. And basically I am OK and that there's something good in all of us really… and made me see my talents and believed in me…I started to see myself differently. (Lemma 2010, p.10)

Lemma describes the importance and power of such a relationship between 'a key worker' and a hurt young person, which she separates from a more formal psychotherapeutic intervention. One such worker described it as:

hard work at times and she got under my skin, but I could see that this was her way of communicating, and you adjust to that and respond accordingly – you have to give them space to do this... years with some of them...but then it's like a switch and they get it... (Lemma 2010, p.9)

Relating the internal world to the external world

The task of a facilitator in the field of therapeutic writing, as in other forms of therapeutic and psychotherapeutic work, is to understand 'the relationship between the real, external, social world and the internal, emotional, representational world of developing children and adolescents...' (Melzak 1992, p.209). To achieve this, the therapist or group facilitator needs to implement a shared relationship encouraging self-fulfillment. The relationship you are forming with each young person is about caring enough so that the young person feels able to make choices and learn that they themselves can eventually be in a position to help others with acts they valued in their own healing.

First steps with Amina, using Dickens's Pip

Amina was part of a small group of trafficked young women with whom I began, who spoke English fairly fluently. I needed a text that dealt with helplessness but ended in hope and that included movement towards a realistic grasp of how to live in the here-and-now.

The session with these young women took place in the centre's office, a small bright colourful room facing an inner-city park. It felt like a safe place to them. We began with an initiative of finishing each other's stories: scraps of paper were handed out on which a person wrote a line and the next one had to add to it randomly. What emerged was full of sadness. I suggested they wrote word pictures of themselves (they had never been photographed at this point). I asked them, if faced with an actress who has to impersonate them, what details they would use to describe themselves accurately so the actress could really portray them as they were. Their responses were naturally guarded – we needed time in which to build a relationship of trust. Amina wrote:

> My name is Amina. I don't know how I came to be named Amina.
> I believe it is just a common name in my village…I never saw my
> mother. I always fantasize that I look like her.

We began the session by talking about Charles Dickens's difficult
childhood and his feeling of abandonment by his mother. The young
women indicated subtly that they had known and felt the same degree
of suffering as children.

Amina wrote down the following:

> Dickens didn't have a mother he liked… He had no real kindness…
> He was lonely… It happened to myself. So I ask: who am I? Can
> I really become something? Dickens wants to make his readers
> know what it's like to be a teenager with no one to help you.

This seemed to trigger a memory Amina had of a neighbour's
humiliation in her village, as a woman with whom she identified, and
that still made her feel angry. She wrote a poem about it that seemed
to relieve her, as if by remembering the hurt of this woman she knew,
and expressing it gave her some control over what she remembered.

> Her eyes seem so distant and [to] beseech
> Her shoulders are a bit sloppy, she
> Walks alone in a narrow path
> Carrying a stack of books
> Her teeth are full of dust and bare
> She seems to have worn the same
> Dress to school for the last five
> Days. She's singing to herself
> While eating a piece of fruit
> She passes by Mr Kato's house
> And stops. She kneels down to greet him
> Though he's about a mile away. She wonders
> Why she can't go towards where he's sitting
> And makes sure he hears her properly.
> Maybe Mr Kato doesn't want anyone near him but why greet
>   him in the first place?

Others in the group did not respond so positively. I learned that absences from sessions and difficulties in taking part were because of personal adjustments, a reluctance to talk or unfamiliarity with the English language.

Indirectly addressing Amina's complex memory of her father through Alice Walker's work

Amina came for a one-to-one session. I decided to bring in Alice Walker's short story, A Sudden Trip Home in the Spring (Walker 2005). Amina could identify not only with the writer as a black person fighting an unfair system, but also with Sarah, the writer's protagonist in the book, who is a strong and talented young black woman and who, like Amina, had a complex relationship with her father. I knew Amina's abuse was part of a memory that would always be with her. Perhaps tackling this indirectly through a character she could identify with and onto whom she could project her inner feelings would allow her to 'word' it as a form of relief.

The story is about a daughter's feelings towards a father, whose cruelty caused her mother's death and in his 'rage of despair' destroyed their child. It concerns Sarah (Alice Walker's alter ego), a black student attending a wealthy white American college, who has to return to her roots in the Deep South because her father has died, a man whose cruelty she cannot forget. Amina identifies with this. Sarah's image of her father is a symbol of a 'closed fist'. Amina comments that this 'stands for his power over his daughter for whom he had felt nothing'. It relieves her to say this.

Sarah's rich, white friend offers her father's very smart car to take Sarah down south to a village that is not unlike Amina's. The writer describes Sarah's white roommate as having a grimy neck and Amina is amused by the idea of a wealthy white girl being unhygienic. She comments with pride that 'when you are on your own in your family and in the world, you have to learn to keep yourself clean'. Expressing this gives her a sense of pride in her self-reliance, despite the long and difficult journey she is undertaking to control the memories of her abuse.

The troubled relationship of the African American writer Richard Wright's domineering father is mentioned in the story, a father who was 'omnipotent, unpredictable, undependable and cruel. Entirely in control of his universe. Just like a god…' (Walker 2005, p.252). The question posed is 'Could he disavow his father and live?' Amina responds: 'We all have the right and the freedom to be ourselves. You can learn to do without a father like that. You learn to depend on yourself.'

The delicacy of the interchanges and what they revealed was based on the beginning of a trust between us – the 'existential engagement in which both partners commit themselves to the task of recovery, in which you bear witness to the truth, bearing in mind that there are boundaries to be kept that tolerable to both you and the young person' (Herman 1997, p.147).

The session succeeded in linking Amina's different aspects of herself in the past and in the present. In this way, through this focused exploration of the story and the main character in relation to Amina's own life, she gained a measure of courage and hope in what she could do with her future (Figley 1983).

Trust within creativity: beginning a relationship with Asoum

Asoum comes from a family with high expectations of their son. His father was on the 'wrong side politically', which meant that Asoum was sent to the UK for his protection from those who terrorised his family. He has a physical disability that adds to his sense of frustration and isolation, which sometimes leads to outbreaks of anger.

He came to the first session wanting 'creativity…to write something original about myself, to make a story'. We must read only a little and slowly.

I have brought with me a small bicycle fashioned from wire by street children from South Africa and a story, *Papa, Snake and I* by B.L. Honwana from Mozambique, translated from the Portuguese. The bicycle triggers memories for Asoum of home and of his parents. With some encouragement, he puts this into words:

> At home in Africa, when I was a boy, I made a nice car, like a jeep with lights. I competed with friends to make the nicest ones. It was lots of trouble to make it. We used one sort of wire. There was a small, light board attached to each side of the car, a red light at the back so you see it stop. My Dad had a car, a Land Cruiser, so we made it like that. This bike you brought along is not perfect, but it reminds me of my own wire car. My car was really done well…

He feels good about remembering his father's car and proud of the one he fashioned himself.

I have chosen the story because it is about a father who is forced to fight an unfair political regime, as did Asoum's own father, and it is about an adolescent coming of age and learning to understand the complex balance between good and bad in any action and in his relationship with his father.

In the story by Honwana a dangerous snake is killing the village fowls. Ghino, the young hero, looks for and finds it in the woodshed. The powerful Portuguese Senhor Castro has a dog, Wolf, who sees the snake. Ghino lets this dog go forward and kill the snake, and the dog dies, bringing the threat of death to Ghino's father. Senhor Castro demands compensation from Ghino's father or a police beating. Ghino's father is poor and powerless. He prays for hope, as even a poor man must have false hope. He says that we grow up with bottled feelings that we cannot express. Asoum identifies strongly with this. The boy admits to his father his guilt in the dog's death. With great tenderness, his father admits he may face death. Ghino suddenly realises he loves his father. Asoum is moved by this.

Ghino's fierce mother is not told of the killing of the snake, or the Senhor's threat. This is a moral act of kindness, which intrigues Asoum. Asoum says the mother in the story

> is just like my own mother. There are incidents in which you feel fear of your mother. Mine was too tall. She walked too fast. I would try and hold her back by her skirt. As a young boy I would walk for hours alone rather than walk with her.

He is relieved to admit this.

I ask him how he feels and thinks about this story. Asoum says the story is political, something he knows about. The snake is like Senhor Castro, a political symbol. But Ghino's father kept putting off killing the snake; he is passive. Ghino begins to understand his father's plight, his difficult choices, which are moral choices – not to 'act like a wild horse' but to keep hold of his feelings. This could be courage or it could be cowardice.

Asoum is interested in this meaning that lies behind a political action. He comments that it is up to oneself, like Ghino in the story, to deal with the strong, even though you are weak. I say that in the book this is a turning point from adolescent to adulthood. The story hints that the boy's future is hopeful; he is sensitive and learns to stand on his own two feet without using anger. Asoum is interested and comforted by this thought.

Asoum, by reading this story and relating to the young hero, could see his own story of loss – personal, cultural and political – through a prism.

Asoum then wrote a story of how he fought another village boy, but learned to control his anger for the sake of family relations in the village. Here is what he wrote:

> I had a real car. I lent it to my friend and my cousin went with for the ride and he had an accident. A motorbike crashed into it. I was not happy. We had a fight. It was about 45 minutes walk from my village. It felt like a long time to walk, barefoot. We cried, we made peace so the families would not fight.

Remembering the value of control over his own anger gave him a sense of himself and his culture as 'good' and valuable. Writing it cemented this.

ENACTMENTS

Children's group
Re-writing memories into a coherent story through a mirroring narrative

1. Read/tell the story of Pegasus the flying horse, who takes his hero-rider through the sky to the dragon who is terrifying the community. Pegasus slays the dragon.

2. Say to the children: 'Imagine you have a horse with wings that can take you on a journey to destroy the monsters you know. Say your feelings, the place where you go, what was difficult for you (tell us about your monster and what he means to you), and what you found hard to handle on this journey. How did it change you?'

3. Say to the children: 'Write down your stories and read them aloud to the group. Draw pictures of the mastering of the monster. Display words and pictures.'

Young adults' group

1. Bring in Achebe's *Things Fall Apart* (2001).

2. Select and discuss proverbs, sayings and oral stories from the book such as 'the earth and the sky', 'the mosquito and the ear', 'the tortoise and the birds'.

3. Ask the young people to describe sayings, legends, rituals, festivals or icons that they 'hold' as a richness of their own cultures. Share.

4. Achebe shows the dignity of the Igbo people – their humanity in meeting problems. Ask group members to describe an incident they remember in their past experience in which they witness how difficult behaviour was countered within their culture.

5. Discuss their ideas of language, community and culture, the ability to balance change and tradition (the hero cannot, and perishes).

6. Does holding on to one's memories help to live in the here-and-now? Discuss, then write down the young people's ideas.

During these many encounters between a young asylum seeker, myself and a chosen piece of fiction, I begin to understand how self-narration works as a means by which identity is re-created and returned to a hurt young person.

CHAPTER 3

Self-narration and Identity

Therapeutic Writing that Reconstructs and Reconnects

The words make me.

Amina

We construct ourselves from the narratives of others in our society and from the changing stories we tell ourselves. Trauma disrupts these narratives, leaving the 'self' frozen, the memory dominated by images of the trauma. When language returns, so that memories are verbalised or 're-told' in a positive way, a restoration of the persona begins. This can only happen after the young people remember and mourn their losses. They also need to take responsibility and control of their recovery – an act of courage against despair in which they reclaim their own history and regain energy and hope. By telling our multiple stories, we make ourselves, and this is what the therapeutic intervention using books attempts to achieve.

'HOMO NARRANS': NARRATIVE THERAPY

The self as narrative achievement

I encouraged Amina to keep a diary: here is how we discussed it:

> AMINA: When you write and you are writing about you, you sit there and read and you think, all those words are me. The words make me.

FACILITATOR: Are you thinking someone else will read it?

AMINA: No. When you are there, this is your mind and everything is pouring out and you think: how did I live it? A lot of things are going on in your mind. You sit and think, and things come out, but when you have written it, you realise you have never thought about this before – for that tiny moment, I was this person.

FACILITATOR: You are finding yourself...

AMINA: I am really enjoying it – seeing that Amina in Africa – that was me, I used to walk barefoot – and look at myself here now, walking, wearing shoes in London. Sometimes I think there are two of me. The other one in Africa, I really want to bring her out.

Narrative therapy: Derrida and the construction of self through narratives

Narrative therapy is rooted in the Derridian post-structuralist theory of literature that examines the construction of stories. 'Narrative and the co-construction of narratives is a useful root metaphor for understanding the ways human beings construct, make sense of and transform...lives' (Speedy 2004, p.25). It emphasises that the psyche is not a fixed objective entity but a fluid social construct – a story that can be revised – and that our life experiences are mapped into 'dominant stories' constructed by language that is written from a particular culture, upbringing, religion and gender. As we develop an identity, we do not so much perceive the world as interpret it. If a child's dominant identity-story centres on traumatic problems, they become spiritual prisoners because threads of hope, resourcefulness and capability are excluded from the 'storied' self (see King on 'Helping self-regulation of thoughts', Chapter 20 in this volume).

A sense of self can be seen as a narrative achievement. We appropriate the voice of 'others' into the self, so our narrative is co-authored by relevant others, and identity is multiple and contradictory (Bakhtin 1981a). We come to see ourselves as we are seen. At a cultural-linguistic level we import these roles and discourses from a given culture into our self-narrative. The individual teller of tales is 'placed in social and political discourses, cultural and historical conditions and "local stories"' (Speedy 2004, p.25).

Narrative therapy emphasises the multiplicity of selves and identities that narrate a story. It also investigates the 'gaps' in the narrative – that which is left out of a story – as being of equal importance to the narrative as told, emphasising the uncertainties rather than certainties within the story. It relies more on talking than on writing. Therapeutic notes are seen as a way of recording the client's words during key moments and are often shared with the client, thus changing the 'power relationship' by sharing the ownership of these documents, and making the process of therapy more collaborative. People are seen as multi-storied, generating many stories at the same time, though they have one main story. Individuals are asked to tell and re-tell stories, to 'unpack' them, and to regenerate them.

We tell stories on three different levels: *personal self-narrative* organises the small everyday events of our life into a single story-line that consolidates our self-understanding, emotions, goals and performances on the social stage – identity on this level is a narrative achievement that is profoundly shaken by traumatic events; *inter-personal story-telling*, in which traumatic narratives are recounted to others, gives social support and a validation of the experience, which helps healing and growth – social psychological research shows the importance of 'confiding' our stories to others in integrating and transcending difficult life experiences (Harvey 1996); *mythic stories*, known by whole societies, provide narrative resources for members of a culture to draw on in order to find meaning in adversity. Neimeyer concludes that 'Of the many literatures relevant to the phenomenon of posttraumatic life, literature concerned with the construction, deconstruction and reconstruction of narratives may be among the richest, but least utilized' (Neimeyer 2004, p.53).

We construct our identities from the stories we tell about our life experiences or write about them. It is our way of exploring ourselves. What is particularly interesting about this process is that we need to make stories from our lives that we approve of. King and Miner found 'that not only can individuals be coaxed into gaining insight into their negative life experiences by positively reframing these, but that successfully doing so has health benefits' (King and Miner in Lepore and Smyth 2002, p.126)

These likeable stories we build that make the 'self' are disrupted by trauma: 'Traumatic life events have the power to disrupt those self-narratives with which people order their life experiences' (Neimeyer, Herrero and Botella 2006).

Therapeutic writing techniques *in which books are used* to help traumatised young people think, question and write about these experiences at a suitable time within their reconstruction of selfhood is a way to help build the safe, original self-narrative. 'Writing and reflecting on traumatic experiences might be more thoroughly and creatively developed to promote integration and transcendence of tragic transitions' (Neimeyer 2004, p.57). Neimeyer points out that asking 'curious questions' to help processing of new themes and plot developments in their life stories and to discover new possible selves is a hallmark of such interventions.

The 'performed' personal story: using literature to discover what is 'left out' of the dominant trauma narrative

Literature has the ability to help us reconstruct ourselves through learning to re-tell our stories in a self-enhancing way. The 'self' constructed by story-making allows a young person to feel safe. In traumatised children this becomes endangered by the overwhelming reality of a world destroyed by war and abuse. Socially, politically or culturally enforced narratives also may marginalise a personal one, because in effect they 'steal the authorship of the individual's life narrative...and colonise the person's public identity and private self-concept' (Neimeyer 2004, p.57).

Traumatised young people are still trying to find their identity and carry within themselves a confused sense as to who they are at different times of their lives, and who they are in relation to others (parents or close family members) and in relation to their cultural-political history, about which they hold ambiguous and fluctuating attitudes that affect their life-narratives. The approach of therapeutic intervention through literature, instead of looking for flaws in children and young people's psyches, helps the young people themselves to find the omissions in the stories they have constructed. Listening to and asking questions about these constructed narratives helps to name and externalise the problem and to discover 'unique outcomes' (small moments when the client is not dominated by his or her story) that helps a child to challenge the dominant story by examining alternate ones that include hope and resilience (Walsh and Keenan 1997).

The facilitator's role: hearing, and mirroring 'the silent story', using their metaphors

The very act of reading and writing is therapeutic as the story told is 'performed' (Speedy 2004). Writing down what has been said allows traumatised young people to see the way their stories, and their positions in them, change over time, thus giving a powerful voice to experiences that were silenced.

The facilitator 'hears' the child's story and uses the child's language, particularly the personal metaphors each child uses, in order to bond and collaborate with the child in re-telling the life-narrative. The technique releases the child from blame and gives the child power over the problem, and allows acknowledgement and expression of their inner self by developing emotions needed to face the problem. As the child talks and writes, the facilitator shares their memories, discusses their thoughts and feelings about the problem and then asks about their expectations and solutions to the problem.

To incorporate positive life experiences into negative ones within a written self-narrative is to find good happenings in the negative ones, so that a traumatised child can grow through the bad events into accepting the positive ones, allowing the self-control that leads to improved health (King 2002).

The danger for traumatised young people is that a 'silent story' comes to exist, because the traumatic memories resist integration into the self-narrative. Neimeyer found that in a safe environment, 'by listening…constructively mirroring…and working with metaphors', which allow expression of feelings, this re-storying of a life was achieved (Neimeyer *et al.* 2006). Clients moved from shame to pride that they had survived.

The survivors' written texts are the spontaneous words, sentence structures and images chosen by them, kept in the original form as valued and relevant choices. These writings are not about 'beautiful' work or the mastering of techniques to improve the quality of writing. They are concerned with the confidence that self-expression in language gives – the concretisation of memory in words that objectify and intensify through metaphor and symbol, so that an internal 'discussion' can begin to take place as the 'inner selves' that are eventually disclosed face the 'outer selves' that must translate them into their practical everyday lives.

The written pieces in the sessions are initiated by discussing certain themes about feelings that concern traumatised young people: anger, shame, loss, disappointment, victimhood and injustice, and self-doubt, which are to be counteracted through reading and writing with feelings around the concept of home, endeavour, hope, survival and resilience. For instance, a consideration of 'anger' in a character in a book read and then written about may cover the ideas of allowing anger, how to express anger, anger denial and learning to acknowledge anger. In discussing victimhood and the fact that the survivors felt they had been tricked out of their childhoods and the natural course of their lives, the session members came up with humorous individual stories of 'tricksters' who tried to pull the wool over their eyes, and how moral choices would include never refusing a beggar out of a moral sense and a sense of your own worth, counteracted by being taken advantage of by a schemer. This writing gave them a good sense of self and of being able to counteract tricksters who show a neediness that tops their own.

In this context, it is well to remember that some cultures 'tell' rather than write stories. As the young people traditionally use the spoken word and story-telling as the means of communicating rather than the written word, sessions may concentrate not only on their written responses, but on their informal verbal responses, often given in a group context. The informal discussions reveal not only unexpected insights and layers of meaning, but also words, images and thoughts of natural beauty and clarity. Both the spoken and written pieces are in English and not in the contributor's first language, so the words and rhythm of the work, though always true to each writer, often holds a flavour of their first tongue. They sometimes read and write about African village life from writers whose work had been translated into English, which remind them of the value of their own backgrounds, family members, customs and traditions held in great affection and regarded as the basis of their formative selves.

Escaping victimhood using expressive writing

The feminist Professor Jacqueline Rose points out that 'Victimhood is something that happens, but when you turn it into an identity you're psychically and politically finished' (Rose in Jeffries 2012). Jacqueline Rose has made a study of victimhood and has come to understand how a person can 'lock themselves into a traumatised identity' and remain there for life, without being able to grow up and move on towards a sane, more balanced way of living. In her novel *Albertine* (Rose 2002), about Marcel Proust's lover in *In Search of Lost Time*, Rose rescues Albertine from Proust's story of victimhood, imprisonment and death by re-telling her story, freeing her and re-instating her in life: 'returning to Albertine her intelligence' (Rose in Jeffries 2012, p.12). The young survivors learn ways to resist being locked into victimhood to get back their 'intelligence' in order to stand on their own two feet and get on with the reality of their lives, no matter how difficult and uncertain these lives may be. The psychologist Carl Rogers's view that human and social values are common to all people and we have an inherent tendency to expand and develop ourselves underlies the fact that a facilitator is there only to give birth to these values, and does so via books that embody this purpose (Rogers 1951). The young people at therapeutic writing sessions are still learning to 'steel' themselves. It is the 'steeling' effect that makes uprooted children more resilient to victimhood (Garmezy 1982). James Pennebaker found evidence that movements towards the development of a narrative in the writing of individuals is 'far more predictive of health than having a coherent story *per se*', and 'the construction of a story may be the desired end point of writing' (Pennebaker 1993, p.546).

REMEMBERING, MOURNING
AND RECLAIMING LIFE

The recovery of traumatised children and adolescents has three stages: the establishment of a safe place; remembering and mourning their losses which is a form of self-renewal during which they express their anger at their helplessness; and taking responsibility and control of their recovery – an act of courage against despair, in which they reclaim their own history and regain energy and hope (Herman 1997, p.192).

Freud, in 'Mourning and melancholia' (Freud 1917), differentiated between those who remain plastic and adaptable through the process of mourning and those who fall into 'melancholia' and become frozen and inflexible (a state of feeling that is not to be confused with depression) (Green 2013). The facilitator's moral stance affirms that of the survivor's, returning dignity to the individual and normalising the survivor's responses by helping along 'naming' and the use of language (Herman 1997, p.179). The aim is to transform the traumatic memory.

The central task of the third stage is reconnection with ordinary life (Herman 1997). Once they have re-narrated their stories to include survival, the young people begin to enter a new country, both literally and figuratively. They now respond to life with a survivor's pride in a new selfhood. They are learning to build survival strategies that include spontaneity and humour, defining a new 'self' about which they can be more objective, as well as forming new relationships and defining what they want and ways to achieve this. This is the stage of uniting their hard-won sense of discipline and knowledge of their survival with a creative ability to imagine. Life becomes both more adventurous and more ordinary. More options open up and choices can be made. Trust and hope become possible, so relationships are formed. The survivors can draw on those aspects of themselves, and their culture, that they value from before their trauma (Herman 1997).

It is at this stage that therapeutic writing is most enabling. The narrative of suffering can be related to a sympathetic listener and reinterpreted through other narratives similar to their own, which include their own culture and history and which can include the idea of hope. The past becomes re-embodied in the present, and a more complete person emerges. They learn about their own strengths and limitations through the way characters behave in a story-narrative. They weigh up society's power and personal freedom and how to balance them realistically, through exploring in sessions an effective story-line, so that they can negotiate their rightful place in their new world.

This is not straightforward, but it is a process that advances slowly as impasses and regressions are overcome. Reading texts, discussing them and writing from them plays a part in helping the recovering traumatised young asylum seekers to 'deal with political, spiritual and existential issues, as the survivors contend with questions of ultimate meaning and core value[s] in integrating more fully the past, present and future parts of their lives' (Gorman 2001).

USING A BOOK OF BEADWORK

I show the Baobab's children's group, aged between nine and 14 years, a bead necklace made by a young African girl who has woven words, including her name and pictorial symbols, into the necklace. We talk about how the women 'write' messages into their beads using different colours – when young men are visiting, a girl may weave a message into their beads saying: 'I am now ready to marry' and give it to a boy she likes. This thought is met with much laughter.

We talk about beads and beadwork as a cultural tradition, both as having specific meaning to the culture as beads can weave cultural meanings passed down from generation to generation, and as being valuable and beautiful so people are proud to wear them.

I suggest the group remember a piece of beading they have known, describe its colours, beauty and meaning, and write a story around them, saying what they mean to them. They may also like to draw and colour a picture of them.

This is my first session with Asola who is about ten years old. She is intelligent and still disturbed by her detention and arrest. She is dominated by her mother. She was badly treated at an asylum centre, which made her fearful. She can become completely withdrawn at times.

Asola draws the beads, colouring them scarlet crimson. They are cylindrical and plaited into the hair. She explains that hair would be braided thickly in the villages, with the beads woven so you see little circles of red. She writes a piece about the beadwork in her tribal history and culture with enormous pride as she belongs to the royal section of the tribe, and only members of this section may use red beads in their hair.

She writes:

Culture: without the red African royalty beads I wouldn't be me. The Ade means royal. I would not have this culture in me if it was not for the red African beads. So they are extremely special to me. The story behind these Nigerian beads – works of art – lie beyond years and years ago before the world wars. Although they may not be in my possession I have them in my blood. These beads hold my heritage and these beads hold tradition.

Her mother told her this story, which she has coloured with her own words and feelings:

Death – that was what was awaiting him. The African king had died. All the wives and daughters mourned him. They had to find an heir, who was going to be the next ruler, the next monarch. But he had a daughter. And in those times daughters and women couldn't rule and so when his daughter heard this, the princess, she was incredibly upset. She was angry so she went to one of the Gods. She asked if the little white beads that they had been selling to make money for the village would not be found so that they would all be upset and so there would be no money in the village as a punishment for not letting her be queen. So this happened for weeks and months and almost a year until she finally got fed up because there wasn't any change. So she went back to the God and said: 'Will you stop them not having any resources!' And so she did, and so they found the white beads again. She went to all the chiefs in the palace to tell them what she had done. They weren't upset but they apologised. So in favour of her, they went to a God to make the white beads 'reddy' pink colour in favour of her as a woman.

Asola was full of pride in telling us her special origins and recognition of her worth and that of her past.

Adra wrote a description of a bead bracelet she was wearing:

> This is my bracelet which says my name. I got it from my godfather in 2009. I really like it because it says my name and it's readable. I really like it because it is from my home country and I feel special and proud when I wear it.

AN ENCOURAGING TALE OF AFRICAN SPOONS

I came to the young adults' group of survivors who were struggling with their past memories and their present needs to persevere despite a frustrating and debilitating present, bearing two ancient carved African spoons that I use myself as salad spoons. This evoked amazement and almost disbelief that I should use one of their cultural objects in my home, but I began to talk about the beauty of the carving and the way the spoons had been worn by usage.

I asked if anyone wanted to talk about the objects they remember that were used at home in their cultures, and how they felt about them and who they might remember using them. I linked their memories with reading and talking about the text of Edmund de Waal's *The Hare with the Amber Eyes: A Hidden Inheritance* (2011), in which the author investigates, uncovers and tells the history of his family through revered and loved objects – a collection of old carved Japanese netsuke. The de Waal's family members survived the Holocaust in Vienna, as did the beautiful netsuke that remain to tell the family story.

The material released an animated and humorous discussion of memories around boyhood and food, how fish were caught regularly in the lakes and rivers and grain was pounded, as well as fond memories of fathers, cousins and grandfathers finding local wood from the surrounding forests to make spears, kitchen bowls and bows and arrows for the boys to use to hunt rabbits.

Here are pieces of their writing from the sessions.

Gersa wrote:

My African jars
These wooden spoons really remind me of the wooden jars that have been used in my house – big ones, small ones. We used the small jar to break chillies and cassava flowers, and we used the big jar to break cassava leaves and to make maize. Our house jar was of a black colour and was heavy to carry.

The noise of the jar – chuip, chuip – if I keep hearing it, it means that the food is not ready. When you see them doing it, you don't come home, you run away.

I remember about my family in this conversation. I miss my family. We had the freedom as kids. The kids don't have it here.

The wooden bowls keep the food hot – open it and it is steaming hot.

Me, I'm not going into the kitchen. I wanted to go but they always chase me out.

Asoum wrote:

These wooden spoons remind me of a sack of maize being broken up in a big wooden jar by my Mom. The jar is 'foumdouk', and the baton is 'armoud' in Arabic. It was made in the villages and you have to buy them. She needed extra helpers. It made a lot of noise. It made a sound like doum-doum for a long time so you have to run away. We used to get fish from the lake – tilapia, perch. It took a long, long time to die. It was so salty and had more meat, less bones. You could feed many people. And there are the tiny little ones, no bones, you eat the whole thing – you put them on a stick and cook them over the fire, or fry them and then add tomatoes, onions.

Ytan wrote:

What I remember most of all is the arrow which was made for me by my grandfather, may his soul rest in peace. Every boy had to have his own spear, a small one. You can use this spear, but they didn't want us to because you could hurt yourself. I used to go with my Dad's brother in the forest. We made spears of wood.

Teak is good for spears – a tall tree. It is dark brown. When you cut it, you can sneeze all day. The wood must be wet when you cut it – when it dries it is as hard as iron.

Finally, I asked the group to select an object from their culture that they enjoyed, and to write about it. Ralymar talked of a carpet he made himself; Ytan chose a bark cloth used as a shroud; Asoum chose wooden toothpicks specially made for the purpose; Gersa chose to remember photographs of his family no longer in his possession.

FACING CHILD ABUSE USING EXPRESSIVE WRITING

Amina spoke of how school was an escape from the 'hell of home' that was her village life under her abusive father and a step-mother who treated her much as a house-slave. She was so demoralised that if she received good grades, she felt this was her father's achievements and not her own, leaving her without a sense of her own selfhood. I encourage her to keep a journal, as writing about her past could help relieve her of her anger and sense of powerlessness, and return to her a sense of control. Here is a passage from her journal:

> My school did not have all the things a school has. But to me that didn't matter because I knew no other school. Me and my friend, always met at the well. I would stay longer even though I knew I would be beaten. She was my friend. In the morning, I woke up to the sound of birds. There is a big tree in the yard. There are birds…making the yard dirty. I had to see that the compound was always clean…or I was punished. My step-mother would say: 'Get up. The birds are awake, why are you still sleeping!' The broom I used to sweep with was made from a local tree. When mine broke, I made another one. But my father, who is a witch doctor, said my broom was bad and he broke it. Only his broom was good. Why did I never question this? I wish the tree was still there. My sisters are still there.

Part of her longs for the continuity of the past. She remembers her sisters whom she looked after, with the guilt of the survivor who escaped. Yet another part of her is angry at her inability to question her father's and mother's cruelty and power over her at home. By expressing in words these dual feelings, she finds a way of admitting them both, which is resourceful and healing.

ENACTMENTS

Young adults' group

1. Bring in copies of extracts from *Tsotsi* by Athol Fugard (2006). It is about an adolescent street boy, with whom they can identify, who has known only violence, poverty and hunger, who is transformed by finding himself having to care for a baby. Through this action, he discovers himself and who he is for the first time.

2. Read together the passage dealing with the flawed hero, Tsotsi, a leader of a street gang in a township in South Africa, who lost his parents during a forced street removal when he was a young boy. He thinks of himself inwardly as 'darkness'. He is so uncared for, he does not even know his own age or name (Chapter 3).

3. Discuss this and his reasons for thinking this. (He does many wrong deeds to others as a gang leader.) Discuss how this relates to their own experiences of feeling inner 'darkness'.

4. Read the passage in Chapter 7 when Tsotsi learns to feel for a legless beggar, whom he has callously threatened to kill. Discuss the need to feel for others and how this relates to what they know and feel about this.

5. Read the passage from Chapter 8, when, having taken home an abandoned baby, he asks a street woman to whom it belongs to clean it and to feed it – to keep it alive. Read the passage from Chapter 9 about the street gang Tsotsi heads. Discuss how gangs work, in their experience.

6. In the next part of the story, the street woman wants her baby back. *The climax of the story is about how Tsotsi 'becomes' the baby he finds he is with – the baby is his lost early self, and this is a turning point because Tsotsi learns to care for someone else,*

and through this, for himself. Discuss the meaning of how liking oneself and accepting what has happened to that self is painful and is the first step to real change that takes one forward.

7. In the story Tsotsi then discovers his name is David Maconda. He is now able to give the baby back to its birth mother. Discuss this naming of the self.

8. Write: The group members can write about a single event that changed their lives or way of thinking about themselves. Read them aloud to the group.

We can find ways of escaping victimhood by writing about it and by reconnecting with ordinary life through reading books that mirror our own experiences more objectively. But consider attempting to live in a strange country, where people do not speak your language or practise customs and religions with which are familiar. I ask myself if presenting language, plots and characters can help a displaced, traumatised young person to live in two cultures at once.

CHAPTER 4

Living in Two Cultures

'I Am Neither Here nor There'

Asylum seekers are at sea in a culture that rejects their own, so that their own becomes a double-edged sword, both as the source of the violence that shamed them and as the culture to which they owe a loyalty. They need to weave their narrative threads back into the social fabric of the society they live in now, through mentors who enhance resilience by encouraging them, once more to 'be themselves'. The literature I bring to the shattered young people is to remind them of the power of the 'ordinary'.

THE CONFUSION OF LIVING IN TWO CULTURES: REBUILDING A CULTURAL IDENTITY

'Culture' is 'the matrix of representation, enactment, communication and meaning through which each individual collectively manages the conflicts of his/her inner worlds, and which he/her internalises' (Blackwell 2005, p.38). This becomes problematic for young asylum seekers and refugees when they find themselves faced with an adopted culture that fails to recognise their original culture as valid. In this situation, some cling to the culture they left behind; others idealise the culture of their host country and choose to assimilate with it, or they may try to balance the two cultures in their lives or condemn them both and lose their identity, making adapting to their new culture even more difficult.

Many of them are not only grieving for their lost culture, but they also bear a sense of deep social loss. This disrupts their sense of continuity in time, their sense of selfhood and identity and the structure of meaning based on attachments to people, places and political entities. To counter this, traumatised young refugees need to rebuild their original cultural identity in order to restore themselves. They need to be culturally integrated to counteract their cultural bereavement (Blackwell and Melzak 2000). 'Perhaps the best way to enhance the competence of young refugees is to help [them] simply to "be themselves"' (Eisenbruch 1988, p.291).

'Culture' is a way of organising life that also includes its dramatisation in story-telling, humour and other art forms. In order to use effectively literature that contains culturally sensitive material to restore selfhood, I need to map the cultural picture of each individual young person – the relationships between children and their families and communities that reflect their past cultural values, and how this affects each young person's sense of themselves. This includes not only being aware of the culture with which each individual chooses to identify, but also knowing how each young person is affected by family background, gender attitudes and religion, together with the problems of specific war conditions, politics and socio-economic situations (Melzak 1992).

A facilitator's goal is to weave their 'long narrative threads' back into the cultural and social fabric of the society they live in, as 'mentors who enhance resilience' (Kohli and Mather 2003, p.205). You also need to take into account their personal preferences, or not, for any literary intervention. Some young people preferred to simply talk about something that happened to them during the day that interested or amused them, ranging from football to street beggars.

THE SOCIAL AND PERSONAL STRUCTURING OF HOPE

A school-based health survey of 11–16-year-old students and their care-givers in northern Afghanistan showed how the impact of violence (both political and the violence of everyday life) is mediated through individual psychology and cultural affinity, and how much culture matters in shaping experiences of distress and resilience – specific cultural contexts frame individual and collective experiences of political violence. They also show that *the anthropology of hope links well-being with social structures* and that ideologies of hope have importance for individual and collective resilience (Eggerman and Panter-Brick 2010). The distinguished Czech playwright, poet and dissident Václav Havel wrote:

> Hope is not the conviction that something will turn out well, but the certainty that something makes sense, regardless of how it turns out...[and] one's sense of the possibilities that life can offer... Its enemy is a sense of entrapment, of having nowhere to go. (Havel 1990)

What is important for a facilitator of therapeutic reading and writing is that this study concluded that the violated young people found that the important element of hope includes a coherent narrative that explains personal and collective experiences. Arguably, hope is what matters most in efforts to promote mental health, psychosocial support and psychosocial well-being in war zones (Almedon and Glandon 2007). It is one of five recommended elements for interventions addressing trauma from mass violence; the others being safety, calm, connectedness, and self and community efficacy (Hobfall *et al.* 2007).

However, cultural values may also be sources of entrapment, and an inability to conform to cultural dictates can cause great psychosocial distress. Culture and religion become sources of violence, causing a sense of shame, frustration and, particularly for women and children, a loss of self-worth, while young men feel 'impotent' because of an inability to find work (Mollica 2006).

STORIES THAT BRING RESILIENCE BY CELEBRATING THE POWER OF THE ORDINARY

The stories I bring to the shattered young people are to remind them of the power of the 'ordinary': 'Resilience comes from the everyday magic of ordinary, normative human resources in the minds, brains and bodies of children, in their families and relationships, and in their communities' (Masten 2001, p.235).

Nomif is interested to read aloud the descriptions of the thoughts and feelings of the parentless street children portrayed in *The Garbage*

King by Elizabeth Laird (2004). They, like Nomif, have been forced to run away from home, and find themselves out on the open road, defenceless, in an uncaring world. Nomif strongly identifies with the character of the young boy, Mamo, who is desperate, alone and exhausted.

The session is about how when things are hard in life, sometimes people can step in and help as part of the 'ordinariness' of life, not as part of its extremities. This gives Nomif a chance to remember a kindness in his own life about which he was very positive. He was saved on the road to Heathrow Airport when he flagged down a car with an Arab driver after drifting hungry and alone for two days.

> The first meal I have when I arrive in the UK was a big burger and a bag of chips and a full cup of Kola and it was real nice. There was a man who drove a van. He picked me up from the middle of nowhere and buy me my first meal and gave me £10.00 and took me where I could get help. And when he drop me there I was going up and down to get help. After two days I get some help. It was the hostel at the airport. They help me and buy me clothes. I had the same clothes unwashed for months. They give me classes. Then after 10 months they send me back to Italy.

We talk about the boy in the book sitting at a table, and having food brought to him for the first time. Nomif described how this only happened to him at Christmas (his family are Christians), when the church fathers waited on the community. He remembered with glee how his mother cooked for the occasion on 'a metal stove with a hollow', in which a pancake mixture was poured, and a fire was lit beneath it so it became hot quickly and 'made many, many eyes in the pancake'. This was the local form of bread that could feed several people.

Nomif seems encouraged by talking about these good memories of his own culture, and how, like the boy in the story, he knew he must persist, make a plan and keep going until he found a place of safety. He tells me he has found a girlfriend and proudly shows me his initial course outline to begin training as a plumber.

'WRITING THEMSELVES' WHILE LIVING IN AN ADOPTED CULTURE

One of the reading/writing sessions for the young people was about how to address, as asylum seekers, an audience at the Royal College of Paediatricians conference in Wales (in March 2011) on 'My right to the highest standards of health', presenting their own stories themselves. Asoum spoke of the love he has of his country:

> So my name is Asoum. I want to talk about my background. I am from Africa. I came from the main city. We were against the government. This led to troubles. I had to leave my country and journey to the UK with agents. I arrived in the UK in 2001 I didn't speak the language. I got asylum in 2002. Before I came, I had a happy life. I had a motorbike. I was going to study at the Sorbonne though this was a dream. I used to love my country. I would to anything to help. No one is listening.

Gersa talked about the problems of age assessment by the Border Agency:

> My name is Gersa and I want to talk about the problem for me, which is age assessment. They were asking me certain questions, but because I was having emotional and psychological difficulties, I lost my confidence to answer them. They say: 'You are an adult here, and must look after yourself.' This was terrible. This changed my whole life as I was on my own and only 16. I had no support, no family. Now I am doing my training to be in the Health Service myself.

The very act of expressing their long-held sense of pain to a concerned and 'listening' audience, using English coherently and effectively, gave them a better sense of self-worth and a measure of dignity.

THE ROLE OF THE GROUP'S CULTURE IN THE EXPRESSION OF TRAUMA

In work done with traumatised young asylum seekers on Josina Machel Island, Mozambique, researchers found it necessary to think holistically about the traumatised individual and how to place them in context, whereas conventional interventions in psycho-traumatology developed in the global north were not found to be useful. What is important seems to be to understand psychological illness according to the traumatised young asylum seekers' own cultures. What a young asylum seeker brings to the therapeutic relationship is not necessarily the same as our understanding of this (Junior and Errante 2002). Under war conditions, the children in the study stopped trusting adults and so experienced the loss of socialisation by their parents and a loss of faith in attachment to their parents. This left them without a sense of how to behave, as there was a taboo on discussion of trauma memories. Their sense of guilt and disgrace had to be hidden. If they were sexually abused, this was used against them. They had no access to schooling. They lost self-esteem and felt abandoned. Further, illness in this community is viewed as an imbalance or as the result of weak social bonds. This is dealt with by the community giving mutual support, conducting healing ceremonies and seeking solutions from the chief or traditional healers and cathartic rituals in which a cure is an act rather than a process that may take years. The community and the young people realise that there is no hope of finding the perpetrators of their injustices. There are ways of enacting public mourning: the South African Truth and Reconciliation Commission (TRC) encouraged post-Apartheid public group mourning for the victimised, by seeing to it that as many perpetrators of violence as possible faced their victims and publically acknowledged their guilt. This spread to other countries and was effective in enabling a form of group mourning that led to not only mourning loss, but also a vital sense of reconnection of the past with the present and the future. However, Beverley Naidoo, the South African children's writer, points out that the *TRC hardly referred to the plight of the children caught up in Apartheid history*. She writes her books for children to redress this and to allow the reader to enter into their world (Naidoo 2004; see the enactment in Chapter 10 in this volume, using her work).

HOW DO YOUNG ASYLUM SEEKERS AND REFUGEES PERCEIVE 'THERAPY'?

Dr Mina Fazel, department of Psychiatry, Oxford, in a study for the Mental Health Therapeutic Service in Schools, questioned young refugees (Fazel 2012). The study demonstrated that even though they were with a therapist, they still felt an overwhelming fear of racism or felt 'shame' at using a therapist, as it would reflect badly on their culture, or denied they had a need to discuss any issues, possibly because this was too dangerous for them. They had issues with the fact that a teacher could insist that they see a therapist and that the therapy may not be confidential – the family often did not want a child to undergo therapy. They preferred accepting help from a facilitator who was 'like a cool nurse'. On the other hand, 80 per cent said that they listened to the therapist and took advice, and as a result felt more 'free'. The therapist helped them to solve problems at home and with peer relations, with themselves and their feelings. The therapist listened, taught them to be happy, was caring and trusting, gave them hope and helped them to take away their sense of loneliness and to unlock the chains of the past to calm them. Their greatest concerns were to blend in with their peers and to be accepted by them, so a command of the English language was key to their lives (Fazel 2011).

There are issues on both sides: the young people need to be 'confident enough to know what [they] are doing' and the facilitator 'needs to be self-aware enough, brave and daring enough and yet secure enough in the space the facilitator is holding for them' (Bolton in Bolton *et al.* 2006, p.17).

ENACTMENTS
Children's and young adults' groups

1. Read aloud together the brilliant descriptive passage in David Eggers's book *A Heartbreaking World of Staggering Genius* (2000) about how he and his brother play frisbee together.

2. Discuss how the throwing of the frisbee is a symbol – as they throw it higher and wider and learn to catch it with more and more skill, it becomes a symbol of the way to strive, enjoy and

take part in life that is give and take – a way to counter 'lostness' and longing. It stands for the heroic act of caring that an older brother gives to a younger one. It is a passionate gift of love from which we can all learn something.

3. Ask the children and young people to write down a 'frisbee' experience – it could be playing football, for instance – and what it meant in terms of sharing, friendship, joy in using the body and getting outdoors.

4. Read these pieces of writing aloud to the group.

The young asylum seekers are shaped by their native culture, so living in a foreign culture exacerbates the extreme losses they have already undergone. I needed to investigate how others have used the intervention for healing in the past, and how practitioners use it now.

PART 2

Mapping the Terrain

Part V

Mapping the Terrain

CHAPTER 5

Healing Words
Have a History

Greeks cherished books as the source for improving the quality of life. *Therapeutic reading* first came into play as a humane treatment in asylums in 1700, but hospitals introduced the idea of prescribing books with *discussion with a facilitator* for depressives a couple of hundred years later. Only by the 1950s was it prescribed for children and adolescents to aid self-identity, and discuss *feelings* through literature. Today the therapeutic writing intervention has come to mean the use of literature to promote mental health by solving problems, and it is widely used in libraries, schools and colleges, hospitals and prisons as a way of 'serving' and 'healing'.

ORAL AND WRITTEN TEXTS
AS 'SILENT THERAPISTS'

Oral and written texts 'for centuries have worked as silent therapists for untold numbers' (Pardeck and Pardeck 1993, p.1). The word 'bibliotherapy' derives from the Greek *biblio* (book) and *therapeia* ('to serve' or to 'heal'). Greeks cherished books as the source for improving the quality of life. The door of the library at Thebes was inscribed with the words 'The Healing Place of the Soul' (Pardeck 1993; Schrank and Engels 1981). The Romans thought patients should read orations to improve their mental health (Jack and Ronan 2008).

In Europe in the 1700s *therapeutic* reading first came into play when it was allowed as a humane treatment in asylums, leading eventually to the establishment of libraries for recreation in many psychiatric hospitals. In the early 19th century Benjamin Rush recommended reading for the mentally ill as a *treatment*. Forty years later, Dr John Minson Galt II had published an early essay on the need for 'the kindly disposition of officers of the hospital' and care in careful selection of texts to suit a patient's needs (Jack and Ronan 2008; Rubin 1978). As an intervention for health, the use of books was first defined in the literature by Samuel Crothers in the early 20th century, when he wrote an influential article in the *Atlantic Monthly* on the prescriptive use of books in helping hospital patients understand mental ailments such as depression (Crothers 1816). Using the idea of *discussion* of a book with a facilitator following its reading was also introduced as useful in healing psychological problems (Jack and Ronan 2008). Finally, children were included in Edwin Starbuck's *Guide to Literature for Character Training* of 1928. It took another hundred years before physicians were advised to use books for children who presented with behavioural and personality disorders (Rubin 1978).

By the late 1940s psychologists, social workers and educators were including the use of books as an intervention through the practice of reading and discussion, and requested training courses, outcome research and a standard nomenclature of the intervention. Caroline Shrodes realised this was a three-way process of 'the dynamic interaction between the personality of the reader and literature under the guidance of a trained helper' (Shrodes 1949, p.11; Hynes and Hynes-Berry 1994). Facilitators using these skills, particularly with children and adolescents, use literature:

> as a tool to help young people deal with...self-identity, independence and self-worth... It can take place in both a clinical, and a developmental sense as it is directed more to the encouragement and reinforcement of strengths than to the diagnosis of problem areas... (Hynes and Hynes-Berry 1994, pp.17–18)

Psychotherapeutic practitioners began to include *creative writing* by the client as a basis for diagnostic and therapeutic sessions.

Rubin, in the late 1970s, gave a therapeutic dimension to this process of accessing people's problems through reading and talking about books, labelled as 'interactive bibliotherapy' (Rubin 1978) or, as it became known a decade later, 'affective bibliotherapy', because of the element of discussion of books that involved feelings 'between facilitator and client to reinforce and integrate concepts, morals, ethics and philosophies that facilitate those gained from reading a particular story' (Gladding and Gladding 1991).

Berry describes 'bibliotherapy' as 'a family of techniques for structuring interaction between a facilitator and participant... based on their mutual sharing of literature' (Berry 1978). A more comprehensive and modern definition includes the idea of literature being used in the treatment of groups of people with emotional problems or mental illness, sharing books as a means of personal growth (Pardeck 1998). Pennebaker sees therapeutic *writing* (the end product of the intervention for health using books) as helping to identify, organise and resolve trauma narrative: 'Good narratives... organise seemingly infinite facets of overwhelming events...[and] writing [them] moves us to a resolution' (Pennebaker 1990, p.103; see also Part 5 in this volume).

MODERN DEFINITIONS IN RELATION TO TRAUMATISED CHILDREN

Today we have come to use the term 'therapeutic writing intervention' to mean the use of literature to promote mental health by solving problems. It is currently used in a wide variety of therapeutic, educational and community settings, positioned as a sensitive, non-intrusive method of guiding people towards problem solving and coping in their personal lives (Mohr, Nixon and Vickers 1991).

In relation to traumatised children, therapeutic writing is described as helping to dissipate their sense of powerlessness, to help them overcome their having been silenced by shame (Bolton 1999; Etherington 2000), to help those who are in inner turmoil who need to externalise their feelings (Riordan 1996). It also serves people who need to disclose and exorcise memories of stressful experiences (Lepore and Smyth 2002). Based on Erikson's psychosocial stages of development that hurt children have problems on a continuum of severity, therapeutic writing as an intervention for their health may address a wide variety of issues along this continuum (Erikson 1950).

The facilitator's knowledge, experience and skill must be adequate to address the type and severity of the individual's difficulty (Heath *et al.* 2005).

Pardeck saw the therapeutic intervention for children using books both as a clinical tool and a practical tool for personal growth, tackling problems such as anger management, fear, foster care, loss and transition, single-parent families, self-concept and interpersonal relationships, coping skills and improved reading skills – all of which affect young asylum seekers and refugees (Pardeck 1998 in Heath *et al.* 2005; Pardeck 1990).

The intervention applies only to specific literature selected for a purpose and used within a therapeutic context. In this sense it is an important method used in helping children to understand traumatic experiences, learn new adaptive coping skills and consider different perspectives. Like other creative activities, using books can 'recall early memories of connection, attachment, and emotional closeness associated with early childhood' (Malchiodi 2008, p.169).

Through books, a child can see how others have confronted and solved similar problems, have encountered anxieties, frustrations, hopes and disappointments, and applied these insights to real-life situations with the support of the helping person, to gain understanding of alternative solutions to their problems. Abused children may find verbal methods threatening and forming therapeutic relationships difficult, so they repress curiosity and independent action. Therapeutic reading, dialoguing and writing from a prescribed book offers an 'innovative' approach (Pardeck 1990).

THERAPEUTIC WRITING IMPROVES SOCIAL RELATIONS FOR SHATTERED YOUNG PEOPLE

The effect of using self-knowledge gained by children through expressive writing about social conflicts can help prevent violence arising from racial, ethnic and sex discriminations. In a study in which children read and discussed relevant literature that reflects social conflicts and then worked on relationships using shared feelings through writing as self-narration and problem solving, it was found that there was a lessening of their reporting their social conflicts (Daiute and Buteau

2002). Narrative writing aids the development of understanding and of control in children, helping them to improve their position in their social world. Writing was used as a support for 'self-determination, social connection and, when necessary, protection' (Daiute, Buteau and Rawlins 2001). 'Being able to rein in emotional impulse', basing this on perception and understanding, is a learned social construct and therapeutic writing has been advocated as a key strategy for promoting children's emotional intelligence and social competence as 'it strengthens insight by pairing literature with mediation' (Sullivan and Strang 2003, p.76).

Zipora Shechtman uses stories – listening to or reading or writing them – as a 'basic human need to discover the truth, to understand, to find an explanation for painful experiences, and even to *challenge injustice*' (Shechtman and Or 1996, p.139; Shechtman 2009, p.26; emphasis added).

In a session, Nomif expressed his anger and aggression at his marginalisation and of the refusal by the authorities to allow him to work. I asked him to tell me about going to the Paralympic Games with a donated free ticket. He talked about how in his country people with disabilities are forgotten and 'are as good as dead'. He was spiritually moved to 'witness' their courage and dedication. This 'dialoguing' on the subject of how his own anger at being hurt could be put into perspective and move him away from it towards empathy with others, and acknowledgement of how hard it is to overcome disadvantage – this was something that he recognised through his own experience. The fact that good will, good spirit and courage existed outside of himself and set him an example, gave him hope.

We read together my dramatisation of Olive Schreiner's novel, *The Story of an African Farm*, charting the coming of age of three young people of mixed descent, growing up in the semi-desert of the South African Karoo in the 1860s, who are trying to exist within a dangerous, shifting and many-layered world (Baraitser 2000). The young people in the theatre piece are bullied by the harsh farm owner and her dishonest lover. One character remains obedient to her 'owners', the others, forced from the farm, struggle to discover their identity through menial work: one responds to unrequited love by withdrawal and the possibility of suicide, but the central character – a young woman determined to win her personal freedom – bears a child and lives independently of her lover. She is the future. The young refugees responded with their own stories of uncertain thoughts and dreams of fulfilment through work and love.

The poet Michael Rosen has written of how his father read Charles Dickens's *Great Expectations* aloud to the family on camping holidays in the 1950s, and the stories affected his life in a similar way. His was a poor family brought up in the grime and poverty of the East End of London, and the story dealt with how to make your own way into a better future.

> Part of the power of stories is the way in which we can see the facets of this or that fictional person in the people we know and the scenes from the fictional world have echoes in the events of the real world. As the book, and my father's reading of the book, and my feelings about the book developed, I felt from him a sense of yearning. Pip is desperate to get away from his old home...[and follow] the dream of a better life. The scenes became part of our daily language... I'd say that there is an added dimension, when books leave the page and become spoken out loud in a room full of people; of course they become live and vivid, but they also become social, they end up belonging to everyone in the room... at that moment. (Rosen 2011, pp.100, 107, 110)

This was true for the young trafficked women. Reading *Great Expectations* was helping them realise that they were not isolated in their ordeal. It was part of the long journey towards acceptance of their past and the glimpse of a way to heal.

ENACTMENTS
Children's group

1. If the group is new, you can play the warm-up game of 'connecting' where the children pair up and chant 'From my heart to your heart, I wish you well', following this with other parts of the body.

2. Read from the story *Matilda* by Roald Dahl.

3. Talk about Matilda's way of comforting herself when her parents are cruel and reject her for being a girl, while they praise her lazy, self-important brother – she imagines wonderful fantasy stories of being rescued.

4. Discuss the idea of bullying. Talk about Matilda's rescue by the good, young teacher who adopts her, and the value of the friendship of a boy in her class who is an 'outsider' like herself.

5. Ask the children to write a story about 'If I could make anything happen' and to share them by working in pairs or groups to enact these stories to present to the group.

6. Ask the children to write a birthday card to a person they love, with all the things on it that he/she loves about the person.

Young adults' group

1. Bring in passages from Dickens's autobiographical *David Copperfield*.

2. Read the passage aloud to each other.

3. Discuss Copperfield's abuse by his father and his submissive mother's loyalty to her husband, his feelings that he has no one to turn to and his self-determination and self-reliance in leaving his home to find his aunt, whom he knows only by name.

4. Discuss the kindness and moral firmness of his aunt, who takes him in.

5. Ask the young adults to write about their own feelings and thoughts at a time when they showed courage under harsh conditions and a time when someone showed them a kindness, or loved them. Ask if this changed them.

The discovery of the history of therapeutic intervention using literature gave me some ballast for my journey, but I soon realised that I needed to wade into the innovative ideas behind the processes that go into the practice of the discipline.

CHAPTER 6

Approaches

The 'affective' bibliotherapeutic approach I use originates from Freudian psychodynamics using the concepts of identification, projection, mirroring and insight. The process involves a triad connecting literature, participant and facilitator, which differs from therapy where the triad is participant-problem-therapist with no intermediary tool. I found that the latest cognitive behavioural therapies using self-help books in therapy, though they are cheap and effective with many adults, are not effective with young hurt people who have known war violence.

SELF-HELP OR USING A FACILITATOR: COGNITIVE BIBLIOTHERAPY OR AFFECTIVE BIBLIOTHERAPY?

There is a major split between two main schools of thought that use books as a therapeutic intervention – the 'cognitive' intervention, based on learning and the 'affective' intervention, based on feeling. Cognitive behavioural therapies assume that all behaviour is learned and so, with guidance, can be re-learned. Because it is evidence-based, it is most commonly used today. High-quality, nonfiction written material is used as the main agent of change. It is largely a self-help therapy using books, with minimal contact with a therapist. It is seen as an educationally orientated intervention with the main goals as mastering information and acquiring skills. Only when a specific programme/treatment exists are self-help books considered as bibliotherapy (McKendree-Smith, Floyd and Scogin 2003). The drawbacks are that it places more responsibility on the individual so the motivation and ability to use books and work independently become crucial. If a person is emotionally or intellectually not mature enough, the perception of the material can be distorted or reading levels may be limited. Because of the lack of contact with a caring facilitator, and the fact that some disturbed children may not be able to learn from reading on their own or have the motivation to change their behaviour or sufficient ego development to control their behaviour, this intervention is seldom used with children or adolescents.

The affective approach originates from Freudian psychodynamic theories. It needs the involvement of a facilitator or therapist who uses written material to uncover repressed thoughts and feelings. It is based on the idea that while a 'character' in a book works through a problem, the reader becomes emotionally involved in the struggle through identification with the literary character's experiences that mirror his or her own and then gains insight from the way the character solves problems. This needs fictional literature of merit 'so that it can mirror a person's dilemmas, and help him or her to connect to the emotions and pain with the minimum fear…bringing the child and adolescent indirectly to the edge of sensitive issues' (Shechtman 2009, p.20). Shrodes, a Freudian pioneer of the therapeutic intervention of books, saw the importance of: *identification* as an unconscious adaptive mechanism of self-regard through affiliation with another admired person or symbol; *abreaction and catharsis*, as a time when the client expresses some emotional release, which is 'important and is unique to the intervention because the facilitator is monitoring the client's emotional reactions to the reading and to its application'; and *insight and integration*, in which the facilitator guides the client to recognise the solutions to the problems presented in the book and to develop new strategies for dealing with it (Shrodes 1949 in Pardeck and Pardeck 1993, p.11).

This is the method that I use with hurt, young asylum seekers and refugees. It is about becoming aware of active wisdom through encounters with 'life's richness and complexity, through the sustainment of tender curiosity, and through the systematic support for more comfortable ways of telling, interacting and being' (Gersie 1997, p.156). With these methods, young asylum seekers using reading, dialoguing and expressive writing are guided to find ways to 'generate a lost sense of belonging and of being in charge of their lives, and helping them find a sense of home...' (Kohli and Mather 2003, p.201). This is not merely a cognitive understanding, but also an experiential one based on the opening of inner self-communication processes, and is a means of reaching repressed experiences. The drawbacks are that the richness and complexity of the intervention may prove overwhelming and provoke anxiety, or may not serve as a good 'model', and may be misunderstood or distorted by the young person's own experiences.

Objectives of affective bibliotherapy

The affective therapeutic intervention using literature:

- shows the reader that they are not the first to have problems

- makes the reader aware that there is more than one solution to their problems

- asks the reader to understand the character's and their own motivations for their behaviour in response to their problems

- helps the reader grasp their problem

- provides facts needed to solve problems

- encourages the reader to face their situation realistically.

(Gottschalk 1948 in Jack and Ronan 2008, p.175)

Here is an example of how this worked in practice with Nomif. He speaks Arabic and Italian, and though his spoken English is becoming more fluent, he finds writing English difficult. The fact that he is learning to write English gives him confidence that he can take part in life here. We had progressed in our relationship. I consider it the right time to introduce him to *When Rain Clouds Gather* by Bessie Head (2010). The writer was of mixed race and having a white mother made her unacceptable to both black people and white people. She fled South Africa for asylum in Botswana. Nomif identifies with her flight – his father was 'disappeared', causing his own flight to the UK. Head uses biblical references that Nomif, a Christian, recognises. Nomif was kept in detention where he witnessed young men taking their own lives in despair, after waiting several years for asylum without knowing what would happen to them, so he identifies with the main character, Makhaya, a young black man who escapes from a South African prison where he is badly treated as a political prisoner. 'He is like me, a survivor,' he remarks. The book's hero has enough courage to climb two very high barbed-wire fences to cross the border into independent Botswana. In Nomif's detention camp there was just such a fence. If you tried to escape, you tore your hands, but more often broke your leg and were taken back in again. Nomif was told he would not be deported, so he didn't try to escape. The hero says he is not sure who is his 'brother'.

> NOMIF: He is like me, coming to a strange place. Not knowing who to trust. This man is in the same position as me.
>
> FACILITATOR: Yet he makes friends, he changes his view. When he was in prison, he was 'a wild man'. He didn't know how to control himself.
>
> NOMIF: Yes, I felt the same when I was in prison. I felt helpless until I learned to control myself. It was up to me.
>
> FACILITATOR: You picked yourself up, you showed determination and courage.

Nomif feels good about this.

Bibliotherapy in relation to psychotherapy: book-client-facilitator versus client-problem-therapist

Zipora Shechtman, who uses books therapeutically with groups of aggressive children and adolescents, defines the technique as fostering a triad connecting literature, participant and facilitator. This is different from therapy where 'the triad…might be designated as participant-problem-therapist. There is no intermediary tool…' (Hynes and Hynes-Berry 1994, p.11).

The process of using literature therapeutically is continuous, with a participant making their own connections between ideas, images and feelings. It is a creative process, a naming or redefining process of self-actualisation bridging the inner and outer world with language in the form of metaphor or imagery that links the text with the individual's lesser known self. The facilitator's role is to bond with the individual, forming a therapeutic alliance with the individual, using each person's own responses to literature to show powerful ways in which thoughts and feelings may be changed through interaction with characters and plots in good stories. It is up to the facilitator to encourage the identification process, to alleviate emotions and express them, and to help the client understand and express these emotions in a non-judgemental way (Shechtman 2009).

The texts used are properly understood and not distorted through the asylum seekers' or refugees' needs. You are sustaining interest and curiosity in life's ways and encourage an encountering of them.

ENACTMENTS
Children's group

1. Invite the children to draw the outline of each other's hands. In each outline, they can name or draw a person or organisation that helped them survive, then outline another hand and describe five ways that they have helped others to survive.

2. Read or tell a traditional African story, *The Great Tug of War*, about the small hare Mmutla who uses his wits to trick the powerful animals – the elephant and the hippo – who rule him, to take part in a tug of war with each other.

3. Ask the children to draw pictures of this, then write about an event in which they (or a person they know) survived, showing courage.

4. Share and talk about these, asking questions about how to organise life experiences and gain strength from them for their lives in the present.

5. Ask them to write a survival diary, focusing on how they face challenges, manage changes in their lives and make sense of what is happening.

6. Share these, emphasising the importance of their stories, acknowledging their impacts and praising the way the child survives it (Echterling and Stewart 2008, pp.196–199).

Freud's guiding work was invaluable in opening up reading and writing to hurt young people, but I knew there were social psychologists and bibliotherapists who had spent their lives developing unique approaches and techniques and publishing them, whose work I could explore and include in my own attempts to formulate effective processes to implement in practice.

CHAPTER 7

Processes

The value of literature in helping hurt young people depends on its capacity to encourage a therapeutic response. Conventional treatment techniques are difficult to use with abused children, who often find verbal methods of assessment and treatment threatening. They have problems forming therapeutic relationships and find it difficult to take independent action. Using books that lead to therapeutic creative writing offers an innovative way forward. 'Bibliotherapy may be seen as a preventive tool' (Pardeck 1998, p.7). If you can use a book as a compass, you can find your way, and if you can find a language for your feelings, you can 'own them and not be owned by them…[you are] enriched as mind and emotion work together instead of against each other' (Winterson 2011, p.144).

STEPS ALONG THE WAY

Arleen Hynes and Dr Mary Hynes-Berry established the first hospital-based training programme in facilitating therapeutic writing in Washington DC in the 1970s.

They identify the order of the steps in the process they forged:

- catching the attention by reading (recognition)

- looking at the issues and the personal feeling response (examination)

- coming to the first level of understanding of deeper issues in the light of new feelings emerging in the dialogue (juxtaposition)

- evaluating the insights and integrating them (self-application).

(Hynes and Hynes-Berry 1994)

They feel that 'a kind of wisdom' comes from these interventions because they address an understanding of the self; the process through which this understanding emerges must not be confused with a 'classroom discussion of literature or in a traditional therapy session' (Hynes and Hynes-Berry 1994). The value of literature depends on its capacity to encourage a therapeutic response. What the individual is feeling while reading a text with others is more important than understanding its meaning – so even a misinterpretation of a text can be considered as useful if it leads to the release of feelings or insights related to self-understanding.

Assigned and shared reading of stories has the effect of not only providing information, but also of stimulating discussion about what is troubling the young people, airing new values and attitudes, and allowing the group to realise that others have similar problems and the realistic means of solving them.

Appropriate stories also offer the young reader a basis for moral judgement that helps them to tell the difference between right and wrong. They provide models for identification – as Bettleheim phrases it: '"Who do I want to be like?" is a more important question to a child than "Do I want to be good?"' (Bettleheim 1977).

A GUIDANCE MODEL: ENCOURAGING THE CHILD TO ASK THE RIGHT QUESTIONS AT THE RIGHT TIME

Shechtman, drawing from Prochaska's work (Prochaska 1999), has devised a guidance model on how to select effective books for the different stages of trauma in angry, hurt and aggressive adolescents and children, so they may gain control of themselves.

In the 'precontemplative' stage, the children are too overwhelmed to see themselves, or anyone else objectively, and they may react defensively. Questions are not asked at this stage. They need to understand the causes of their position, which they often repress, so they need books that deal with others victimised in a similar way so they can identify with them and apply this to their understanding of their own lives.

The stage of *preparation* begins when the child is motivated by the facilitator to explore the possibility of change because they are able to incorporate new understanding and values and feel empathy. At this stage, the children ask: 'Why did this happen to me and why is it important to make a change?' Books used at this stage may be about victimisation to help their difficulty in trusting others, to identify feelings and develop empathy and to encourage discussion about their fears, anxieties, helplessness and sorrows.

At the *contemplative evaluating and clarifying stage* the young people begin to understand the *motives* of a character with whom they are identifying. They ask: 'Why was this done to me?' The texts used here involve the children in exploring their feelings and what triggers them, to see how these feelings lead them to behave in a certain way and the results of their behaviour. Books may concern the perpetrator of their feelings – how to manage feelings and to examine power issues.

The final, more complex and difficult 'action' stage occurs when the *young person realises he/she must make an effort to change*, using the facilitator as a secure model. Books are chosen to deal with the young people's insecurity and their lack of trust in their own ability to change. The question they ask at this stage is: 'How do I overcome the obstacles to making my behaviour change?' The literature here uses displacement that reflects their own problems and ways of thinking about them. Praise and reinforcement of positive behavioural shifts that come from discussion of the stories and poems around this helps to achieve an understanding that may move them forward.

The *maintenance stage* is about the young person sustaining this change, though relapses may occur.

Finalisation of sessions takes place with clients knowing they can turn to other relationships in their lives, which can lessen their reliance on the facilitator to outline their positions using texts (Shechtman 2009). Shechtman's stages of involvement take about six months to complete, whereas those with war-traumatised, displaced children may take much longer, as their burden is greater and more menacing (Prochaska 1999; Shechtman 2009). Jonathan Detrixhe finds in the work of Shechtman 'a true believer and an empiricist' (Detrixhe 2010, p.61).

PROCESSES IN MY WORKING
THERAPEUTIC MODEL
The reading: encouraging active listening

The listening asylum seeker listens not only to the voice of the one who reads aloud a relevant passage from a selected inspiring book, but also to their own inner voice – they are *hearing* their own response to the words.

Most young survivors come from an oral tradition in which listening to stories is customary. Ben Okri describes how, as a child growing up within his Nigerian culture, it was a natural, everyday occurrence to listen to, and invent, stories and then tell them to amuse other children. His memory of this oral story-telling came to be part of his writing much later:

> I was told stories, we were all told stories as kids in Nigeria. We had to tell stories which would keep one another interested, and you weren't allowed to tell stories that everybody else knew. You had to dream up new ones… And it never occurred to us that those stories actually contained a unique worldview… [It was] only after a period of loneliness and homesickness away from Nigeria, that slowly all those old stories came back to me with new faces and new voices. And I saw that all human beings have their signatures stamped in the stories they tell themselves in dreams, the stories that are embedded in their childhood. (Okri and Emeagwali 1992)

Listening in a group when literature is read aloud is a shared social experience, so the listening process becomes even more powerful as it allows a social experience of intimacy and intensity. Jane Davis, of The Reader Organisation, describes how, in a reading group, 'the public exposure of some customarily unadmitted truth…seemed almost dangerous, as if the air…was cracking with human electricity… The fact that it is being performed, means people can identify with the characters more easily, and feelings can surface more readily, yet they can remain anonymous' (Davis 2011, p.133).

The facilitator, too, listens

The elicited enunciated response to a text is a kind of collaboration. To listen accurately as a facilitator is a learned skill. It is easy to miss the full significance of what a hurt child or young person is saying because of your own unconscious emotional responses. You also need to listen to what is *not* being said. In a reading and writing session, we are all listening, together and alone, to a *written* text that is read aloud, which contains transformational elements. This joint 'listening' draws us together in a communal process, involving complex thoughts and feelings, even though we are listening separately to each other.

Each young survivor's vulnerability is ongoing. Their past remains to haunt them: many have been told by their torturers that no one will believe them; others are left feeling ashamed or cannot speak about what happened to them as they are not used to discussing problems with strangers. You continue to act as a witness to these problems, by listening with empathy and understanding, and this becomes an act of empowerment for the survivors who are doing the telling in response to a story. These are safe boundaries in a safe setting.

So listening becomes a flexible and open collaboration, painstakingly built. By initiating mirroring and projection through other people's stories, you encourage a new way of taking hold of the re-enactments of a disturbing past that continues to disrupt ordinary life. They may see you as too powerful and think that all relationships are possibly dangerous. So you can expect some breakdown in the relationships you are building, and there should be a support system for reviewing your work.

Now you're talking

The young asylum seekers become involved enough in the hearing of the story to begin a discussion. This time, the listener hears thoughts and opinions from others that modify the inner voice, learns from the group, seeing, hearing him or herself in relation to others in a similar position. Revelatory moments happen when the young people begins to *talk* about their thoughts and feelings through those of the literary characters they have discussed. By openly talking about these 'characters' in an appropriate book, and how they reflect their own setbacks, knowledge of violence and helplessness that they, like the character in the text, have known and felt and to which we in the group bear witness, so they begin to allow the final processes of healing: they begin to see their position and their life differently, learning how to be flexible, how to counteract unfairness, develop judgement,and finally, gain insight and be able to re-story themselves. At last, their stories link past, present and future in a way that tells them where they have been, where they are and where they are going (Taylor 1996).

Therapeutic conversations

Shechtman stresses that before the therapeutic process can be initiated at all, a bond must be established that allows 'therapeutic conversations'. The young people must sense that this relationship is different from the destructive relationships they know, because the facilitator cares about them (Shechtman 2009).

Ravi Kohli, writing on social work practice with unaccompanied asylum-seeking children and young people in the UK, writes that his key finding was the need to establish a complex and robust relationship with each young person that is 'honest, clear, realistic and precise', which takes time to establish and needs emotional engagement with the young person's story. He found that the relationship should lay foundations for reciprocity, so the young person would in turn become honest and realistic, too. The relationship aims for 'cohesion, connection and coherence' in which you are a collaborator and a companion holding the 'permeable line between friendship and professional assistance' (Kohli 2006, p.5). You are trying to connect events, people and feelings that help them to experience containment and safely connect their inner and outer worlds. You become 'memory-holders' for the lives of the young people, who fear these memories will be lost. Your role is to deconstruct, and reconstruct life stories of asylum and trauma giving a sense of a fresh start and the rhythms of ordinary life.

Expressive writing of their stories: becoming their own listening reader

In the wake of the reading, listening and talking together about a piece of literature, when the person is no longer afraid of acknowledging their fear or pain I encourage them to write their own stories. It is this process that is most valuable because, as we have seen, it is a way of recreating their identity – a more likeable identity in which the self talks to the self and hears it – they become their 'own imagined reader, a listening, watching presence', finding meaning in the words being written (Hunt 2000). 'Expressive and explorative writing is really a process of deep listening… You listen to yourself *after* you write, rereading' (Bolton 2011, p.18).

The beauty of writing as a therapeutic intervention (apart from the practical fact that it costs so little) is that young survivors can pick it up any time, which gives them an added sense of independence and self-reliance and an awareness that they can work towards their understanding of themselves independently.

Buchi Emecheta, the Nigerian writer who was married to a violent man (chosen by her father) by whom she had five children in six years, tells us that if something worried her and no one was listening to her, she put it on paper, then read it to someone, and this was therapeutic (Emecheta 1974). Anne Frank, in her war diary, tells us: '…the brightest spot of all is that at least I can write down all my thoughts and feelings; otherwise I'd absolutely suffocate…' (Frank 1954, p.151).

Writing allows young survivors a chance to hear themselves more clearly for the first time, and to think more clearly about themselves and their situation in the past and in the present.

> Writing creates tangible footprints which can, and probably will be followed… The process of gaining insight is three-staged: first the dash onto the page, then rereading to the self, then…reading and sharing with a…chosen other [or others]. (Bolton 2011, p.19)

But expressive writing is also different from talking. It gives confidence in a different way:

> It can allow an exploration of cognitive, emotional and spiritual areas otherwise not accessible, and an expression of elements otherwise inexpressible. The very act of creativity – of making something on the page that wasn't there before – tends to increase self-confidence, feelings of self-worth and motivation for life. (Bolton *et al.* 2004, p.1)

Part of the process of using books therapeutically is about this final releasing self-expression in writing. No word written by a survivor can be wrong. It is a process to release deep feelings and memories – a series of choices that are entirely in the hands of the young survivor. It can be a form of private, inner healing, which may be shared with a group.

Although the informal discussions that arise from the readings often reveal the most telling thoughts and feelings about past traumas and present lives, it is the linking of these *discussions* from *the reading* of the appropriate text with the *writing* from them that cements the process. It can take any form: a poetic phrase, a story, a symbolic image, a diary entry – the choice is theirs. Writing arises *because* of the discussion we have shared, and it is this writing that has the greatest effect. As Danny Abse, poet and doctor, wrote: 'Whatever else poems do, or do not do, at the very least they profoundly alter the man or woman who wrote them' (Abse 1998). This is the process when the deepest thinking takes place, when the past self faces the present one using a bridge of words.

Sheila Hayman, director of the writing group Write to Life for adult asylum seekers and refugees, comments that the process is a:

> …tricky business needing constant sensitivity. What do you do when somebody writes an account of an event which is vivid and detailed except for the violent death at the centre of it which is dismissed in one blank sentence? We know that the reason may be the self-protective way memory can strip out emotion and only leave the bare facts. But it is the emotion we need to get to… There are no rules for these situations; only mutual trust and knowledge, and attention to instinct, can steer us safely through. (Hayman in Bolton 2011, p.166)

In our sessions, the hurt young people write expressively to a subject that comes out of their reading of the text. I praise whatever they write, accept it gladly as a gift and an achievement that concerns their growth and self-worth. 'The focus of therapeutic writing is on the process not the product' (Bolton *et al.* 2006, p.21). This ability to think from having written something about themselves gives them independence – a sense of control over their past experiences. The choice to take part in the acts of reading and writing always come from the troubled young person and not from the facilitator. It gives back the responsibility to the individual to make the gesture towards creativity, self-growth, spirituality and well-being that come from reading and writing.

Traumatised young people often feel incompetent in their ability to feel and they, especially, need to hear, to tell and to write stories so they may think about what they feel. Reading, telling and writing stories are extremely useful tools for traumatised children: they help them to release emotions, provide possible solutions to their own problems, encourage them to talk about their own problems, allow them to witness cultures different from their own, provide them with other interests to follow and give them grounds for self-reflection (Pardeck and Pardeck in Pehrsson 2005).

Finally, showing

We arranged an exhibition, for an invited audience, of the young people's written work from several sessions accompanied by their photographs of the 'geography' of the places where they live (see the Introduction to this volume). This went on to be shown at the Group Psychoanalytic Society conference, 'Cultures, conflict, creativity', in London in 2012. Both exhibitions of their written work gave the young people a sense of self-confidence in their creative ability and self-worth.

STORIES AS MEDIATORS

'With their playful character and their closeness to fantasy, intuitions and irrationality', stories can be used as mediators in therapy – the more fantasy in the story the better (Peseschkian 1986 in Shechtman 2009, p.200). Individuals can identify with characters but at the same time feel protected and associate with the story, and so talk about their conflicts and needs, but the facilitator can suggest changes in a position 'which has the character of a game', so the person sees his 'own-sided' position (Shechtman 2009).

I brought to a session with the young adult's group Sholem Aleichem's story *Today's Children* (1987), which is about Tevye, a man with one horse and a cart and a couple of cows (a background familiar to the group) whose sense of humour crosses boundaries. Tevye's daughter begs to marry the man of her choice. Tevye thinks he's 'a nothing' (*nebech*), 'a tailor boy'. 'Do you plan to feed your wife on matching vests?' he asks. Instead, he has chosen for her a rich, widowed butcher to marry. But after she breaks down in tears and begs him to allow her to marry the man of her choice, Tevye finally gives in, removing his chances of ever becoming a rich man. 'My daughter, she is crying and kissing me until we are both wet all over.' What took me by surprise was that on hearing this end to the story the group burst into spontaneous applause, approving Tevye's difficult but moral choice.

It is necessary to keep in mind that some cultures expect children to contain their feelings, so being asked to 'express' them can be interpreted as intrusive and counterproductive to producing a safe environment. So hearing a story can be comforting to them, rather than risking exposing their feelings to others by writing them. Their parents may feel that long-term creative interventions may be intrusive or merely 'playing' and so do not help their children's problems to do with their trauma. I had to learn to take note of the implications of a story from another culture. At a session with the young adult's group, we read together from copies of the story *A Handful of Dates* by the Sudanese writer Tayeb Salih (1985), then head of drama at BBC Arabic. It is set in Egypt and is about a Muslim boy who respects his grandfather until he begins to realise his grandfather's greed has driven him to cruelly wrest the land from his neighbour, Masood, who is poor and weak. Dates are grown on the land, which his grandfather is gradually appropriating, from which he is becoming wealthy. His grandfather gives his grandson a handful of dates to eat, which, when he realises they have been gained at the poor neighbour's expense, he spews out as a sign of his new awareness of his grandfather's greed.

The story was read with great interest and there was much discussion of the boy's sensitivity and ability to change. The wealth earned by greed is suspect. I was taken aback by one young man's reaction to the story. He felt that all grandfathers, no matter how badly they behaved, were only to be tolerated and respected. Supporting the boy rather than the grandfather went against his own deep cultural values.

USING WRITING AND READING AS HUMOUR AND 'PLAY'

Writing can sometimes be a form of play, a way in which a young survivor can act out a sense of buoyancy, humour and fun, in which experiences, thoughts and feelings can be 'acted out' in words. It helps to normalise past experiences by recreating them more positively. It is a form of self-soothing that enhances support and enriches relationships. It helps the young people to take heart (Malchiodi 2008).

Here is Amina's description of the pillow provided for her by her foster family – a moment she describes with great humour in her journal as a way of objectifying her anger about her 'difference' from the foreign culture that she sometimes feels is suffocating her. The writing also reflects her confusion as to how to deal with her dilemma – whether she should try and accept the new cultural mores or reject them as foreign to her. She projects these feelings onto the pillow she finds on her bed: it is a shape-shifter – a symbolic double character, a dubious friend or foe. The piece also expresses Amina's confusion about her inner and outer selves that she is trying to connect with one another. The writing brings her a measure of relief and pleasure. She can hardly wait to read it aloud to me.

> This pillow won't leave me alone. It wants to be friends with me. Why won't the pillow go away and find a place at the end of the bed? I don't mind which side really. As long as it is not near me. I don't want to smell it or ever feel its smooth silky cloth near. But alas! Every night when I toss and turn in my dreams, the pillow's

right next to me. Sometimes I get so angry at it, then I'm forced to open my eyes, get hold of it and throw it as far as I can away from me. However much I try, I think that maybe it gets lonely at night because it looks different from the other pillows and there's no one on my bed that looks like me, so then the pillow feels like maybe we can become friends. On my bed there are pillows that look like the same – like two look the same and the other two look the same. Something really bad happened this morning. I woke up and right next to me was the pillow. I think I should really give it a name. I will call it 'Wiggy Pillow'. The thing is Wiggy Pillow!

When I ask Amina to talk about this piece of writing, she says:

I get so angry with this pillow. I want to get hold and throw it. At night, it's different from the other pillows. Like me, it's different. It's Wiggy Pillow. I'm different too. So we can become friends. I like it. It's soft. But when I'm sleeping, I don't want it. I didn't choose the pillow.

Writing about her anger and pain with such wry humour allows her to accept the limitations of her 'real' situation, acknowledging the good within it too – a true development.

TAKING SMALL STEPS ALONG THE WAY

'Titration', or helping to release troubled feelings and memories little by little, is one of the aims of the therapeutic writing intervention with traumatised children (Rothchild 2000).

The next step in my journey with Nomif was undertaken at a further session with the help of Elizabeth Laird's *The Garbage King* (2004), about street children in an African town and their means of survival. Nomif's past experiences were reflected in those of the street children, to the point where he was able to recognise the name of towns he knew, which gave him confidence in the book. I suggest he builds his own word-list by going to the library and looking up the new words from the story, which gives him a sense of purpose.

The passage from the book we use this time deals with a boy who is wealthy but bullied by an ambitious father who plans to send him away, so he runs away. Nomif, too, had to flee his country, and he identifies with the pain, loneliness, exhaustion, hunger and isolation of the boy in the story.

I suggest he writes down his own survivor's story. He writes:

> I was holding on under the lorry going on the motorway, and when it stopped on the motorway my friend and I escaped from under the lorry. We had to walk and we don't know which way. We are walking all night. My friend, he dropped. Someone phoned the ambulance who came and took us to Oxford. They checked my friend, they feed him and give him some injection. I didn't want them to see me so they don't feed me. So then I begged from the people in the streets of Oxford and I go to Birmingham because they tell me there is a community of my people there. They tell me to go to the Home and they send me back home… But I came again.

ENACTMENTS
Children's group

1. As a warm-up, pass an endearing stuffed animal around the group, with each child saying how they are feeling and what they would like to talk about.

2. Create a safe place in the room and ask them to create a pose, then tap each person to ask them to show and tell the group what their space looks like, what it contains and what they are doing there.

3. Ask each person to make sculptures, using 'characters' that threaten them. Then ask them to step away and make changes, telling their feelings to the group. Or they may create a wax museum containing characters from their past that reflect their feelings and situations about a theme such as anger or hate, and the others can walk through it.

4. Enact these 'characters'. The rest of the group should question them. Write stories about them.

Young adults' group
Reconnecting, establishing safety, empowerment with humour

1. Read aloud together Sholem Aleichem's story *On Account of a Hat* (1953). It is about a young man from the *shtetl* returning home on a train anxious not to be late for his wife's celebratory dinner, who finds to his horror that he has by mistake picked up the hat of the important official sitting next to him on the station. Everyone treats him with a deference entirely false to him. He is forced to return to the station, replace the hat and arrive home late for dinner, to an enraged wife.

2. Ask the group to talk about their own humorous incidences of frustration within their everyday lives that involve their need for finding a safe place.

3. Write about stories they know about how to face dangerous and frustrating situations realistically, and how to find workable solutions that give a measure of empowerment.

4. Read these aloud and share.

5. Enact them.

I was on my mettle – after a lifetime spent with literature, I needed to sift and sort the books I knew that were of great truth and impact, to find appropriate texts that applied to, or transformed, traumatised young people's problems in a way they could absorb and use them effectively. This meant trawling through not only English literature, but also world literature in translation.

CHAPTER 8

Transformative Books

A Key to Unlocking Trauma

There is a difference between resilience and developmental growth in relation to trauma: resilience is about being able to go on with life after extreme hardship, whereas post-traumatic growth is harder to achieve because it is transformative – it changes self-understanding and so the quality of life. This cannot always be achieved: the book and the facilitator's use of it need to give the individual a realistic sense of hope, not a false one, and to give information about the problem being presented. Therapeutic reading/writing groups that persist are composed of self-selected people who are naturally drawn to reading and writing and who are able to put their emotional experiences into words more readily (Pennebaker 2002a).

SELECTING BOOKS THAT TRANSFORM

It is important that a selected text presents complex emotions, thoughts, character development and morals about the dilemmas of being human under great trial, and always includes an element of hope. It should be literary, in the sense that the book itself as a structure and a work of art moves us with the quality with which it is composed and written – in itself a courageous and moral act that reinforces a sense of life humanely lived. The books should be about universal values: fairness, moral choices, a belief in freedom and the value of each individual and the ability of characters who live by these values to survive (Chavis 2011).

Encouraging the imaginative creation of identity

A book should encourage imaginative interpretations, allowing a hurt young person to imagine or free-associate about what they would do in a character's circumstances, *allowing them to identify with themselves.* 'The story and the fantasies it inspires become like a transitional space, a special world of play and exploration that is exciting yet safe, because it exists both outside the individual and reality' – a form of play before identifying, or taking responsibility for a problem (Winnicott cited by Caspary in Detrixhe 2010, p.69). Books can be the middle ground that excite feelings, which can flow into the interchange between you and the young person (Detrixhe 2010).

Themes projected by the selected text need to include universality, power and simplicity (rather than being simplistic), with the structure of the text not being too complex or too long. The themes should be explicit enough for the purpose, and positive, though the material can also be used to help identify negative feelings that can lead to change. The book should enhance the value of personhood, enlighten interpersonal relationships and orientate the young reader towards a grasp of reality. Level of vocabulary is also an area to consider, otherwise the young refugee may simply be cut out from 'imagining' by lack of a means to understand the text in the first place.

Comfort and reassurance from appropriate books

To use a story so that it transforms a life of a traumatised young person, a facilitator needs to judge the level of projection and identification that is comfortable for the individuals concerned at each phase of their development. You want them to understand the fictional characters in terms of themselves *as they are at that moment in time* and to learn from what the characters feel, think and do. Sometimes a hurt young person cannot yet empathise with anyone, or a young person may intellectualise the problem revealed in a text, rather than gain insight from it. If the text represents a young person's hurt too closely the young person may refuse responsibility for solving the problems within his or her life situation, feel threatened and withdraw (Pardeck and Pardeck 1984a). Stories, symbolic characters and metaphors (and the use of 'play' in relation to them) encourages indirect discussion of the young people's problems, by providing an indirect, safe way to talk about them that gives comfort and reassurance (Malchiodi 2008). As an adolescent, Jeanette Winterson watched her mother burn all the books she revered and had secreted under her mattress, because they were 'of the Devil'. But, with her great resilience of spirit, she realised that the books were already imprinted on her mind and her soul, and that they could never be eradicated. She memorised whole passages from these books to keep up her spirits, especially when she was locked in the freezing coal-hole all night long. 'What they held was already inside me, and together, we would get away' – what the stories and characters meant to her had a transformative effect on her being (Winterson 2012, p.42). This is what therapeutic interventions using books is about.

Context: readiness is all

As a therapeutic facilitator using books, you are with children and young people at different stages of their development. The individual's readiness for such an intervention is key: you both need to agree on the presenting problem that has been explored in depth in sessions with a therapist, and the book should reflect this readiness of the young person involved.

You should also know the adolescent's reading level and interests so you are able to suggest a book rather than prescribe it. In matching the story to the disturbed young person's life, there is the danger of oversimplifying the process or reducing the range of the discussion, though books with uncertain endings can lead to open-ended discussions offering alternative solutions to problems (Pardeck and Pardeck 1984b). The reading of the book is followed by discussion and interaction, together with other art activities such as creative discussion and role-play (Pardeck and Pardeck 1993). In using selected books, the opportunity for interaction and relational factors with the young people can be seen as more important than the gaining of insight (Caspary 1993). You also have to be aware that books are complicated, and people's reactions to them are even more so (Detrixhe 2010).

The young refugees are in cultural confusion and may feel more at home reading a text about their home country that has been translated into English that reminds them of and reconnects them with 'home'. Cultural relevance and applicability of theme and characters to each person's or group's level of development and their current situation is also important.

The role of age and gender in book selection

Age and gender matter in the selection of a book. Young children like more concrete situations in the books they read and enjoy reading about sibling problems or difficult parents, whereas adolescents are concerned about social problems and areas around friendship and relationships, respect and fairness. Boys are interested in the nature of power, but girls of a similar age are interested in intimacy. Young children like to have stories read to them; 10–12-year-olds love fantasy. Older adolescents prefer war stories and romances that reflect their lives, whereas late adolescents like stories that deal with values, society and unusual human experiences, and stories about transition to adulthood (Pardeck 1998).

The role of books is a *developmental* one at a stage when a young person is able to be objective enough to their problems to be able to incorporate change that involves learning to confront personal feelings, self-identity and self-worth. It requires a responsiveness to words and their meanings and a need to link this with feelings, thoughts and memory. A hesitancy to write occurs more in a group of young men than in one composed of only women. Some of the young women ask for sessions on their own, as they feel more inhibited in their writing and in saying what they feel when witnessed by a group of young men who have retained their own cultural attitudes towards women – there are usually twice as many male refugees as there are female asylum seekers.

Bringing in The Soul Bird

I gave a session with a mixed group of 10–13-year-olds who had recently been through several emotional upheavals such as moving schools or coping with problems of puberty (not having their own space, gender issues), managing difficult feelings towards carers, feelings about absent fathers and distracted mothers, family breakdown or evictions.

The session is about understanding and acknowledging powerful hidden feelings.

I bring in *The Soul Bird* by Michal Snunit (2004), a children's book with bold line drawings of the 'soul bird'. The symbolic bird contains a person's soul: it reacts to the way the person is treated by responding with a set of feelings hidden in locked drawers deep in that person's soul. When a person is hurt, the bird is restless and suffers pain, but when the person is loved, the bird hops about and grows and makes the person feel good. A person is encouraged to unlock their 'soul bird's' drawers once in a while, and to look into his or her emotions, like happiness, frustration, jealousy or hatred. The book, by displacement, allows the children to become aware of the complexity of having strong feelings, and sometimes mixed feelings about the same person, and ways of dealing with this. It is also a way of revealing their inner self-image.

I begin by asking the children to write down in a short time anything that comes into their heads – a form of 'freeing up' – to read aloud. I mention that the 'soul bird' turns the drawers upside down so all the rubbish at the bottom is turned out and that 'rubbish' can be different and interesting. Kei say he sometimes feels as if he's 'rubbish' – 'kind of dirty'.

From the free writing, Adri has written a kind of poem made up of single words with great spaces between. Adri often blocks her true difficulties and feelings about her situation as a coping mechanism: her mother is considering returning home, they are being evicted and Adri misses her television.

We read *The Soul Bird* aloud together, each person taking a page of the text and showing us the pen-drawn pictures they have made of the 'soul bird'. The language is at the right level for this group.

I suggest the children write a second piece about what they like about their soul bird – what it looks like, and what it feels like to be inside it: 'What it is saying to you? It could be letting a feeling, a secret or a dream out of one of your drawers.' The poem below shows the effectiveness and appropriateness of the book.

Erit, the youngest class member, wrote:

My soul bird is a giant bald eagle…
My soul bird cares
Never tears its beak
Sometimes it sheds tears
It loves you
My soul bird is very lazy
It makes you feel special
It never turns its back on you.

We write down their feelings, and the opposites of these feelings, and we talk about the fact that we can sometimes feel both at once towards one person – perhaps a carer – and it is acceptable to do this. Making the children aware of how normal it is to have complex and difficult feelings relieves them of suppressed feelings of guilt and inadequacy.

AIMS OF BRINGING BOOKS INTO PLAY

Drawing out responses

In working with children and adolescents, along with structured activities, the important skills of drawing out necessary responses by asking questions is used more than in other therapies (Leichtentritt and Shechtman 1998). These responses may be about the content of the books used so that the young people understand the dynamics of the characters and events in the story or poems. Or they may relate to the children's experiences, helping them to explore their own issues and directing them to self-understanding. Questions must be open-ended, encouraging self-reflection.

The skill of reassuring

Reassurance, approval, encouragement and reflecting feelings are all necessary skills. Being able to interpret responses and behaviour, and challenge the young people to take decisions in behaviour change in a constructive way, are key skills in achieving insights into the cause and effect of their problems. The aim is the encouragement of a private response more deeply felt and thought about that also can be shared as a public admission of feelings and thoughts (often in a trusted group), to gain self-awareness and self-discovery.

Therapeutic or creative writing?

Gillie Bolton believes that there is no real distinction between therapeutic writing and creative writing. People write because they need to write: 'Much creative writing is deeply therapeutic [and] therapeutic writing is creative. Its very creativity is one of the therapeutic benefits.' However, the point of therapeutic writing is not to make art that reaches a wider public. 'Writing…is a skill and an art. Therapeutic writing is deeply supportive, self-illuminating and personal.' It releases deep fears and memories that may be painful, but are never wrong. Once it is outside yourself, it can be shared with others (Bolton *et al.* 2004, p.2).

MATCHING BOOK TO INDIVIDUAL

Primarily, a facilitator will need to match the book to the needs of the individual – this is often an educated guess, though you will need to know about the issues each person presents, their state of mind, emotions, level of trust and past traumas. The therapeutic stories you bring in, whether to a group or in a one-to-one session, will be in relation to each young person's age, racial and ethnic background, stage of development, gender needs, sexual orientation and literacy level. The selected text needs to encourage the stories the young traumatised person wants to tell, but bear in mind that many of the young people find self-expression too frightening, or their cultural mores do not encourage this form of dealing with trauma. The story in each book should encourage a sense of the possibility of survival in new circumstances, empowerment and hope, despite the difficult odds. It is also important that they realise the telling of their stories is purely for them or for those in a similar situations, and to reassure them that no one is going to judge, ignore or deride the writing they do from the books.

To see how this works, we return to Asoum and Nomif. At this moment in time, they have gained in confidence. British Rail has provided Asoum with a guide because of his disability, so he can now catch the train to go on the annual therapeutic retreat at the seaside. He is troubled by escaping into drink and drugs, but is working through this and hopes to apply to college to study international politics. Nomif, too, is to go on the retreat. He admits that he has never been taught how to put his face underwater and the sea is too full of salt, but I encourage him to have a go in the sea, which he does. He works (and finds himself clothes) as a volunteer for Oxfam. He is continuing to try to improve his ability to read and write in English.

I have brought in Bessie Head's *When Rain Clouds Gather* (2010) for us to read aloud together. Asoum giggles because the old woman in the story insists that Makhaya, the hero, is 'handsome and not a black dog'. This is how wants to be seen, though the reference to the black dog is not about skin colour but about depression. In the story, Makhaya admits to the old woman, the 'good mother' in the story, that he blames the whole world for his own troubles, but that he must become responsible for himself.

FACILITATOR: Like you have done, by applying to study.

ASOUM: Oh, I dressed up in a suit, I filled in the forms...

FACILITATOR: But it was you who decided to reach out and change things.

ASOUM: At home it was illegal to study – the president would only allow you to find 'work'. They bullied me. Now I got to university, but no one will give me a job because of my handicap. The old woman in the book has faith and trust, but the young man has none. There are always people who will try and stop you.

Nomif suggests that you can trust God, but that it is very hard to trust in human beings, and Asoum adds that they let you down.

I say that the hero in the book, Makhaya, slowly learns to trust a young immigrant agriculturalist who helps the community improve the growing of crops. He is also learning to trust himself and his judgement. I ask Asoum if he trusts himself more. He says: 'I do now. I was drinking too much. It doesn't work.' I say: 'That is a great achievement.'

In the next session we will go into the matter of dealing with that 'black dog' depression.

ENACTMENTS
Children's group
Making a coherent narrative of their lives

1. Talk about making a book together: word-pictures connecting our memory-feelings.

2. Ask the children to choose word-pictures that are memories of things that are funny, good, difficult to understand, secret, thrilling, important, things they are good at and a place from their past that is special (its smells, sounds, people, what they did there and their feelings about it).

3. Ask the children to write and share these word-pictures. These can be in a child's original language, which can be translated.

4. Make drawings for these word-pictures.

5. Ask the children to use them to write their own life-stories in a few lines.

6. Print the words, stories and images to form a book. Read from the book and show it to others.

The task of selecting appropriate books with which to approach devastated children and adolescents is challenging and complex. Creative interventions, like any therapeutic approach, require a rationale, an understanding of basic principles and experience. I needed to find out if any formal guidance was available in this task.

CHAPTER 9

Core Competencies

Training and Organisations

If a facilitator is a practising creative writer – training in his or her own right – they bring to the sessions an understanding of the working of the imagination and the use of words as a way of self-expression. Training in literature and group management, and in psychology, are also important. The emphasis of the work is that of an intervention rather than a therapy (Flint, Hamilton and Williamson 2004). Chavis tells us that 'We are providing a venue where they [the young people] can process their initial responses, to make order out of chaos' (Chavis 2011, p.231).

SUPPORT ORGANISATIONS AND COURSES FOR HORSES

The Literary Arts for Personal Development (Lapidus) is an organisation founded in the UK in 1996 to support and develop literary arts practitioners promoting creative writing and reading for well-being for individuals and communities. The organisation serves writers, medical and healthcare professionals, therapists, artists and social care and educational professionals. It sets out 'a toolkit' that clarifies structures, policies, procedures and research programmes for practitioners who are working in the literary arts in the UK in healthcare, as well as key points about professional recognition, which include the role of writer in residence. It also supports training for staff in working in health and social care and training in literature development (Philipp 2004).

Little formal training is in place in the UK for creative writing specialists interested in using literature as an intervention for health. The National Federation for Biblio/Poetry Therapy (NFPB) in the US is an independent organisation that offers qualifications either as a certified applied poetry therapist (CPT) or as a registered poetry therapist (PTR); both are qualified to work with clients in clinics and hospitals and with individuals with 'adjustment problems'. In their summary for training requirements, the poetry therapist completes an advanced level of training and fieldwork, 'commensurate with the highest levels of clinical practice' and 'poetry' designates 'all forms of the interactive use of literature and/or writing to promote growth and health' (www.nfbpt.com). In addition, personal qualifications necessary include 'self-understanding, emotional stability, patience, tact, flexibility, good judgement, and respect for boundaries' (www. nfbpt.com). An approved mentor/supervisor may work with a student via audio-visual taped sessions, email and written reports if the student is not in their geographical area. At present only a few therapists in the UK have qualified through the NFPB to take on international trainees for them.

The Metanoia Institute (UK), an educational charity specialising in the professional training of counsellors and psychotherapists (including training in trauma and trauma stress), implemented an innovative part-time MSc in Creative Writing for Therapeutic Purposes in 2013, as well as a two-year Postgraduate Diploma in Creative Writing for Therapeutic Purposes. It is validated by Middlesex University and based in London and Bristol. Currently in development is an MSc in Cyberculture: Online Therapy and Coaching, to be launched in October 2014 (www.metanoia.ac.uk).

Skills for facilitating therapeutic writing can be learned by experience and practised by a facilitator who has a combined training in writing, literature and psychology, together with experience in group leadership. The facilitator needs to work in conjunction with a psychotherapist, counsellors and/or art therapists who deal with asylum seekers' and refugees' special needs. The clinical centre at which I work as a writer in residence giving sessions in therapeutic reading/writing provides discussions in staff meetings, debriefings and a series of open lectures by associated professionals.

In tutoring literature sessions over many years at Birkbeck, London University's Extra-Mural Department, I subliminally became aware that the texts we examined, laughed and wept over, evoked extraordinary glimpses of the suffering in the covert traumatic lives of group members. It sometimes felt as if I had my nose to a vast cauldron, heaving with the shadowy figures released from books by these readers – figures that hummed, whispered, sighed, laughed and cried out to be freed. People were coming to sessions not only to learn about great books, but also to use the discussions and written work as a way of accessing their own buried hurts through characters and events in the texts we studied. Over and again, I was experiencing in these sessions the power of literature to transform.

I also knew this terrain as a writer. The main characters in *Mr Bennett and Miss Smith* (my first performed play) are two writers who, like many newly arrived young survivors, found it difficult to 'speak' – Mr Bennett (Arnold Bennett) stuttered badly, and his pupil, Miss Smith (the South African writer Pauline Smith), suffered from a facial neuralgia so intense that she hardly uttered a word. But they wrote wonderful, moving letters to each other, sometimes three times a week. I set their younger selves on stage to voice their traumatic stories and to explore their master–pupil relationship through books and writing.

I realised that the hurt young asylum seekers, too, could be encouraged to find the words as expressive writers themselves – to unconsciously and freely find those small, rough symbols to 'tell' their anguish and guilt, to rewrite their harsh memories and so to escape them.

I brought to the young adults' group Sholem Aleichem's comic story *On Account of a Hat* (1953) about a poor, lowly train passenger who, in error, dons the hat of a high-ranking official sitting next to him, and is from then on, mistaken for him. People bow and scrape to him on the train journey, until he is so uncomfortable at this dishonest and ridiculous grandeur, that he returns all the way to the station bench to put back the hat and pick up his own, arriving late home to a scolding wife. This went down well with the young asylum seekers. In the discussion they identified with the symbolic character of a humble and honest young man, and vented their scorn in words about the society that patronised and excluded him because he was not wearing the right hat, so like the cultural exclusion they themselves experienced. For once, they could laugh at the situation they found themselves in with their adopted society, talk about it openly and voice their sense of hurt at the exclusion they felt here. It felt therapeutic.

Practitioners of the therapeutic arts intervention that use books with hurt children need guidance and the formalisation of study, but we also need to know about the ethics of good practice. I turned to the rich field of written accounts of this subject by experienced practitioners.

CHAPTER 10

Aims, Ethics and Good Practice

Facilitators can use concepts such as 'helpfulness', 'holding and containing' and 'bearing witness', rather than 'treating'. Therapeutic expressive reading and writing considers the person as a whole, including their culture, history, development and experiences, both before and after their trauma.

ETHICS OF BRINGING BOOKS TO GROUPS WITH DIFFERENT BELIEFS AND CULTURAL ORIGINS

It is necessary to be aware of the ethical problems of introducing literature that might hold messages unacceptable to the way a young asylum seeker is being raised within family mores and beliefs.

Michael Davies and Elizabeth Webb's survey of Somali war refugees in Wales in 2000 found that child-rearing practices were different from those in the global north – there was no concept of emotionally or psychologically based childhood disorders in the Somali culture, for example. They also found agencies in the global north responsible for these children's education could be inflexible and unwelcoming to children from families who often did not want their children to attend school, thus compounding the young people's sense of alienation.

This dilemma of how to remain ethical to both the standards of the global north and those of the group you are working with, while using world literature, needs to be taken into account.

I brought to the group of young adults the poet Jackie Kay's autobiography *Red Dust Road* about her adoption by a Scottish childless couple, her mother being white and her father black (2010). We talked about her feeling that she did not know who she was, as she felt she was neither black nor white, and knew neither her Scottish birth mother nor her Nigerian father. She seeks and finds her father in Nigeria, a highly intelligent scientist, who is also a flamboyant born-again Christian who accuses her of being the cause of her own illegitimate birth, saying she was a malevolent force for bad. Despite this, Kay feels at home in her native landscape. It was interesting that the young men in the group sprang to the father's defence, saying it was most unusual for a father in their cultures to say this, and that she had been unlucky.

I brought Chinua Achebe's *Things Fall Apart* (2001) – the title is taken from Yeats's poem – to a small group of young men, which included Muslims and Christians. The book shows the workings of traditional Igbo tribal life that are overcome by missionary Christian beliefs and British colonisation. Achebe himself, was raised a Christian in the village of Ogidi in Eastern Nigeria, a centre for Anglican missionaries, so he would say prayers at home then hive off to his great-uncles' compound for a local meal. Out of these dual memories, Achebe made his book. 'The story-teller creates the memories that the survivors must have – otherwise their surviving would have no meaning' (Achebe in Bandele 2001, p.x). The book is written in English that includes the loving use of many of his tribal sayings, words and descriptions of customs.

We discuss what 'fall apart' means. 'It breaks down like a relationship,' says one person. In the book, the village life breaks down when another 'people', the white Christians, come into the village and establish a presence. The aim of the session is to show the fair-mindedness of the author to two factions, both of which were in his life. We talk about how each person in the session has a 'self' of the past in a village and a 'self' of the present in London, and that this is like the writer's position – he has to learn to make both selves work together, taking the good and the bad things into account in both situations, as does his book, by respecting the differences between them. The young people talk about their pasts. Nomif is both bitter about those who took his people's land and his detention and cruel treatment by the new 'people' to which he must belong on reaching England. He feels that he has no country, that he is lost. We talk about the fact that Okonkwo, the hero who cannot adjust to the fall of his village and to the new ways of the Europeans – ultimately destroys himself. Nomif talks about how being brought up a Christian has allowed him an inner base he still refers to, and that he feels akin to many things that his African culture gave him in the past.

ENACTMENTS
Children's group

1. Read aloud an animal story.

2. Ask everyone to choose an animal they would like to be. Ask them to tell the group what animal they have chosen and why they did so.

3. Ask the children to work in pairs, saying what it feels like to be this animal, its secret feelings, what it finds difficult, what makes it sad and happy and what is important to it.

4. Ask the children to write a story together about their two animals in which the animal performs an act of kindness or frees someone from being trapped. Ask them to enact their animal story to the group in small 'tableaux', 'freeze frames' or 'snap shots', using body gestures and sounds.

5. Ask for the group's responses to each story enacted.

Young adults' group

1. The group contains some several members who are trained and creative African drummers and often give informal performances of drumming as a proud expression of their cultures. Ask them to bring their drums with them.

2. Ask the group what the word 'home' means to them. Discuss this and write down these meanings of home. Ask the young

adults to write about a place where they do or do not feel 'at home' (i.e. they were uncomfortable, sad or pretending).

3. Read passages from Beverley Naidoo's *The Other Side of Truth* (2000) describing the lives of the brother and sister as asylum seekers in London, whose father is held as an illegal immigrant.

4. Discuss how the author bases her story on that of Ken Saro-Wiwa's fight for the Ogoni people's fight against the environmental disaster of the Niger Delta.

5. Read the passage where the young boy uses drumming as a way of getting rid of his anger at his and his father's treatment as an asylum seeker. Ask what feelings the group has when drumming or listening to others play the drum, and what drumming for yourself or for others means to them.

6. Look at some of the images Naidoo uses in her book. The young girl loves the word 'wood' (rather than 'forest' which frightens her) because it reminds her of the wood behind their house in Nigeria, which she associates with her mother who has died.

7. Ask the group to write down a list of words, metaphors or sayings they love that are associated with their past, saying why they love them, where they heard them and what they mean to them.

8. Ask the group to write a letter to one of the children in Naidoo's book.

9. The children in Naidoo's book go on television to publicise their father's plight and he is released. Ask the young adults to write another ending.

Now I was to take up the cudgels of the trade – language itself – words, symbols and metaphors, both in the stories I was using and those the hurt young people stumbled upon instinctively, playfully or from the heart, through the telling of their own stories, both verbally and in written form, in response to the literature we were reading aloud together and discussing.

PART 3

Derring-do

Entering the Symbolic World

CHAPTER 11

Trauma and Word-play

Give sorrow words: the grief,
that does not speak,
Whispers the o'er-fraught
heart, and bids it break.

WILLIAM SHAKESPEARE, *Macbeth*, Act 111, Sc. iv, l. 24

Words live in the mind.

VIRGINIA WOOLF, 'Craftmanship' (1937)

The spoken word is close to immediate, emotional meaning, but writing becomes a concrete statement that is negotiable between a traumatised young person and a facilitator, which places them on an equal footing. Discussing individual words, symbols or metaphors around trauma or resilience that arise spontaneously from reading, discussing or writing is a way of encountering memories held in language. Objects and paintings, too, can evoke the imaginative and release spontaneous feelings about memories and the objectification of feelings and thoughts: young people can insert themselves into the painting or see themselves through the painter's eye.

LANGUAGE IN DEVELOPMENT
The innate content and structuring of language
We make words and they make us, as they are burdened with memory and experience: 'Words [spoken or written] contain aeons of human and perhaps pre-human experience in them… As much as we shape them they shape *us*…' (Steinberg 2004, p.44). In addition,

the mind makes structures that govern words, and these structures exist independently of them. The brain can make sentences never made before: it can be endlessly creative, and this is true only of the human brain. This is innate, instinctive and universal to all languages (Chomsky 1956; Lehrer 2008).

Finding the individual voice that communicates

The child psychoanalyst Winnicott argues that the young child first communicates in a way that is 'not non-verbal…[but is] absolutely personal. It belongs to being alive' and is a kind of private communicating. At this stage of development of the child's self, language becomes a 'potentially terrifying maternal object'. Winnicott links the second form of the child's communication with verbal language, which he considers to be 'shrewdly' indirect but explicit. The third type of personal communication, which begins to develop at adolescence, is a compromise 'between language and silence', linked to Winnicott's belief that humanity tries to stay '"isolated" but not "insulated"' by developing a protected, inner identity. Winnicott notes that adolescents tend to want to avoid psychoanalytic treatment as they are preserving their identity and discovering a way of communicating that does not violate their 'secret' central self. They are not yet ready for invasive 'language'. In *Playing and Reality*, his final book (1991), he writes that the transitional search for an individual voice is a form of creative discovery or 'playing' that is healthy (Winnicott in Phillips 2007, pp.146–148).

The development of 'the true self and the false self' in relation to trauma: the role of language

One of the battles for a traumatised person is to find their identity – their best self: a self that gives them confidence in who they are and a self that they can trust to cope with problems in a way that takes them forward. Winnicott links the idea of the development of an individual's 'true self to infancy, when 'the spontaneous gesture' that is creative and bound up with bodily 'aliveness' in the developing child is incorporated into the psyche, and is the beginning of existing, of feeling 'real', and of authenticity. This is in contrast to the 'false self', which is a protection, a reaction, a defence against 'that which is unthinkable, the exploitation of the true self which would result in annihilation'. The false self protects and hides the true self, allowing it a secret life. At its most extreme it 'results in a feeling unreal, or a sense of futility' (Winnicott in Phillips 2007, p.148). An example of a life lived in terms of the false self rather than the true self lies in a letter from T.S. Eliot to John Middleton Murry in April 1925: of the trauma of living with his first wife, he writes that '…gradually and deliberately – I have made myself into a *machine*. I have done it deliberately – in order to endure, in order not to feel…have deliberately died – in order to go on with the outward form of living' (Eliot 1925).

Empathy in a relationship is a strong force that can allow the early creative, 'alive' self to emerge. Communication through using language and its tenuous relation with psychoanalytic intervention is relevant in achieving this goal (Phillips 2007).

I bring in this idea of being forced to live with a false self rather than a true one in the next session with Asoum and Nomif. Reading together *When Rain Clouds Gather* (Head 2010), Asoum immediately identifies himself with the hero's description of himself as 'the black dog', which they interpret as referring to their being African. In the ensuing discussion, the two young men express their sense of hurt and anger about racism, and how deeply they need to be seen as equal to others. I point out that the hero is also calling himself 'a black dog' because he is depressed. He feels the force of a dark sense of 'badness within him because he has rejected his belief and his culture (he does not want to be known by his Zulu tribal name and he can never forget the poverty of his childhood). He also cannot forget the breaking of his spirit by his white torturers from whom he escaped, but in his adopted culture he feels confused. In short, he is living by the rules of his 'false self' and guarding his 'true self'. In contrast, the old woman he finds himself talking to says she is 'pitch black too' and has lived all her life in a harsh world, but that she has kept her sense of self-worth, and she recognises the hero of the book, Makhaya, as being a worthwhile person, too – she senses his 'true self' that is hidden because of his trauma. Asoum remarks that because the hero

Makhaya could not think of himself as 'good' or 'true', he could not move outwards from himself towards others.

I SAY: He does eventually.

ASOUM ANSWERS: I must read this book.

The writer describes Makhaya's black arm in his black shirt, resting on the table (as does Asoum's in our session) as being 'in the form of a question mark'. Asoum feels he, too, is 'a question mark'. Makhaya fears he will destroy himself if he remains shut behind his wall of silence. Asoum fears this too. We talk about how life forces us to move back and forth and that nothing is simple, but that Makhaya (and Asoum) can learn slowly to move outwards towards others. Eventually, as his trust in his new environment develops, the hero discovers what it means to have empathy for another person – he walks for miles through the bush to bring back the body of the child of the woman to whom he is attracted, even though their relationship remains patchy and incomplete. He is slowly, and with difficulty, admitting his true self into his life as he gains confidence.

As we leave, Asoum says that the novel reflects his feelings and his problems. He has been writing down most of our comments to think about. The session has moved him. Maybe he, too, can find a way towards allowing himself to be with others in a way that is less defensive.

Using spoken or written texts

Plato tells us in *Phaedrus* written in 370 BC that Socrates argued for the spoken word as being more immediate and closer to an original meaning than the written one: 'The living word of knowledge has a soul...of which the written word is properly no more than an image' (Plato 2005). The 'living word' is often close to meaning that is immediate and emotional, but when writing is used as therapeutic self-expression, because it is concrete, it is there as a statement that is negotiable between a person and facilitator, which places them on an equal footing, and as such, is especially valuable (Steinberg 2004).

In a collection of puppet texts I edited, I wanted to show that the written text (eventually performed or voiced through the medium of the puppet) is an essential part of a classic puppet theatre piece. The poetic, condensed performed language (often playful, political or satiric) adds to and transforms the 'animation' of it. Furthermore, a good text can be published, 'read' and studied in printed form (Baraitser 1999). I brought one of these written puppet texts – *Faustus in Africa* – into a session with the young adult asylum seekers. The text is based on Goethe's *Faust* (performed by Handspring Puppets of *War Horse* fame and directed by the artist William Kentridge). We looked at the poetic words of the scene 'Gretchen walking across the landscape', which deals with the words 'mother' (as whore), 'father' (as thief) and 'sister'(who takes Gretchen's bones), all being 'laid out in the sun', and becoming the wings of doves that fly. The group considered these words and concepts as debatable and as issues that needed to be worked through in their own lives. The words bore the weight of their cultural associations, memories and experiences, and exploring them at the right time allowed the group to talk about them and release their memories and feelings. Kentridge drew the powerful charcoal backdrop drawings that were part of the performances. They, and the puppets themselves, were symbols of the suffering and destruction brought about by colonialists – art forms of the highest value, which we discussed as hard-hitting political statements in their own right.

'Personal' words

In looking at how words form us, in the next session with Nomif, we were reading and dialoguing around *When Rain Clouds Gather* by Bessie Head (2010), when he opened up in a discussion on the word 'soul' that comes up in the relationship between an old Tswana women (who holds Christian values, as does Nomif) and the confused young hero who is angry and closed in on himself. Nomif had not come across the idea of the human soul before: as a Christian he thinks maybe God has given him a soul, but he finds the notion of being able to create the contents of his own soul by his experiences and how he responds to them, a new idea that is empowering.

Amina and I explore the word 'identity' in a session – identity as having a number of selves both good and bad, one's changing self, seeing the identity of others in different ways and choices that lead to an identity. We read together sections of the book *Mister Pip* by Lloyd Jones (a book that plays with Charles Dickens's main character Pip from his 1860 novel *Great Expectations* (Jones 2008). This represents a step forward for Amina on her journey towards selfhood, as she becomes able to externalise her sense of self as good through the main character Matilda.

> AMINA: Everything happens 'to' Matilda until it reaches a climax... With me, I knew I had to do something soon. Safety was the most important thing. You don't think of anything else. It's about you.

> FACILITATOR: Survival.

> AMINA: Matilda begs for the pig-food when she has nothing. So she survives... What if you had taken the other road, the voice in me keeps asking. Matilda made a mistake, she took the book *Great Expectations* that Mister Pip was reading and hid it for her own needs, and that is why the others suffered.

> FACILITATOR: She needed it so badly to learn from it, to comfort her, so she took it for herself.

> AMINA: Yes, the mother lets Matilda sacrifice her... There is a part of yourself you don't want. That little part of yourself – it was imposed on you – it isn't you. When you're fighting for survival, that's the one you have to be.

> FACILITATOR: Then take yourself further.

> AMINA: That's when you find you have a lot to offer in you.

> FACILITATOR: And so Matilda manages to stay alive. Like you, she comes to England and becomes a teacher. She throws off the depression by deciding to write her story, like you are doing in your journal.

> AMINA: But the person you unravelled frightens you.

> FACILITATOR: You have to contain that past person and work on the new one like Matilda does.

> AMINA: This is a very clever writer.

ENACTMENTS
Children's and young adults' groups

1. Spontaneously write down words associated with: 'home', 'puppet', 'dreams', 'control', 'escape', 'anger' and 'helpless'.

2. Put the chosen word at the centre of a word-wheel with the participants adding related words radiating from the central word.

3. Create a 'character' that inhabits one of the emotion-words discussed. This 'personality' has a dialogue or interchange with another group member, who is impersonating the opposite emotion. Ask the rest of the group to comment or to make suggestions.

4. Hand out copies of the graphic novel *Home Number One* (Baraitser and Evans 2006) about three teenagers in the Holocaust, two of whom survive Terezín, the Nazi transit camp.

5. Discuss the words in the title *Home Number One* and the cover drawing of two puppets being manipulated by a pair of hands.

6. Read selections from Anne Frank's diary (Frank 1954).

7. Consider ways round being controlled. Study the pictures and 'speech bubbles' of extracts from *Home Number One* for the theme words: friendship, group solidarity, kindness of carers, the necessity of art and self-expression to survival and the power of education (forbidden to the children in camp). Discuss these.

8. Draw and write using graphic novel speech bubbles and 'stick drawings', about a time when group members helped a friend or person in difficult circumstances.

9. Use puppets to 'tell'/enact your story, fears and fantasies (as the children do in the graphic novel). Tell a story of a monstrous bully and three brave children who defy him (an opera written in Terezín has this theme).

10. Discuss the ending: the graphic novel ends with the Russians freeing the few survivors in the camp by the end of the war;

one young girl no longer has a home but is cared for by an aunt. Ask the group members if they would like to write their own ending.

11. Get the group to dress up as characters in the graphic novel, particularly the characters from the scene where the girls help dress someone for a 'date', using boot polish for eye makeup, etc.

Images, symbols and metaphors are of great significance to an individual, whether spontaneously written or spoken. In accessing these words that encode relevant emotional events for a traumatised young person, a pathway to 'seeing' a problem in a new light is imaginatively created.

CHAPTER 12

Accessing Trauma Through Images, Symbols and Metaphors

Metaphors make covert comparisons whereas symbols become interchanged with actual experience (Shrodes 1949 in Rubin 1978).

The use of personal metaphors and symbols are necessary as forms of language that allow hurt young people to express their feelings in a way that can represent their trauma. When emotional experiences associated with violence and victimisation are not connected to language, emotional disorders may follow. Pennebaker tells us 'Health gains appear to require translating experience into language' (Pennebaker 1990, p.100). The feelings around trauma held in repressed and fragmented 'pictures' can be retrieved by putting them into verbal symbols or metaphors. Displacement from the child's inner world to the outer world of reality can be achieved by way of 'symbolisation'. It is important that young asylum seekers are encouraged to find metaphors and narrative symbols to describe a feeling so that they may make some order or meaning out of the chaos of their experiences.

Objects also stimulate traumatic memories and connect with metaphors and symbols. Paintings can evoke the imagined and release spontaneous feelings about memories. Place, too, may serve as a metaphor that can join hurt young people's past and present lives by allowing them to compare where they were (their difficult past) to where they are now (the here-and-now).

THE USE OF METAPHORS TO ACCESS FEELINGS ASSOCIATED WITH TRAUMA

'Speak memory': reconnecting with trauma feelings through metaphor

It is necessary to understand that 'Human *thought processes* are largely metaphorical' (Bolton and Latham 2004, p.117; original emphasis). Victims of torture, in the early stages of their recovery, live in 'a world beyond metaphor' – a world that lets in life only as 'reality' (Herzog 1982 in Bolton 1999). Jean-Claude Métraux, a child psychiatrist working with migrants in Lausanne, having worked in the 1980s with communities affected by civil war in Nicaragua, calls this 'closing or denial' when 'narrative identity is amputated', preventing true memories (Métraux 2004).

Metaphor, with its power of truth, is an essential aspect of our mind that accesses our memories, allowing them to speak. It is 'the currency of mind, a fundamental and indispensable structure of human understanding. It is by means of metaphor that we generate new perceptions of the world...[and] organise and make sense of our experience' (Modell 1997). It is T.S Eliot's 'objective correlative', words that 'shall be the formula of that *particular* emotion... The artistic "inevitability" lies in this complete adequacy of the external to the emotion' (Eliot 1951, p.114; original emphasis). When metaphors emerge during a narrative, 'a seminal past experience is couched in imagery that embodies significant meaning and emotion in the present moment' (Chavis 2011, p.174).

Gillie Bolton, who has worked extensively in the field of expressive writing for health, came to the understanding of the importance of this process because she found herself writing wildly and manically about her own trauma as a child. In secret she played with metaphors such as the house key she was unable to fit in the lock or the little red shoes that had to dance to Daddy's will. Using these metaphors to dialogue with her different 'selves' (Bakhtin 1981b), she 'heard' her trauma and finally 'knew' it.

I brought in to a session with Amina's group my short story *Tiekiedraai* (Baraitser 2010). The *tiekiedraai* is a South African dance in which couples hold each other around the waist at arm's length, whirling and lifting their knees waist high. The metaphor linking the action is that of 'shoes'. In the story the young girl dances the *tikiedraai* with her father at a wedding, though she has no dancing shoes because of her mother's refusal to let her buy a pair, despite her mother owning a cupboard full of shoes. Jealous of the daughter dancing so well with her husband, and angry at her for questioning her authority, the mother locks her daughter in her shoe cupboard. In the session, the young women talk of shoes as a 'metaphor' for their own experience of doing without shoes – some of them did not own shoes until they came to England. They also talked of the power of the mother – Amina was used by her step-mother as a servant to her step-siblings. Talking through the metaphor of shoes in their lives released their anger at their past experience of helplessness under the control of oppression.

ENACTMENTS

Children's and young adults' groups
Playing with metaphors

1. Warm-up: ask the group members what weather would reflect their inner feelings at the present moment.

2. Talk about this, write it down and share the responses.

3. Food metaphors: ask them to describe the worst meal they have had and they best one (include the place, the people associated with the meal and the sounds they remember).

4. Grief metaphors and self-expression: turn the space into a television interview between two group members talking about their fears. For traumatic grief, a pair could enact or they may project the enactment into the past or the future or enact a farewell scene, each time showing a different feeling: anger, sadness or fear. The group should suggest new strategies or different options to ending the scene.

5. Creating the metaphor of a safe place: the group should build a safe school, parent or family.

OBJECTS AS METAPHORS RELEASING IMAGES THAT COMFORT

Objects, too, can serve as metaphors that link feelings with memories. Bringing in an object or a collection of objects to a session can be a fruitful way to access both good and bad personal memories that help the young people to focus on something outside themselves (Kopp 1995 in Chavis 2011). We have seen how bringing in a bead necklace stimulated Asola's empowering memory of her family as being distinguished as 'royal' by the beads woven into their hair, and how Asoum, when shown a small bicycle fashioned from wire, was reminded of home and of his mother who was 'too tall' (he is very tall himself) and of walking alone because he was unable to walk along with her great strides.

It is good to bring objects that hold importance for individuals to a writing session, for example objects that have appeared in dreams or were given as a 'gift'. They can be made concrete by fashioning them from materials to share with a group who can describe them or write about them. These are powerful weapons to use in contacting the past and reconnecting with complex feelings (Bolton *et al.* 2006). They can link with chosen texts that evoke themes that thread through the dominant feelings of the traumatised young people: anger, fear, loneliness or humiliation.

A session using food and people associated with its making, as metaphors for 'home' and 'safety', with the young adult group of survivors evoked animated conversation about good feelings and memories rather than bad ones. I brought in my own objects – two old, carved African spoons that I use as salad spoons. I linked these with pictures of Edmund de Waal's family heirlooms of netsuke carvings, which he uses as metaphorical objects to inform himself and his readers of *The Hare with Amber Eyes* of the tragic story of the persecution of his Jewish family over generations (De Waal 2011). I ask the group to remember and describe old familiar cooking utensils that they held dear and that are used in their culture.

In addition to Gersi and Asoum, Noy chimed in:

It is a long time since I have eaten from the bowl made of wood. You cut the wood in half and dig it out. Sometimes they use stones, very sharp stones, white in colour. Certain leaves they rub it with to make it smooth. I remember – wooden spoons, bowls, 'muhawo' [flat spoons], spears, photo frames, chairs and benches. But what I remember most of all is the arrow which was made for me by my grandfather, may his soul rest in peace.

Finally, I ask the group to select an object that stands for something from their culture that they enjoyed, and to bring it in to the next session. One talked of a carpet he made himself; Noy chose a bark cloth used as a shroud; Asoum chose wooden toothpicks specially made for the purpose; Gersi chose to remember photographs of his family, sadly no longer in his possession.

ENACTMENTS WITH METAPHORIC OBJECTS

Children's and young adults' group

Literary picturing and symbolic memory: being your own 'decent hero' in your story

1. Warm-up: ask the children and young adults to bring in a much-loved object. This may be a favourite piece of clothing or jewellery. Ask them to describe it, what it means to them, who gave it to them and how they have made use of it to help them.

2. Talk about 'heroism' in everyday life. Ask the group to describe a moment they think is an example of this.

3. Ask them to write a story about their 'best self'.

4. Objects from dreams are powerful. Ask the young people and children to describe them and the effect they have.

5. Objects as gifts: good memories can be evoked by re-experiencing in writing gifts made to them, recalling the givers and the gifts. Let each person choose a box from a collection and ask them to say why they have selected the box, what is inside it, where it comes from, what it can contain and what could be released from it.

6. Ask the group to speak, then write about, personal objects (special or ordinary ones, or those belonging to a person special to them).

7. Ask the group to find natural objects outdoors, like the small park they can see from their window, or objects found on visits to places like Hampstead Heath, and ask the group to write about them. They can write about a place of peace they remember.

8. Ask the group to write about objects they would put in a suitcase when they leave a place they know.

9. Objects from the Museum of the Past (an imaginary collection): ask the group to select objects to make up their Museum of the Past, to share and describe them.

Children's group
Objects and creativity

1. Bring in two old pots.

2. Ask about pots the children have known. Ask if they can remember who made them, who used them, the meals cooked in them or the places from which water was drawn to fill them.

3. Tell the fable of *The Cracked Pot* (Anon in Chavis 2011, p.107) in which an Indian water carrier has two pots, one of which is cracked and leaks water, causing him to feel ashamed and as if he is a failure. Only when the pot bearer points out that the leaked water has made flowers grow, adding beauty to the household simply by being himself, does the water carrier feel able to value himself.

4. Ask what the story is saying to the children about feelings they have experienced themselves.

5. Make a word-tree about 'feeling hopeless and ashamed' and another about 'creativity'.

6. Role-play, using two chairs for two 'characters', a story about feeling ashamed and escaping this feeling.

7. Can there be another ending to *The Cracked Pot*? Ask the children to write this and share.

8. Choose an image from the story and draw it.

Using paintings as metaphorical objects

Paintings can evoke the imagination and release spontaneous feelings about troublesome or good memories. I used Marc Chagall's painting *The Fiddler on the Roof* as a way to discuss the expression of good feeling through the playing of a musical instrument – as creativity that communicates and is also a way of counteracting anger. I began the session by asking the group, many of whom were drummers, what the picture of the fiddler on the roof meant to them.

Here is Ytan's response:

> When you play an instrument, this can make you feel like you are in the happy days. This painting gives me memories of my own country Uganda. People used to play almost all the time to make the village a happy day. Things like drums and many more. When I play the drums I think you play what you feel – the rhythm, your hands, what they do. And just enjoy it. This man is enjoying it. That's why he is dancing. It is a celebration because of the lights. He is not religious.

Ege says:

> You can see by the way the fiddler is standing, the player was sad, but now he is happy. He is trying to get the best out of his violin. I think he is dancing. People are hearing him playing from their houses. A sad man who expresses his feeling through violent playing. The sound of his instrument changes his mood and he starts dancing.

Others say:

> The yellow piece on the violin shows he is happy. Then there is the white.

> He has got nice music to attract people to listen. He is looking out at the river.
>
> This guy is sitting on top of the hill, using his imagination.
>
> Maybe he is just practising outside.
>
> This guy is poor as well.
>
> The tree is flowering. There are two chickens underneath.
>
> It's cold. There are people watching. You can't see them.
>
> He is playing to bring the people together. He is making an income out of his playing. That is why he is not so cold.

Chagall's metaphoric dream world overlapped with their own experienced world in a way that released their sense of their being akin to it, and acknowledged the use of music to access ways of thinking and of being, which countered the memories that haunt them.

Using place as a metaphor that comforts

Place is a metaphor that can join hurt young people's past and present lives by allowing them to compare where they were to where they are in the here-and-now.

We take the young people to Hampstead Heath for its calm and beauty, to counteract the crowded and often challenging conditions under which they live in the city. It reminds them of their natural environment 'at home'. Their response to Hampstead Heath is to examine everything in great detail, picking up feathers, spying small animals in the undergrowth that I would never have noticed and responding particularly to the trees, so much part of their own past stories of foraging for wood.

Here is Amina on visiting Kenwood, part of Hampstead Heath:

> The Heath made me realise that the most natural things are the ones that we feel most comfortable with. When we were at the Heath, it reminded me of my home because it had a lot of dried trees. When I was at my home, I always had to collect wood, so I was always looking for firewood to bring home and if I didn't find

any, I was punished. At the Heath, I don't feel any disturbance. It is natural. Firewood is out there.

By way of contrast, we also visit the Law Courts and Asylum Courts as a way of remembering and thinking about the circumstances that they have survived. This releases passionate writing, expressing their anger and humiliation at their treatment by officials and the asylum court procedures.

A young man wrote:

...suddenly I remember when I went to the Court, how I feel is very scared – my whole body was shaking and my interpreter was holding my hand. As well as this, my head is always looking to the floor.

Another wrote:

I felt she was telling the truth but that the lady from the Home Office is not believing her, just asking, asking questions. After we left, I was very afraid to be in her situation.

A third person wrote:

I realised that on the board they had written 'The Royal Justice Court', but there was no justice at all.

ENACTMENTS
Children's group

1. Ask each child to bring their toy pet and describes to 'the vet' its sickness, worries and feelings. These often reflect their own situation. Identify what the pet needs to get better and then empower them to give the pet what it needs to heal.

2. Read Hans Christian Andersen's *The Galoshes of Fortune* about the chances of a happier life (Andersen 2004).

3. Look at maps of the children's journeys from their original country to the UK. Talk about them together.

4. Ask the children to write a story about magic shoes that take them where they want to go and give them one wish. Tell them

to describe the place, who they meet and where they arrive. Ask them how it compares to being in the here-and-now and to give their feelings and thoughts about how they see their journey now.

THE USE OF SYMBOLISATION IN TRAUMA NARRATIVE

Allowing the creation of selfhood and self-communication

Psychologists working with disturbed children have long realised the importance of understanding the nature, use and meaning of symbols embedded in language, in terms of the workings of the psyche and its development.

Jung saw symbols as giving meaning to the unknown, differentiating them from 'signs', which stand for something known (Petocz 1999). Freud regarded symbols as universal and instinctual, appearing in dreams, myths and folklore, fixed in their meaning in the unconscious, which may leave the user mute in the face of them (Freud 1920). Marion Milner, British psychoanalyst, educationalist and artist, sees symbols as an intrinsic expression of primary creativeness. Using 'image' and 'symbol' as interchangeable terms, she also develops Jung's idea that we express ourselves in pictorial symbols that are part of our selfhood. She felt that 'images are "truly real", striding the gulf of the inner and outer' (Milner 1987). She asks *how* we create, rather than Freud's question of *why* we create.

The psychoanalyst Hanna Segal (again using 'symbol' and 'image' interchangeably) tells us that the word 'symbol' comes from the Greek term for 'integrating', so to her the process of symbol formation is a continuous process of bringing together and integrating the internal with the external, the subject with the object, and the earlier experiences with the later ones. 'A displacement from the child's inner world to the outer can only be achieved by way of symbolisation' (Segal 1957, p.396). Segal jettisoned Freud's need to 'translate the symbol' to understand it – and maintained that there is no dictionary of symbols (quoted in Henley 2008). She writes that 'the capacity to communicate with oneself by using symbols is, I think, the basis of verbal thinking…' (Segal 1957, p.396). Segal saw symbolisation as involving a three-way relationship between:

> the thing symbolised, the thing functioning as a symbol, and a *person* for whom the one represents the other… Anxieties that could not be dealt with earlier on, because of the extreme concreteness of the experience…can gradually be dealt with by the more integrated ego, by symbolisation. (Segal 1957, p.396; emphasis added)

In relation to disturbed children, Segal's mentor, Melanie Klein, found that children's play, a form of sublimation, is a symbolic expression of deep desires and wishes (Klein 1930). Once more, the facilitator can use words, symbols and images drawn from the client to allow indirect exploration of issues that disturb and so release them.

These ideas of how symbols, reality and selfhood interact are necessary to a way of working with traumatised young people. Evoking, drawing out, discovering and discussing the images *they create*, especially from an objectifying text that evokes relevant symbols in their descriptions of their inner selves, their experiences and their memories, is part of the function of the therapeutic writing facilitator.

Winnicott's words acknowledge the difference between 'apprehensive knowing [non-verbal] and comprehensive knowing what we can allow ourselves to *formulate in words*' (Winnicott 1991; emphasis added). He describes how 'the process by which the inner becomes actualised in external form becomes the basis of perception… Perception itself is seen as a creative process' (Winnicott 1991).

As a young girl, Amina was expected by her step-mother to look after her siblings and to cook and clean for the family, as well as to help with the hard labour of farm work and walk miles to school. She was also ruled by an abusive, autocratic father. Amina's symbol for him was 'the King's throne', the chair used by her father for his meals (other family members ate apart on the ground as there were no other chairs). 'He was His Highness, you know, like when the Queen is visiting. When I put up the chair [and table] it meant he was going to sit.' Only Amina carried 'the throne' from the hut, and she alone cooked and served him his food when he sat in it.

> So when I put the chairs and table outside, what it meant was, it time for him to come and eat the food I had made, and stop what he was doing…. So putting the chair and table out each day, they stood for me. I was the one doing it.

This gave her a perception of herself as her father's selected handmaiden from whom he demanded 'rights'.

When Amina *worded these image*, which continued to haunt her in these therapeutic expressive writings, she was able to externalise her anger and guilt and find a truer identity. Bollas called this 'the unthought known…a space for the arrival of news from within the self' (Bollas 1987).

CHAPTER 13

Writing Traumatic Dreams and Fantasies

DREAMS REFLECT TRAUMATIC FEELINGS OF DISTURBED CHILDREN AND YOUNG PEOPLE

Freud thought of dreams as a communication between the unconscious fantasy and the conscious mind, allowing him to 'translate' the contents of a dream to a patient. He considered that dream analysis should be a research endeavour, not a therapeutic one, and concentrated on dreams pertinent to the current phase of a patient's therapy. In contrast, Hannah Segal thought of dreams as 'getting rid of mental content', so in working with disturbed children and their dreams, she emphasised the need to understand what a child is *feeling* when they dream, rather than seeing dreams as wish-fulfilment (Segal in Henley 2008).

Dreams of traumatised children and young people need to be understood and processed to reduce repetition of the traumatic material (Dieckmann 1986). Traumatic dreams containing replicated trauma imagery may disappear in a few days or weeks of the event or they may recur. Dreams may be remembered only when aspects of the trauma have been worked through. Only then can children communicate their concerns and fears that their traumatic experiences will recur. Traumatised children may dream of their helplessness in preventing the horrors they have witnessed or of their trauma connected to grief – for example, a boy who saw his father killed dreamt of being reunified with him. Cultural and political factors may shape traumatic dreams – Bedouin, Irish and Israeli children, for example, have twice as many conflict dreams as non-conflict ones (Nader 2001).

Kathleen Nader, a specialist in understanding and assessing trauma in children, writes that the degree to which traumatised children and adolescents have dreams or nightmares about their experiences depends on factors such as the nature of the threat to themselves or their perception of threat to significant others, the phase of recovery they have reached and their personality. This dreaming may be associated with somnambulism, difficulty in concentrating and problems with memory (Nader 2001).

Traumatised young children and adolescents dream in different forms. Between the ages of three to five, children's dreams do not have a story-line, human characters or feelings, though they usually incorporate animals and monsters, and they are very briefly reported. Between seven and nine years of age, the dreams refer to the children themselves, their thoughts and their feelings. At ages 11 to 12, they may be too fearful to report their dreams at all, or they may omit details, but they do begin to construct a dream narrative (Nader 2001). Traumatised adolescents have 'monster dreams' (though these may occur at any age). One study reported findings that 43 per cent of children's dreams contain encounters with monsters, though this could be a prepubescent fascination with death (Terr 1990 in Haen and Brannon 2002).

Ways to confront dream monsters

One of the ways to confront monsters in children's dreams is through using characters from a book in which warrior heroes outface monsters with magic and power, making a child feel safe. A 'dream monster' can be tamed by a facilitator listening to the dream and reframing and expanding the child's sense of self that can tame the monster, with the idea of safety being introduced by the characters in the book – a monster can love flowers or can wish to be human or a character in a book can want to befriend the monster (Haen and Brannon 2002).

In Maurice Sendak's classic role-playing book *Where the Wild Things Are*, a child uses his dream world or fantasy to assuage his sense of guilt and return a sense of his own power after his mother denies him his supper for misbehaviour. He creates a world of monsters or 'wild things' in a wild place where he can fearlessly dance with fierce and roaring monsters as their 'hero king', thus identifying with them and acting out his inner rebellious 'monster'. Thus empowered, he can return to the reality of his position of a child who acknowledges the reality of his need for love and supper (Sendak 2000).

Troubled young people may be encouraged to write the dreams or dream fragments they may remember and then rewrite them in a imaginative way that empowers them, rather than being asked to try to explain them. Care must be taken, as this sideways leap into chaos may be overwhelming to them (Bolton 1999). Geri Chavis writes of an abused young woman who constantly dreamt of her abuser attacking her in the form of a monster. Chavis asked her to write the words she wanted to tell her and to imagine what she wanted to do. The young woman read and reread these words, which she eventually incorporated into her dream until she warded off the monster in her dream, diminishing her nightmare (Chavis 2011). Orlando Tizon, of the Survivors Support Coalition, Washington, writes of a young woman survivor's dream of a man rummaging through her clothes, taking the best items, while she protests but feels she can do nothing. The dream pictured the moment when she was arrested and the house she was in was raided by military men, who went through her clothes. She felt stripped, physically and spiritually. By talking about her dream, she realised how much anger pervaded her life about her helplessness, which was expressed in the dream. She felt that writing the dream and talking about it gave her an active role in her own healing process within a safe relationship. She was able to 'swim freely in the "normal" world of relationships, yet was not left entirely alone' (Tizon 2001, p.467).

Amina's dream

Amina's experience of fear and abandonment came up in a recurrent dream she had of feeling afraid of a vast space like a tube-tunnel, in which she was overwhelmed and felt tiny. This came up spontaneously in a discussion of the scene in *Jane Eyre* when, as a child, Jane is locked in the terrifying Red Room. Amina identified with the hurt and helplessness felt by the child, so we celebrated Jane's and Amina's brave, instinctive spirit of resistance to the cruelty and unfairness shown to them, despite knowing 'dread as children only can feel' (Brontë 1966). The knowledge of Jane's courage and final finding of her true self helps to counter Amina's dream.

ENACTMENTS
Children's group

1. Read Maurice Sendak's *Where the Wild Things Are*, showing his drawings.

2. Ask the children to write a dream-story. Share.

3. Talk about 'monsters' that appear in dreams, and the self that can tame them, as does the character in the book. Telling others can help this.

4. Ask the children to put into one word what they would like to do with the monster in the dream. Ask them to look at the images, colours, place and sounds of the dream.

5. Ask the children to draw the dream or a picture from the dream in storyboard form.

Young adults' group
Rewriting dream images

1. Ask each person in the group to write a dream they remember.

2. As them to give it a title and then make the characters from the dream speak. They should give details of colours and images that appear in the dream.

3. Ask the group to rewrite the dream from the point of view of a different character in the dream. The dreamer can become a character in the dream, as a powerful person.

4. Share. Ask the young person to find a way of linking the dream to their everyday lives, asking about its message or what it

means to them, why certain characters have appeared, and what events the dream reminded them of.

5. Look at the images in the dream. Discuss these.

6. Suggest that the young adults keep a dream-journal (Bolton 1999).

PSYCHOLGICAL REALITY OF TRAUMA: FANTASY OR ACTUALITY

Oliver Sacks reminds us that Freud believed that the psychological reality of the abused child might be the same, whether it came from actual experience or from fantasy. Psychologists now listen more carefully to what hurt children tell, to try and decide if it fantasy or reality. Sacks, admonished for 'remembering' a bombing incident he never saw, concludes: 'Frequently, our only truth is narrative truth, the stories we tell each other, and ourselves – the stories we continually re-categorize and refine' (Sacks 2013). Fantasy is one way of imagining a longed-for memory you have never had.

Here is a fantasy of Amina's (which I included in the exhibition of writing of the young people to build her confidence) about the need to find peace in the form of a new self. This fantasy was a constructive survival tactic: it allowed her a form of release by writing the imagining of a deep need.

One day, I was in Lucy's office and on her wall there is a picture of a boat. When I looked at the picture, I immediately wanted to get in that boat and go far away where nobody can find me. I think in the middle of the sea it is so peaceful. It can make you become someone else, a new person is what I want to be. I am tired of this person I have been. A boat will take me to a better world.

The psychoanalyst Stephen Grosz, in *The Examined Life*, tells of a person who throughout his analysis refers to his 'safe house' in France – an isolated farmhouse set within fields and forest. It is a house to escape to when reality becomes intolerable. He mentions that in his childhood he would hate it when his parents would get drunk and his mother would have violent tantrums, beating him until he cried out to God to keep him safe from her. He tells Stephen Grosz the house he has built has a special door through which he can escape, if necessary. Finally he admits that his house is a fantasy. He created it as a place of escape from his harsh past, and it helps him to survive in the present (Grosz 2013).

Trauma fantasies as revenge

The resistance to mourning loss in traumatised young people may be disguised by a revenge fantasy in which the role of perpetrator and victim are a 'mirror image of the traumatic memory' (Herman 1997, p.189). The person fantasises they can force the perpetrator to admit they have harmed them, but repetitive revenge fantasies only increase the hurt and make the person feel degraded. Further, some survivors fantasise forgiveness of their punisher to empower themselves. Others fantasise that they will be properly compensated. The only way through these fantasies is to go through the process of mourning. Far more constructive to selfhood is allowing or encouraging the feeling of 'righteous indignation', which allows the hurt individual a measure of freedom to begin a quest for justice.

This is why, when Amina relayed her fantasy that her father could be apprehended for his abuse of her, my reply was that this was unlikely but that she had found other ways of countering his hold over her, which were about writing about her past situation with a view to expressing what she felt.

ENACTMENTS
Young adults' group
Controlling revenge fantasies

1. Warm-up: ask the group members to create their own fantasised safe places in the space used for the session by marking sections of the room designated as 'safe' with tape.

2. Ask them to imagine a magic box into which they can dump their revenge fantasies where they can be kept safely.

3. To transform overwhelming images into safe ones, ask the young people to use an imaginary television remote control button to change channels from violence to good viewing.

4. Empower them to say who hurt them and in what way, then get the whole group to push the person out of the room as a way of ousting their damaging internal imagery (Haen 2008).

Writing session on fantasy

1. Warm-up: ask the group to write a line of a persistent fantasy on a piece of paper then to cover it up and hand it to the next person; they should continue this until the group has created their own fantasy story.

2. Ask the group to share this and to talk about their fantasies and whether they regard them as productive to their present situation. They should discuss what would be a more useful way of facing those who appear in their fantasies.

3. Ask each person to imagine they are faced with an actress or actor who has to impersonate them. What details would they use to describe themselves accurately so the actress or actor could really portray them? This allows them aspects of themselves that are grounded in reality.

The next step in my journey was towards a particular form of story-telling with which children and young people are familiar – fairy tales. The problem for me was that many such tales are violent and sometimes even hold within them a form of licensed child abuse. I needed to know if I could safely use fairy tales with those children who had experienced abuse in actuality.

CHAPTER 14

The Therapeutic Use of Fairy Tales and Myths

Fantasising Empowerment

Fairy tales and myths involve the psychological processes of distancing and wish-fulfilment, serving as transitional objects that reassure children that they can overcome dangerous obstacles by identifying with the common person who is transformed into a hero. Fairy tales also have a social function, showing metaphorically how children relate to others and how humane social codes need to be in place. Recently, a study of fairy tales showed that they contain other elements that may be counterproductive to children who hold within them memories of loss and terror (Young-Bruehl 2012).

FAIRY TALES AS REASSURING TRANSITIONAL OBJECTS

Enduring fairy tales and the myths of all cultures can be used to unravel the psychodynamics of calamities experienced by children. They are like dreams, and are sometimes even derived from dreams, which are retold and elaborated because they portray universal conflicts and fears. Dreams, fairy tales and myths portray symbolisation, condensation, displacement and distortion. They serve as transitional objects, reassuring children that they can overcome dangers, that their fears are taken seriously and that they can take hope in the recovery of loss through the story and comfort in the fact that the story-teller continues beyond their loss. Freud's essay on fairy tales in dreams tells us that these childhood stories can even replace memories 'because they help us cope with the dark side of ourselves' (Freud 1913). They allow traumatised young people to identify with the ordinary person who must struggle to regain a life of stability and, in doing so, become heroic. On the other hand, if more than half of fairy tales show cruelty to children, we need to question if they are, in themselves, sometimes abusive to children.

THE THERAPEUTIC USE OF FAIRY TALES

Fairy tales can be used therapeutically for healing because they help to objectify deep psychological fears and problems. They are archaic and primal, unlocking the unknown that we try to know by giving 'form to the unformed, speaking the unspeakable, and shap[ing] the chaos' (Dieckmann 1986, p.101).

Fairy-tale figures give children someone to identify with and a plot that includes the conscious and unconscious existential dilemmas of children, providing them with reassuring cohesive structures and a possible happy ending that is not found in play (Bettleheim 1977). Children's fantasies based on fairy tales are an extremely important element in their psychic lives because of the dangers the tales describe of abandonment, mistreatment and 'being belittled...or being threatened' (Bettleheim in Dieckmann 1986, p.v). They involve the processes of distancing and wish-fulfilment. They serve as therapeutic transitional objects, reassuring children that they can overcome dangerous obstacles, that their fears are taken seriously, that they can take hope in the recovery of loss through the story and take comfort in the fact that the story-teller continues beyond their loss (Goldberg 2008). Jung thought they were part of the collective unconscious with its mythical language incorporating the deep emotional layer of primordial images. The Jungian Gertrud Mueller Nelson used the reading and analysis of fairy tales to help a group of adult women come to terms with the issues in their own lives as a way of healing and transforming them. She found that by engaging in the pain of the fairy story, the traumatised can 'engage [their] own "stuck" places, the blocks, the wounds, the fears, the passions, the possibilities' – leading them to realise that 'only *dis*enchantment can transform us' (Nelson 1992, p.43; original emphasis).

STORYING THE 'COMMON PERSON'

Fairy tales need to give the listening traumatised child a free space in which to imagine, while at the same time allowing a feeling of being safe from dangers that exist in real time (Tolkien 1938). They are also the child's way of managing aggression (Dieckmann 1986).

A traumatised young person can identify with the ordinary self transformed into the heroic self who must struggle and face obstacles and feelings of overwhelming fear and sadness, by using his wits, stamina and courage to escape, together with the help of magical creatures or animals to recover him, and console him, to help him towards a catharsis and to finally become king. In reading of the hero, the traumatised are offered hope, resurgence and survival (Wester 2009). In fairy tales the powerful and nasty are punished by the 'small' people, and though some tales end tragically, most bring happiness and a sense of cooperation and hope to those who struggle, bringing a sense of social justice (Zipes 2008).

FAIRY TALES AS THE MORAL COMPASS OF SOCIETIES

Fairy tales begin in oral form, but once they are written down they change to incorporate different cultural and religious values. The Brothers Grimm for instance, added Christian elements to please their educated audience and to serve their interests – fairy tales were not meant for the ears of children until the late 19th century, when they were adjusted to be what adult readers of the time thought was appropriate.

Jack Zipes sees fairy tales as timeless and appealing to all ages, serving as a moral compass for groups across societies. At best, 'they constitute the most profound articulation of the human struggle to form and maintain a civilising process' (Zipes 2008). They offer counter-worlds – perhaps a form of escapism in which there is always justice – to our real worlds where justice is scarce. Societies need and use them as part of the sense of what Freud calls the 'uncanny', because they tell us 'what we need and they unsettle us by showing what we lack and how we may compensate for lack' (Zipes 2008). They include a 'hint of happiness' or 'anticipatory illumination' – they map out ways to know happiness and to expose and resolve moral conflicts. They show us that 'we are all misfits for the world, and yet, somehow we must fit together' (Zipes 2008). Fairy tales are a form of 'dreaming ahead' in which our projected fantasies represent our radical urge to restructure society – the hero shows the way to overcome demonic evil (Zipes 2008).

A fresh look at fairy tales reveals that they contain other elements involving the rationalising of what amounts to child abuse. Almost half of Grimms' fairy tales entail cruelty to children. A recent study on the work of the psychoanalyst Elizabeth Young-Bruehl, political activist and biographer of Anna Freud and Hannah Arendt, in her book *Childism: Confronting Prejudice Against Children* (Young-Bruehl 2012) demonstrates how people and societies mistreat children in order to fulfil their own needs, to project conflicts and to stop their authority being questioned – and that these ideas are included in many fairy tales. In the current socio-political context, many societies may not ratify the developmental needs or the rights of children. In the anatomy of this prejudice against children, Young-Bruehl shows how this works *against children* in fairy tales. She examines Greek myths to demonstrate their inclusion of slavism, sexism and racism, and what she terms 'childism' (crimes against children), asking that societies finds acceptable what is enacted in the tales, rationalising them as a form of authoritarianism, because the abuse is forgotten in the 'successful' outcomes of the tales. Fairy tales do not question the rights of adults to discipline their children with cruelty – the adults judging the tales see their cruel behaviour as justified by the gods, or a God (in both the Bible and the Koran) (Young-Bruehl 2012; Zipes 2012).

HANDLING CRUELTY WITHIN FAIRY TALES IN THERAPEUTIC SESSIONS WITH DISTURBED CHILDREN

In therapeutic reading and writing sessions with young asylum seekers within a wide age range who adopt a variety of approaches to their identity within their own cultural tales and myths, great care needs to be taken in selecting and presenting these stories.

A member of a group of mixed-gender, young adult asylum seekers was encouraged by a therapist to select and share a folk story from the asylum seeker's own culture as a form of remembering and celebrating it. He told the story of a young girl placed in a cave until she reaches puberty, for fear she will be abducted by a great beast, who lurks in the outside world and lies in wait to 'swallow her up'. The girl rolls back the stone against the cave entrance only to receive food and water three times a day from her mother, who sings to her daughter so she recognises her voice. A member of the group was encouraged to sing the African words and melody of the mother's song. The beast finally succeeds in learning to imitate the mother's voice and lures the girl out of the cave and swallows her whole, but the mother takes a knife and slits the beast open and rescues her daughter. The ancient folk tale is about the preservation of virginity before marriage – young girls living in a village culture rely on parental authority and protection to survive into adulthood sexually 'pure' before marriage, a form of cultural and religious obedience. The young man telling the story and others in his audience from the same culture enjoyed a wry knowingness about both the temptations of being ruled by lust and their parents' responsibility in controlling this. At the same time, there was a sense of irony – everyone subliminally knew that among the listeners were a homosexual young man (homosexuality was not tolerated in his country of origin) and young women who had been cruelly trafficked – the folk tale needed a discussion coming from the young people themselves to explore ways of encountering their sexuality, in both old and new ways.

To allow a discussion of how to manage self-reliance and sexuality within the adopted culture of the global north in which they find themselves, a book like Toni Morrison's *Sula* (2005) could introduce the idea of freedom of action (including sexual choice) in contrast to the need that society has for a sense of morality and consideration of the needs of the other. The story looks at the personal, self-loving, expressive life force in the perspective of the ability to nurture, forgive and love; the nature of 'aloneness' in contrast to loneliness; the meaning of life-long friendship between two young black women from a poverty-stricken valley despite betrayal; and the need to understand more deeply the nature of what is 'good' in terms of responsibility versus individualism. The book asks how the imagination can work for a destitute community. The writer in her foreword alludes to 'the creative strategy for survival' of the oppressed (Morrison 2005). These are the areas for discussion and from which to write that will give strength and maturity to young asylum seekers facing their new culture in socio-cultural terms dealing with difficult issues such as sexuality.

I may also use a subtle and aware book that incorporates fairy tale or folk elements of heroism and the dark, overwhelming forces of evil, which overlaps with the young people's experiences of dislocation and their resulting difficulties in displacement from one culture to another. An example of this is Beverley Naidoo's *The Other Side of Truth* (2000) set in Nigeria and England in the 1990s, and written for young people. The author, an anti-Apartheid activist in South Africa who came into exile in the UK, sets the story against the assassination of Ken Saro-Wiwa who tried to help the Ogoni people protest against the environmental oil disaster in the Niger Delta. It involves two children, Sade and Ferni, whose mother is assassinated when their father sides with Saro-Wiwa. 'Overnight, these two children – who have been brought up with the idea of the importance of speaking the truth – find they are illegal and the truth is dangerous' (Naidoo 2004, p.7). Their story mirrors that of many of the young asylum seekers. The children are smuggled out of the country to their uncle in England. Their surrogate 'mother' deserts them at the airport and their uncle disappears and the children are left to wander the streets until picked up by the police and handed to social workers, fearing all the time they will be found out and sent home – a situation that mirrors those of many young asylum seekers and refugees. Their father flees to England but is held as an illegal immigrant.

The point of the story is that the children, in their moment of desperation, take their survival into their own hands. They raise a public outcry by appearing on television, leading to their father's asylum, though this is temporary. To the reader/listener, the two children are like heroes in a folk tale, overcoming all obstacles with courage and ingenuity, asserting eternal social, moral and ethical cultural values that counter cruelty. This approach will only work with children or adolescents who have reached a degree of inner stability that would allow them to identify indirectly with the characters. Many may not be ready for this.

ENACTMENTS
Young adults' group

1. Ask the group to suggest a suitable myth or story from their individual cultures, which celebrates folk heroes or heroines and evil and good spirits.

2. Discuss their idea of the effectiveness and use of folklore and folklore characters, myths and magic and traditions in their societies.

3. Select a myth that brings in issues or themes that are important to them. Ask someone to 'tell' it.

4. Ask a group member to become the story-teller and describe the hero and the person opposing the hero. Ask the story-teller to give his or her opinion of the key issues of the story. Let others give their opinions.

5. A group member should enact the hero character, while the group asks him or her questions. A second group member should enact the second character.

6. The two 'characters' may enact a dialogue in which unconscious attitudes or issues emerge. These may be discussed and explored by the group.

7. The group could sing, dance or ritualise the story, encouraging a sense of their cultures' strengths through the story – humour, love, dignity and legitimacy.

Having found a way to select appropriate texts with which to approach children whose own life stories had been interrupted or silenced, now was the time to grasp how to help children to respond most effectively to them – to encourage both inward listening and outward expression of what they had heard.

Fairy tales, we have seen, allow children and young people to fantasise empowerment, escapism, heroism and wish-fulfilment, using magical powers as a way of managing their aggression. But because these are young people whose past lives have been destroyed by the actuality of violence, trafficking and cruelty, fairy tales can also be used as stories in a way that increases their ideas of how to incorporate these past experiences into their present and future lives with hope.

It was time to turn to the extraordinarily rich and valuable resource of poetry and short stories as a reservoir of metaphors, symbols and images with which to work. I would need to search for those written with an awareness of the vulnerabilities and special needs of a group of traumatised children, so that they would release the natural and instinctive poets within themselves.

CHAPTER 15

Using Poems and Fiction for Developmental Listening/Reading/ Writing

Poetry is 'a facility for expressing that complicated process in which we locate, and attempt to heal, affliction' (Hughes 1995). For children suffering trauma, poems and short stories work well as a resource to access their hurt and to develop their identity and confidence. A poem may be used to open up for discussion a theme or problem, but their most relevant stories sometimes cannot be talked about directly because some young people may not have the words. 'Ruminating' with others by listening to poems, and writing them, or telling their stories, is a process in which emotional events are shared in a surprising intimacy, often bringing in listeners who become part of the sharing. Writing poems and stories that integrate social-cognitive-emotional life is healing to young people living under stress that they cannot control. Writing unsent letters or keeping a journal are other forms of writing that light up new possibilities of self-expression that lessons inner tension.

USING POEMS AND STORIES
TO ACCESS TRAUMA

'Poems are like dreams because you write into them what you do not realise that you unconsciously already know' (Rich 2002). They 'profoundly alter the man, or woman who wrote them' (Abse 1998, p.364). For young people, finding the words to form their own poems or short stories about their personal traumatic experiences may come from reading aloud together someone else's story of coping with suffering that echoes their own. It is a way of telling themselves and others, in their own words, about their past.

Poems special to hurt young people

The poems that work best when read together or performed with traumatised young people are short and condensed and contain repetition, rhyme, rhythm and patterning of sound that work like song, which helps to release thoughts and feelings. They should be funny, poignant and relevant to the difficult lives of the young people, both past and present, like the poems of Jackie Kay, Michael Rosen and Ted Hughes, which deal honestly but indirectly and often playfully with issues of race, trauma or loss.

The poems selected should not be too difficult to grasp in terms of meaning, vocabulary or theme.

One kind of poetry that works – both listening to or writing – is 'rapping', which uses a language that is both personal and cultural to 'speak' the realities of racism, street warfare, police confrontations, poverty and absent parents with which the young refugees can identify. This works best in a group where professional musicians and poets can be invited in to help this along.

The lives of young asylum seekers and refugees are so restricted by circumstance – difficult parents and siblings, puberty, combating racism at school and their own overwhelming feelings of fear and doubt – that to be free to express their feelings any way they choose is releasing for them. I asked a children's group to write a poem saying anything that came into their heads. Each poem was scribbled over the page with sentences in random order.

Here is part of one:

Hungry Me Rubbish Music
Animal
HELP!!!
Family me
Must Homework Do.
Film-------want to play
Tired...
Me thinking
Hmmm...

The poems that follow need to overlap with their problem, giving them a new perspective or consciousness of this and surprising them with new, vivid images without upsetting them. The young people should be guided to identify with the poem's subject and explore it and be able to apply what they have gleaned to their own situations.

I may bring in poems as material to start off a discussion around a theme that is troubling the children, but the choice of poem needs to give the children some objectivity to their trauma-related emotions. Distance is necessary for traumatised young people to process their difficult memories (Van der Kolk 2003). They need to look at a problem from a place safely removed from reality (Haen 2008).

A poem may be used to open up for discussion a theme or problem. I brought a poem to a group of young asylum seekers who were struggling with unreliable parent figures about whom they had confusing mixed feelings. To stimulate the imagination, we read the poem *The Magic Box* by Kit Wright (Wright in Rosen 2009). It explores an imaginary world through the senses, in which anything can happen: odd animals and objects are linked together on a rollercoaster journey of the world. Then I ask the children to choose and describe a box from a collection of small boxes. I tell them the myth of Pandora's Box of bewildering feelings that she unwittingly releases and that she can never catch and put back in her box – not forgetting that 'Hope' is left right at the bottom and released last of all. I ask them to open their chosen boxes on the count of 'three' and 'catch' and name their own feelings released from their box and name their opposites. We explore the idea of having opposite feelings for a person.

We read Jackie Kay's poem *Kimberley* from her book of poems *Three Has Gone* (1994, p.67). Its theme is of how feelings can surprise and confuse you, but you can learn to be influenced by the feeling that helps rather than hinders. The poem is about a girl who is teased at school for being black and different. She feels bad and ashamed about herself because of this, until a Chinese girl arrives in class, who is teased in Kimberley's stead, and Kimberley finds herself joining in. But her feelings quickly change to shame and sadness that she has done so. She apologises to the new girl. We discuss that it is normal to feel different feelings, sometimes even at the same time, but it is best to listen to the 'good' feeling inside yourself, as did Kimberley.

Later, I worked with a young asylum seeker whose language is Nigerian Pidgin English, a form of English that is condensed and pictorial. I needed to increase her confidence in herself and in using English at college. I brought in a selection of Nigerian Pidgin English poems, and asked her to translate them into standard English with me. The poems were full of wry humour about the state of her own country and its rulers, as viewed by one of its poets writing in her language. With gales of laughter, we proceeded to translate, and to discuss rules of English grammar and spelling in relation to that of Nigerian Pidgin English, and to debate and understand the wit of the poetry in each other's language.

ENACTMENTS
Children's group

1. Hand out printouts of Kit Wright's poem *The Magic Box* and ask the children to read it aloud, giving a line to each child.

2. The poem is about a box made of ice and steel that contains memories and vivid images of the world, like how a Chinese dragon's nostrils look or memories of ordinary experiences like touching a sore tooth with the tongue, along with wishes and cowboys on broomsticks.

3. Ask the children which images excite them.

4. Ask the children to imagine their own box, big enough to surf on. Let them imagine surfing to another world. When they get

there, 'a moment of change' happens that is difficult but leads to them doing something that makes them proud of themselves.

5. Ask them to write these stories. The children should then read these to the group.

READING FICTIONAL STORIES TO CHANGE PERSONAL STORIES

Finding the words to face the past with compassion

According to the writer, Nicholas Wroe, 'Fiction is related to ethics in that you step out of your skin and become someone else...and it is a short step to extrapolate from that to the teaching of compassion' (Wroe 2013, p.17). The psychotherapist Stephen Grosz's work is sometimes about disturbed people who come to him with the story they cannot tell 'and us working out how to tell it' (Grosz in Henley 2013). This is because for the disturbed story-teller, the present is the only time that is real: 'The past is alive in the present...the future is an idea in our mind now' (Grosz in Henley 2013). They live in the present because 'all change involves loss...we lose ourselves when we try to deny those changes' (Grosz in Henley 2013).

Listening to their own trauma stories in the 'potential space' between reader and fiction

Listening to stories read aloud or told by another is a creative act, a transaction. Celia Hunt points out that when a person is no longer afraid of acknowledging their fears and hurts, they can become their own imagined reader – a listening, watching presence; only then can a person write their story (Hunt 2004).

This takes place in what Winnicott described as a 'potential space', that is, an internal, transitional place where psychic reality and the real world can be accessed at once – a 'holding framework', a safe enough place within which it is possible to confront the chaos of the imagined (Winnicott 1991). This is also Marion Milner's 'framed gap', where the reading/listening self can hear the writing one, perhaps for the first time, because it is safe enough to do so – safe enough to allow what has become 'the known' to become 'thought' (Milner 1952).

Here is a discussion with Amina on this subject:

AMINA: When you write, and you are writing about you, you sit there and read and you think, all those words are me. The words make me. For that tiny moment I was this person.

FACILITATOR: You are finding yourself.

AMINA: I am really enjoying it – seeing that Amina in Africa that was me… I used to walk barefoot, and look at myself here now, walking wearing shoes in London. Sometimes I think there are two of me. The other one – I really want to bring her out.

'RUMINATING' WITH OTHERS: A FORM OF CO-CONSTRUCTION IN SPACE: A THERAPEUTIC CONVERSATION

'Ruminating' with others by telling personal stories is a process in which emotional events are shared in a surprising intimacy, often affecting listeners who become part of the sharing. These 'ruminations' in a group involve making sense of things, problem solving, memories and anticipations. Within them, each survivor, despite still being emotionally uncertain, develops a narrative with the trauma as the turning point, which involves thinking about disengaging from unattainable goals of the past – the regretted 'lost' goals – and formulating new ones for the future. This is a new kind of thinking that involves 'meaning as significance' as an intermediate step to posttraumatic growth (Lutgendorf and Ullrich 2002). Using texts to evoke this indirectly is useful in providing alternative schemas related to growth and empathetic acceptance of disclosures. Rumination is about the ability to question more openly the fundamentals of life. It is a process and an outcome (Tedeschi and Calhoun 2004). It is a form of therapeutic play that explores stories as a co-instruction in a space and within a supportive relationship or a sympathetic group, which encourages the exploration of ideas and thoughts. Meaning is given in the act of doing this together.

The stories created in this playing space may not be 'true' but often will be genuine and powerfully felt and expressed…the facilitator lets each individual story this until something coherent, or a new pathway of interest opens up. It is a therapeutic conversation. (Engel in Malchiodi in Cattanach 2008, p.213)

It elicits interpretations giving meaning to experiences that perhaps did not exist before.

Expressive writing of narratives for an audience as 'play': defining the social self

Expressive writing for 'an audience' or group is another complex way in which hurt young asylum seekers are allowed to 'play' and yet define themselves at the level at which they can cope. Writing that integrates social-cognitive-emotional life is healing to young people living under stressful conditions they cannot control.

In a sample of young people (7–8-year-old and 11–12-year-old girls and boys who came from a range of racial and ethnic backgrounds with poor income), Daiute and Buteau (2002) looked at 158 assigned fictional narratives and 158 autobiographical narratives about a social conflict that the children had experienced, coding them for narrative structure and narrative social relations. They examined these in relation to problem behaviour measures, to see if over a year there was an increase in socialisation and resolution strategies in relation to expressive writing.

They found that expressive writing as a process helped young people to negotiate conflicts within social issues like racial threats and racial, ethnic and sexual discrimination, particularly when the young people considered and wrote about the consequences of conflict on their social relationships.

They identified narrative writing as making personal meaning, 'because it is a symbolic process by which individuals control cultural tools, including language and values, for social and personal purposes' (Daiute and Buteau in Lepore and Smyth 2002, p.58). They found individuals grow and develop as a member of their culture through symbolic means such as writing (Daiute and Buteau 2002). Symbolic processes mask as well as express intentions and behaviour (Billig

1999). Yet narrative is also a context for critical reflection and resistance (Daiute 1998). Young people can craft self-representations in narrative writing, trying on and revising identities that are about ongoing self-reflection and motivation. The very act of writing a personal narrative positions the individual as someone whose experiences are worth recounting. By writing yourself, you are 'preserved into the future... someone who can be imagined, interpreted, and even revered through readings by others, as well as the self' (Daiute and Buteau in Lepore and Smyth 2002, p.57).

In their violence prevention programme, their group read and discussed high-quality literature about social contexts that included discrimination conflicts, and then discussed the characters' ways of dealing with this in relation to their own lives. The conclusion of this study was that writing about strategies that might resolve problems was an important focus for children and young people: 'Socially protective processes are integrated within the narrative. Narrative expresses references to real...events and evaluative meanings' (Daiute and Buteau in Lepore and Smyth 2002, p.56; see also mask work in this book, pages 181–186).

WRITING A JOURNAL: 'THE STRAY MATTERS ARE...THE DIAMONDS OF THE DUSTHEAP'

Virginia Woolf described keeping her diary as a 'rapid haphazard gallop' rushing her along without pause for thought, which 'sweeps up accidentally several stray matters...which are the diamonds of the dustheap' (Woolf 1978). The 'stray matters' – the most informal and spontaneous thoughts written in her diary – were the most informative and precious to her.

Marion Milner regarded the journal she kept as part of her discovery that writing is a way to learn how to live. In answer to Freud's question, 'What does a woman want', she replied that she could discover this by a form of self-analysis using the active imagination.

Amina's journal was a way to face her past traumas with honesty and clarity by describing them and knowing that she would not be punished, to comfort herself by privately admitting the strangeness and loneliness of her new life and to be able to form a new relationship with herself, 'talking' to herself through her diary.

Here is an extract from Amina' s journal about her everyday life in her village:

> Every time it had to be him. What about me? We were planting coffee. We would all go to work in the fields. One day the bicycle broke down, that meant that all the heavy loads had to be carried on our heads – I mean me and the two boys who helped around the farm. I always prayed for the bicycle. I asked God to keep it safe, I begged Him because when the bicycle broke down, those were some of the worst days of my life. My three step-sisters always had everything done for them by me. Sometimes I would be so tired and wouldn't have the energy to wash the plates. I wished that one day they would stop treating me like that. I wonder what went through their minds. Was I invisible? Was I a naughty child? Maybe if I had asked them I would have known the reasons why. I think someone knew but chose not to tell me.

Here is how we discussed keeping a journal:

> FACILITATOR: What does writing a journal mean to you?
>
> AMINA: It helps me to put memories. Things that's happened to me in a different perspective. It forces me to find the line. Talking doesn't help at all. When I write, I'm having a relationship with my journal, on my laptop. Talking is a one-sided conversation. Writing is like having a conversation with your 'self'. I'll love myself in writing. I tend to be more honest pick up on things like deeper. But sometimes there'll be stuff I want to say in English but I don't know the words. And I write it in my own language. Writing it down helps with the pain. It helps, seeing me there, and seeing me now and I try to comfort myself.

Journal writing suits those young people who are already connected to writing positively, like Amina. Her journal entries show how the voices of the survivors are empowered by writing their own story, *for themselves*. Amina is privileging her own voice over her father's destructive voice. She becomes able to recognise what was done to her, unwitnessed and unacknowledged, as traumatic, so that she can 'own' it, integrate it and move on. The fact that the journal is written over a period of time gives it continuity and a sense of the self developing, continuing in time.

A journal is a 'process of integration', a therapeutic space for containment and a safe place to put experiences and feelings, no matter how difficult they are, that can be reviewed in safety, later, when the writer has perhaps moved on. It can also be seen as another 'play space where the writer can be explorative' (Best 1996).

Keeping a journal or diary is a metaphor for a productive relationship with the self – a reflective process that helps psychological healing and a way of getting to know yourself: 'A journal is a journey, a way of finding a voice' (Thompson 2004, p.73). It keeps at bay the sense of isolation that threatens to overcome a traumatised young asylum seeker. The development of intimacy with the self can also lead to feeling less inhibited about talking about trauma to a facilitator or to others in a group. It makes the lived experience real and confirms existence as an accumulative record or map of the psychological healing. Consciousness is expanded and integrated in the writing of the journal – you get to know yourself. It can access previously inaccessible material – by giving the troubled mind a definite task the unconscious comes forward – so new realisations are learned. Talking about the process of keeping a journal can be more productive than simply reading extracts aloud. It also becomes a place of catharsis, containing the immediate expressing of deep emotions, which validates experiences (Thompson 2004). Gillie Bolton tells us that:

> The boldness this sort of writing requires is also based on self-respect. This in turn is based on a generosity to myself: the gift of time, materials and focused solitary attention, and a putting on one side the sense of my own inadequacy. (Bolton 2011, p.52)

In sessions I use journal writing as a self-directed method of personal development rather than the journal therapy devised by Ira Progoff, the doyen of journal writing in America in the 1960s, that uses structured sections (Progoff 1975). His method is beyond psychotherapy. One of his journal-writing ideas was for a client to choose a person, dream or meaningful event and have a conversation with them in order to discover what is important to explore in the self (Hynes and Hynes-Berry 1994).

WRITING UNSENT LETTERS

Among famous unsent letters are those of Kafka to his father (Kafka 2008). He attributes his self-loathing to always having been put on trial and found guilty by his father's unpredictable and dictatorial rule, which Kafka represented in his novels as a system of chaotic social control, not unlike that experienced by many asylum seekers.

Writing a letter that will never be sent, addressing a person with whom they feel helpless or angry, allows the expression of raw feelings and uncensored thoughts. As Katie Thompson reports, counsellors who used this technique with a client found 'the unsent letters circumvented [the woman's] defences and allowed her to begin to recognise this. The ensuing fruitful work in our counselling sessions would not have been possible without her writing' (Thompson 2004, p.78).

Writing unsent letters to a younger self is particularly useful for young survivors of sexual abuse in order to heal the split self by telling their abuser what they think of them without fear. For those suffering loss of a person close to them, writing an unsent letter can help to process overwhelming feelings. It is a form of dialogue in which a person can intimately talk to themselves to discover why they are behaving better in a particular way.

ENACTMENTS

Young adults' group

Encouraging letter writing and keeping a journal

1. Read *Jane Eyre* with the group (Brontë 1966).

2. Ask the children to write a short letter to the author, to Jane Eyre's bullying aunt or to her blind suitor. Read these aloud and ask for comments from the group.

3. Suggest to the children that they keep a journal of day-to-day difficulties, feelings and thoughts about them, and ways to take them forward.

A two-day workshop

1. Warm-up: ask the young adults to write a sentence on a piece of paper, fold it and pass to the next person, who should do the same. Read the completed 'story' aloud (the wild juxtaposition of 'events' will make the young people laugh).

2. Read the Hans Andersen story of *The Red Shoes* (Andersen 2004). Talk about the issues it deals with.

3. Tell the young adults to imagine they have a pair of shoes that walk them to a place they want to go. They have one wish. Ask them to tell the group where they took them, what characters they met, what happened to them and why?

4. Share and discuss, relating the stories to the here-and-now of each person.

5. Ask the group to get into groups of three and use props to enact to the group one of the stories that captivated them.

Working with a group over a period of time, managing both the group dynamics and several different life stories at various phases of development, is another skill I was challenged to develop.

PART 4

Social Dynamics

CHAPTER 16

The Value of Commonality and Community

The goals of therapy are to be
able to love and to work.

SIGMUND FREUD, 'Analysis Terminable and Interminable' (1968)

A traumatised young person's self-realisation and growth in perception and understanding about their trauma is best achieved through interaction with others if the verbal and written response to the group interaction comes largely from themselves. Groups are complex and need to be managed as they develop and change. Abused young people feel they can belong in a group of others like them, as they no longer have to hide their secret. It is the *experiencing* of literature within a group that is most helpful. Personal strengths are identified and shared with social support and trust until a sense of belonging and social competence among its members is developed. Therapeutic work with books comes into play when symptoms are under control, social support is in place and a desire to reach out to others is stronger than an inner dread.

COMMUNING: RESTORING A SENSE OF CONNECTION

Commonality is about belonging to a society and the playing of a public role within it. It is also about being 'known' by taking part in a community's customary and commonplace activities and accepting the smallness of one's own place and one's troubles in relation to the community as a whole.

A social bond means one is no longer alone. A sense of self-worth depends on being connected to others. Trauma destroys the bonds between a survivor and their community. Group solidarity protects and bears witness against terror, which isolates and shames. A sense of connection is restored when another person show generosity, decency or courage to those who have been traumatised. Herman writes that 'The survivor who has achieved commonality with others can rest from her labours. Her recovery is accomplished; all that remains before her is her life' (Herman 1997, p.214).

Being present in a group is a powerful therapeutic tool for those who, like child soldiers and traumatised young asylum seekers, have felt isolated by 'shameful secrets'. Survivors of extreme situations particularly need groups, because each person is with others who 'mirror' their experiences, so they feel they belong, as they no longer have to hide their secret abuse.

The process in which group acceptance increases the individual's self-esteem is an 'adaptive spiral'. Growth in perception and understanding can come through interaction with others.

Here is a poem written by Amina describing what the community meant to her:

> It is so amazing because we all have different
> Backgrounds but we don't feel different at all.
> We understand we are one family at Baobab. And
> When we all cook our favourite food this is a way of uniting us.
> And when Ytan and sometimes me play the drums everyone
>   feels the
> Music even if they don't understand what
> The song means it doesn't make any difference at all at
> Baobab we are one.
> At the community meeting is when you will have a
> Chance to meet everyone, to congratulate each other's
> Successes, new babies, birthdays etc.

This poem describes a community that is a safe place where creativity can help to counter the traumatised young people's massive anxieties and their heightened awareness of injustice by explicitly offering space and time to explore and process their experience of violence, loss and change and a place where they can work towards integration of fragmented aspects of themselves. The Baobab Centre's name and logo is the baobab tree. This was chosen by the young people, as it has many different symbolic meanings in different communities especially in the southern hemisphere (though it is mentioned in Saint-Exupéry's classic *The Little Prince* and one grows at the Eden Project in Cornwall). There are many traditional stories connected to this tree – it is often used in communities as a place for meeting, shelter and storage of water in the rainy season: 'It can grow large enough to shelter and protect many community members at the same time' (Melzak 2012). When reading/writing takes place in such a therapeutic community it becomes part of their group experience.

Promoting collective cultural identities is healing

The Centre for Torture and Trauma Survivors, in Decatur, Georgia in the USA, runs therapy groups for Somali women (among others) using community healing via social clubs and organisations that promote the values and cultures of the group. They point out that trauma dynamics of collectives differ from those of individuals who are traumatised (Kira *et al.* 2012, p.70). Collectivistic cultures use the resources of family and community elders as groups that deal effectively with individual traumas, encourage adjustment within the communities to a new culture and help to increase family cohesion and reduce child neglect (Kira *et al.* 2012, p.73). Shared activities (including reading/writing sessions) further the traumatised young people's understanding of the reality of their own position in their new culture and encourage ways of re-seeing the value of their own mores within this position. This modulates the intensity of talking about painful experiences and promotes levels of self-expression and feelings of being productive. Group work focuses on present stress as well as past trauma using flexible but structured sessions to explore political and religious issues and community networking (Kira *et al.* 2012, p.74). Groups are organised around a theme or activity, with each session ranging in topics from immigration experiences to financial difficulties, cultural differences and loss, grief, rage and loneliness (Kira *et al.* 2012, p.78). Addressing discrimination and oppression is important in a community group, as is working with traumatised collective identities and anger about oppression and members' feelings that their survival lies in their political and religious beliefs, as well as in their natural survival strategies and strengths.

One of the cultural themes discussed for a writing session with the young adults' group was their responses to the idea of 'tricksters'. We talked about oppression and its opposite – kindness, charity, empathy – and never refusing someone who is in a worse position than ourselves. The young men came up with a rich variety of humorous stories they could share with the group, which strengthened their individual sense of being. One young survivor told of how he tricked a visitor in error, by spooning brown rice instead of brown sugar into his friend's cup of tea, and how they laughed together on discovering this 'innocent' trick. Ytan wrote of his friend's cross-dressing, which he no longer regarded as a 'trick', so demonstrating his own ability to change and grow.

The facilitator needs to make it known that the group will allow everyone to show their abilities equally and that the discussions around the material brought in by the books are open and offer opportunities for learning from one another and for co-operation. Personal strengths should be identified and shared with a sense of social support and trust until a sense of belonging and social competence among its members is developed. Peer interaction, support and adult affirmation and reinforcement of hope are curative (Kohli and Mather 2003).

Expressive writing with others helps traumatised young people to socialise

Pennebaker noticed that people change in how they communicate with others after taking part in expressive writing paradigms. He found they talked more and expressed more positive feelings towards others. He concluded that 'Writing has the power to change the ways we think which, in turn, can affect our entire social world' (Pennebaker in Lepore and Smyth 2002, p.290). The traumatic experience and the writing paradigm itself are all a part of a complex social system.

Writing exerts 'its effect on people's social lives' (Pennebaker in Lepore and Smyth 2002, p.290). He also noted that those who come to expressive writing groups for well-being are self-selected as naturally suited to working with language (Pennebaker 2002b). It is only when a therapeutic writing/reading approach can be incorporated into the ordinary everyday life of refugees, creating the right conditions and circumstances for their recovery in their newly adopted culture, that such services become part of therapeutic encounters.

Writing with others is more beneficial to traumatised individuals than writing alone. The process of writing about trauma, and sharing this, makes others aware of the person's psychological state whereas keeping it secret has adverse biological effects and blocks thoughts that would help the individual come to terms with the trauma, thus distancing the person from friends. Upsetting experiences that are transformed into stories shared with others makes individuals happier and more able to communicate with others, and physically and mentally healthier, as well as able to make closer social bonds. Scientists Wenz and McWhirter tell us 'Creating and sharing writing seems to improve and increase self-disclosure, self-actualising behaviours, and self-acceptance of feelings and experience' (Wenz and McWhirter 1990, p.38). The role of expressive reading/writing for health in a group has been described as including improving communication skills, learning new coping behaviours, increasing insight, self-awareness and self understanding, providing solutions to problems, airing taboo feelings and so providing meaningful release and orientation that facilitates new learning and helping a young person to stay focused and accomplish goals (Pardeck 1998).

THE EXPERIENCING OF LITERATURE AS A COMMUNAL ACTIVITY

It is the *experiencing* of literature within a community that is most helpful. It helps the hurt young people to realise they are not alone in their feelings of fear, anger, sadness or guilt. By using the action and characters on which to project problems, a freer and more open and creative discussion develops. The give and take – the sharing of a text that takes place in a community – can help individuals to find other meanings and purposes in their own choices and actions. Using mirroring and projection of their own problems onto the text, they learn to express themselves through expressing their problems to others, and the validation of their experiences by others is of great value to them as it heightens their sense of self-worth and may lead to reality testing a new attitude to others.

I helped to lead a two-day, mixed, group, community mask/mime/ language workshop, together with an art therapist and a number of asylum seekers and refugees. The group ranged in age from 15 to 25 and came from several countries. It included young people who knew each other well and newcomers still frozen by their trauma, two of whom could hardly speak English and were accompanied by translators. Some of us spoke French to those who spoke it as their native language.

We aimed to work by indirection or displacement, with participants fashioning masks or 'characters' that represented both their outer social self and their hidden, inner self. We had in mind Jung's idea of the 'persona' – the public self as we see ourselves – and its 'shadow' – our suppressed, creative self that emerges from the shadows.

We also wanted to explore the idea of the 'social' mask – how others within the group perceive our 'outer' self. We used group sound and word games, dramatic enactment, movement and gestures, and sound and words, finally developing these into enacted group story-telling.

Knowing the sense of confusion, loneliness and frustrations many of them felt about adapting to their present culture and coping with their inner divided selves, we began by talking briefly about the theme of the mask we wear on the outside as our public self, and how different this is from our inner private self that hides our true feelings. We also mentioned that masks can be frightening and anyone who feels this should make it known to us. One young Afghani said he was too afraid to make a mask and decided to make a hat, creating not the policeman's one he knew so well but the simple hat worn by his friends and relatives – substituting this unthreatening one as his mask 'character'.

The warm-up exercises aimed at 'playing' to encourage a reaching towards their child-self and releasing their creativity, together with a sense of going on a journey. As facilitators we felt like part of their 'family', holding and containing these child-selves. An older member – an ex-child soldier – felt he was moving into being fatherly towards his sibling who had just joined the group.

We began with the whole group running and then freezing a pose, which we regarded and admired and asked the young people to remember for later mime sessions. We sat in a circle and, asking them to keep in mind the idea of the masks that they wanted to make, to pass round a movement, each person adding to it and changing it and then giving each movement an accompanying cry or sound appropriate to the mask character and, finally, a word that expressed what their mask was feeling. They came up with: 'presenting', 'expressing', 'protection', 'silence', ' faking', 'mirror', 'protecting others' and 'camouflage'.

Everyone then fashioned their masks, with quiet concentration, from a plethora of materials ranging from feathers to wool, with a choice of making both the 'inside' and 'outside' masks together, possibly writing into the masks their 'feeling-thinking' words or writing them down on paper, describing the scene.

Several young people made masks that reminded them of folk characters from tribal tales. They wanted something familiar to them from their own cultures associated with their masks, and many of them enjoyed dancing around and performing behind these masks that represented power and control. Others wanted a mask that would allow them not to come to terms with their inside persona.

Amina took an innersole from a shoebox, painted it black and white and fashioned and attached a 3D eye, also in black and white, saying: 'It is the foot that makes the journey – the foot is the seeing eye, isn't it – it has an eye – it is the way.' One member said he was making the mask to be part of the group – for company – as he hated being alone. A young Afghani who had taken up acting and whose mask was a clown who was happy outside but sad inside, and was also the Lion Tamer, wrote me a piece:

> Hello my dear Mrs, I am doing a piece about Musa, the circus performer. He is someone who can make people laugh and smile,

that is why I am happy to do this mask, because I like this man who does not want to smile but likes to make people smile, and I am happy to make this today, and also happy to come here and to say Thank You.

Another made a 'jungle mask', saying the masked one is an evil, all-powerful one who has controlled the jungle for thousands of years, yet his mask is saying: 'I am in the wrong place in this community.' A young woman new to the group, who had been used as a servant and raped, when asked what she was feeling in her mask wrote: 'I am in England. I don't know what is going on around me. I feel like something would happen tomorrow, I can't do anything without God. I am so grateful for my life.' Another wrote: 'I am walking – it is very hot – I have blisters all over me – I want water – it's a long journey ahead.' Another wrote: 'I'm who I am. But no one knows who I am really. I'm next to the sea and my only friend is the wind.'

Finally a young man who had painted the inside of his mask white and the outside black with no additions, explained that in Yoruba belief, a strong person who wants to lead is pure inside but outside it is devilish and bad. Only when the clean, pure inside comes out and transforms the outer 'evil' does the powerful one transform into the good 'king', yet this young man said his mask 'is looking for a girlfriend… I'm thinking how I can make more friends. I am thinking about life.'

One young man who had been arrested and tortured by the police made a policeman's mask and uniform, complete with policeman's hat with a giant gold coin imprinted with a skull and crossbones. An 18-year-old made a mask that looked like himself, but the eye holes and the mouth were left closed, indicative of his feelings about his recent past trafficking. He was cared for by his grandmother whom he adored, and he wanted to care for elderly people as a mark of his gratitude. His mask said: 'I am over the moon!'

After lunch, we donned our masks and, in a circle, uttered words and mimed actions expressing feelings from within the masks. These included 'Colonel Gaddafi', 'enemy', 'searching', 'scary', 'ready to kiss', 'watching', 'hope', 'danger', 'comedy' and 'forest'. We then swapped masks with the person next to us and looked through these masks at the others, giving them a sense of someone else's 'character'.

On the second day, we warmed up by using dance and song, freezing movements as mimed mask poses, then sat in a circle and shared a discussion of what 'masking' ourselves meant and why it was necessary to do this. Wearing masks, we spoke a line that expressed what the mask was thinking or feeling, using the phrase 'I am...', each person sharing their responses with the group. The young people came up with 'I am me', 'a witch-man in the jungle', 'innocent', 'the seeing fool', 'Mr Lion Tamer', 'El Diabolo – all powerful', 'safe and protected', 'honest' and 'fearless'.

Finally, working in threes using their created and imagined mask characters, the refugees wrote a story-play. They used cloths to create a 'theatre', costumes and props (drums and a penny whistle provided the divisions between stories) and, with great brio and glee, enacted their tales using mime and words.

Amina summed up the day: 'We were free – we didn't have to think all the time, or listen to instructions.'

This shows how a group setting is therapeutically valuable, releasing insights that might not emerge in a one-to-one interchange. Interactions between peers may be easier than with a facilitator. In the group, each recovering person needs to be able to function in relationships with others in order to encourage self-affirmation, and the reaching out to others in the group encourages acceptance and unifies the group. Group members are there to support each other and to be able to be open about their feelings. It helps each recovering person to come to know the ways in which they relate to others. Each member helps to build the group by learning to be aware of 'otherness', bringing their own responses to a theme or dialogue, which tackles ideas on our ways of feeling that we hold in common or understanding how one issue can be seen from several different perspectives. The group can also genuinely provide an answer to a person's problem with a workable strategy and can respect different opinions and how to disagree or reaffirm a position. The young people learn to see how they are seen by others, which leads to greater self-understanding. Many hurt young people do not have the skills to be precise about their thoughts and feelings. Using language therapeutically in a group setting helps to give a focus for interrelationships.

SOCIAL ATTITUDES TO GENDER AFFECT A YOUNG PERSON'S RESPONSES TO TRAUMA

Mixed gender communities may not work as well for women from some cultures, as the men are reluctant to enter into women's gendered experiences, such as their exposure to violence in paternalistic societies. In communities within the host culture, there are about twice as many male as female asylum seekers and refugees (Haen and Brannon 2002). Perhaps this is the reason that some of the young women asked for sessions only with a community of other women, as they felt more inhibited in their writing and in saying what they felt when witnessed by a challenging group of young men.

A facilitator of a reading/writing group should be aware that society still teaches boys gender socialisation emphasising strength, courage, success and a wariness of feminine traits (showing emotions and a caring, vulnerable side). If a boy does not conform to this, he will experience gender role strain. He is taught to suppress feelings of vulnerability, sadness, grief, insecurity and affection – a role system that is 'unbalanced and unintegrated' (Haen and Brannon 2002). Many boys feel ambiguous about their undeveloped counter-roles. This can lead to boys who feel weak, internally defending themselves by creating a false distancing mask behind which they retreat in silence – a sign of dysfunctional role-playing, as the role masters the player and the boy concerned appears not to need us when the opposite is true (Landy 1993).

This is reflected in the difference in fantasy and play, as reflected by young boys and young girls. Traumatised young boys who experience rage, sadness, violence and helplessness are able to imaginatively identify with, and play the role of, the monster who is also heroic as a form of self-expression. A young boy in a group of children who suffered neglect, abuse and abandonment, but were unable to harness their impulses or emotions, took the role of a mean and powerful monster who destroyed everything good or human. Another boy, in a desire to be recognised by the group, played the role of a caged panther poisoned by his family who had abandoned him and, in revenge, he was going to infect all the other animals – a mark of not being able to distance himself from the feelings flooding him. A third boy in the group fantasised he was a 'monster-serpent who ate the eyes and organs of a family out camping', displaying a need to identify with the aggressor-father, or as a mark of anger at victimhood. This may serve him in his attempts to gain power and express rage, it can help him distance himself from the group when it is perceived as threatening or it may be an expression of a boy who feels unlovable. 'By embodying the monster...the [boy] child already is diminishing its fearful aspects' (Jennings 1999, p.59). The traumatised young boys needed to identify, by projection, with a hero portrayed in a book who, unlike themselves, is powerful and respected. Through discussions that arise from a book, they can be made aware that they can make a transition from their fantasy of being 'heroic' to being heroic in real life in small ways, such as by helping others: 'The roles of superhero [and] monster...are not just roles that our clients use in fantasy play, but they are also real life roles that can be both affirming and detrimental, adaptive and maladaptive' (Haen and Brannon 2002, p.32).

Haen and Brannon found that when girls were added to a group of disturbed boys, they played heroes and monsters less frequently. The girls played the roles of singers, models or kittens, and brought a family component into their role-play. Maccoby maintains this is because of the importance of a social context – boys aged five to eight years show six times more aggression in role-play than girls of the same age and with the same problems. She finds groups of boys are more cohesive, sexist, exclusionary, vigilant about gender-boundary violations and separate from adult culture (Maccoby 1990 in Haen and Brannon 2002). This has been called the Boy Code (Pollack in Haen and Brannon 2002).

READING/WRITING COLLECTIVES FOR THE STAGES OF DEVELOPMENT

The sense of collective empowerment based on common interests is important for development of disturbed young people, but different kinds of collectives are appropriate at different stages of development:

at the beginning of their adjustment programme, individuals need a collective that securely establishes a person's safety and self-care; they then need a collective to which to tell their trauma stories in which resourcefulness, imagination and humour of the other survivors is invaluable; finally, they join a group that concentrates on the restoration of connection and integration of the survivor into the community (Herman 1997).

The intervention of therapeutic reading/writing can play a useful part in the second and third groups, when symptoms are under control, a social support is in place and a desire to reach out to others is stronger than an inner dread. Working with books in a collective at this stage is part of the process of focusing on the past and of helping each individual, using the collective's input, to outline a personal goal related to the trauma. The young people drawn together by a sense of commonality are able to tell their own stories to the group as a form of recognition that emphasises relationships. It is relatively unstructured, and the therapeutic task is to focus on the here-and-now. It aims for diversity to increase each member's sense of belonging and commonality. It allows conflicts and difficulties of relationships as part of gaining new insights and of resolving problems as part of rejoining the wider world. The young people at this stage have learned that trauma can be surmounted in active engagement with others (Herman 1997).

Here is an interchange between two young women in a group session using *Mister Pip* (Jones 2008).

A member of the women's group spoke of enjoying reading Ntozake Shange's book *For Colored Girls Who Have Considered Suicide When the Rainbow Is Enuf* (Shange 1977) because it released her own feelings, allowed her to cry and to let out her anger. It made her 'gasp for air, cry, but you get it off your shoulder'. She showed concern about the character who is raped by someone she trusted, and that this happens in life. 'I say to her: "You need to take back what has been stolen from you – your self-esteem and confidence."'

AMINA RESPONDED TO THIS: I always read novels that have the same background as me. That helps me. You cry. You are released. It might upset you, but it reaches a stage that you can accept it.

ANOTHER GROUP MEMBER ADDS: God is the only person the young woman has, so she writes to him.

AMINA ANSWERS: You read a character and you ask: if it was me, would I have done the same thing? I read this story of a girl who was raped, she had a journey, she didn't break down, she was so strong. You ask yourself: would I have done this?

HER FRIEND REPLIES: Being raped makes you selfish because you must protect yourself, you put yourself first.

FACILITATOR: In *Mister Pip*, rather than be raped herself by the soldiers, the girl sacrifices her mother. She realises she has to save herself. She wades into the sea and clings to a log and is picked up by Mister Pip in his boat.

The group decides that the moment of choice comes, and that is when you should 'have your conscience'.

There are several ways in which communal life is encouraged at the centre at which I work: there are football teams, music groups, a theatre group that mounts the Christmas show; there are educational outings to films relevant to the young people's lives or to places around themes that concern their feelings and experiences; a therapeutic community lives together for a time during the holidays, which includes experiences the young people may not have had before such as swimming in the sea or horse riding, cooking and eating meals together and sharing food from their cultures. Story-telling and role-play have an important part in exploring problems within this communal experience.

Every six weeks, there are community meetings with staff and clients coming together to air issues. It is 'a community...or somewhere between an extended family and a community' (Blackwell 2011). Some of the members of this group have been together for several years; others may be recent arrivals, uncertain and attending with a translator. There is no agenda, rather subjects for discussion (both conscious and unconscious) arise spontaneously from the concerns of the members. Any individual, including staff, is free to raise an issue or to turn the discussion in any direction. It is a lifeline, encouraging tolerance of opinions about beliefs and cultural practices, and it often ends in sharing ethnic foods that the young people have cooked themselves.

Meetings can be about awareness – members spontaneously contribute their ideas and their mistakes, airing their frustrations with one other and with the conditions under which they live. There are often long silences, but these are valuable as people chew over ideas, so, in a way, these community meetings are a training for life, reinforcing a sense of the young people's abilities to hold their own, to know who they were and to test it out against a group of like-minded people who have each others' well-being and advancement at heart. It is sensitively monitored by experienced facilitators, who 'translate' and encourage group members' tentative responses.

'SOCIOMETRIC' EXERCISES: 'MENTALISATION', USING BOOKS, TO HELP SHATTERED YOUNG PEOPLE TO EMPATHISE WITH OTHERS

Haen (2005) uses what he calls 'sociometric' exercises, which emphasise commonalities and connections, such as asking traumatised young people to go to a part of the space according to their feelings and then discussing why they are there. He works at encouraging them to create a sense of connectedness with others. Young people learn to think and feel about the self *and others*, which leads to an ability to learn from others, known as 'mentalisation', which trauma inhibits. It includes learning to be empathetic, self-regulatory and self-protective, articulate feelings and develop a personal agency and an integrated sense of self that includes discovering how actions affect others. These qualities help the young people to deal with their trauma (Bateman and Fonagy 2004; Fonagy and Target 2000).

These reflective functions can be developed by a facilitator using books that allow the group members to externalise aspects of themselves to examine, organise and understand. The young people can also learn to think about the perspectives of others through looking at how different characters that are distant from their own respond and take action in a book, often reclaiming their own voice through the safety of metaphor and character, both by dialogue and role-play. Learning to link outside and inside reality and to test out different possibilities in groups using dramatised 'play' allows them to externalise aspects of the self so they can understand and organise them. Taking on roles from books in group play allows them to think about other people's feelings and thoughts (Haen 2005). You might ask a young person to represent or act out the story or feelings of another by using a puppet, or use doubling to express what another is feeling while they stand behind one another and the person doubled is asked to share how close the person has come to their reality.

ENACTMENTS

Children's group

Developing a sense of commonality through collective story-making

1. Warm-up: ask the children to make a list of and describe who they grew up with, what they meant to them and why. What made them feel at home with themselves? What is 'home' and when do they not feel at home?

2. Read poems from Jackie Kay's *Three Has Gone* (1994), a collection for children that deals with bullying.

3. Discuss her responses and ways of dealing with racism, unkindness and hurtfulness. Does this happen to them? How do they feel about this? Do they listen to their 'inside voice' or their 'outside voice'? Are there other ways of coping?

4. Write a group story. Begin with a magic shoe that can walk the character anywhere, who has one wish. (One person starts the story and if they get stuck, the facilitator can offer three alternatives for the story-teller to use and then the next person continues.)

5. The group can change the story when it is collectively replayed. The group should write down the story together. Metaphors and symbols that arise can be enjoyed and discussed as meaningful in terms of place, feelings and ideas.

6. Group members should enact one moment from the group story.

7. Ask they group if they can hold on to the bits that make them feel 'this is how I feel at home with myself'. Can they face the bits that are difficult – that tell us about ourselves – and learn to deal with them?

8. Ask them to write a letter to Jackie Kay about this. Share.

Young adults' group
Integrating, bonding, sharing and promoting psychosocial well-being within the group; learning things about yourself that change your attitude

1. Warm-up: ask everyone to give a sense of their culture's meaning to them.

2. Read passages from Bessie Head's *When Rain Clouds Gather* (2010) about an African political prisoner Makhaya, who escapes over the border and has to find a place in a new culture.

3. Read the passage about the local people using mud to build tobacco sheds – a group activity that is productive and bonding. The hero helps. Discuss the value of this.

4. Describe the developing friendship between the white agriculturalist and Makhaya – the young white man has married and settled in the new culture and finds new ways to improve the local agriculture. Makhaya learns and takes part. Ask about the value of friendship in a new place and of a community in terms of their own everyday experience.

5. Ask the group to write five lines on friendship and their sense of a community. Share.

CHAPTER 17

The Facilitator's Group Skills

Helping the individual's return to self-expression is key to group work. It needs patience to build the cohesiveness of a group. A facilitator needs to activate the group and interact personally with each group member, be supportive and help members to gain support from each other and form relationships within the group. The social roles that group members play serve as clues to their inner emotional landscape – being in the group is a form of play or self-expression. It is a safe place where people learn to establish their boundaries where continuing inner trauma memory can be calmed. Group work also encourages the young people to be comfortable in their body again.

FORMING A WORKING GROUP THAT COHERES

Groups are complex places concerned with hidden dynamics of motivations, transferences and projections – processes that are both conscious and unconscious. Yalom defines the aims of a therapeutic group as including the installation of hope, giving a sense of universality, imparting information, being concerned with altruism, developing socialising techniques and discovering how to learn from others. He regards group cohesiveness and interpersonal learning as of the greatest importance to the young people's development (Yalom 2005).

A group needs active, engaged leadership by those who define the group task. A climate of safety needs to be created, in which group members' stories can be heard. To encourage spontaneous communication, the group should be non-directional (Rogers 1955 in Rubin 1978). The British psychoanalyst Wilfred Bion, serving as a captain in World War 2, was placed in charge of groups of discharged officers, many of whom were suffering from PTSD (shell shock) and in need of regaining their self-esteem. To achieve this in his experimental programme in group therapeutics, Bion understood that the group worked best when it was 'a framework enclosed within transparent walls in which each individual could move freely and undisturbed by "outside interference"' (Bion 1961, pp.14–15). His aim was to further personal relationships, and to give the individual a sense of 'detachment…a first step to therapeutic seminars' (Ibid.). The group would give each person within it a new ability to make contact with reality and to regulate their relationship with others, within which was a sense of both facilitator and group member being engaged in the same 'worthwhile and important task'. The facilitator needed to be intuitively sympathetic, and group members needed 'free expression of the person's private enterprises' (Ibid.). Each group had a primary task to accomplish, which kept it anchored ('the work group'), but underlying this were also tacit assumptions on which the group behaviour was based ('the assumption group'), which the facilitator needed to take into account (Bion 1961, p.21).

At the same time, the client must *want* to see their past in a way that allows them to survive better – only they can change the world of suffering imposed on them – and to attain what they really want, they must change. This will not work until the individual person's relationship with the facilitator is working well. 'Everyone is born again, born together in the group…[there is] personal mastery through explanation… *It is far more important to the process of change to construct plausible, meaningful, personal narrative*' (Yalom 2005, p.183; emphasis added).

MANAGING STAGES OF DEVELOPMENT IN A GROUP

Yalom puts the stages of development within a group succinctly as 'forming' (the group), 'storming' (group members establish status), 'norming' (working for group cohesion), 'performing' (insight emerges) and 'adjourning' (bringing the group to a close, discovering what the group meant to each group member) (Yalom 2005).

Group members need to shift towards empathy and communication, focusing on the present. It is important that the group experiences the facilitator as a human being who, despite imperfections, is trying to help them. They must know that you speak the same language and that they can comment, as equals, on the approach and processes of the group.

Initially, group members should be screened as being able to function together and to ensure they have similar kinds of problems and vulnerabilities, as well as age, sex and experience, so the group is largely cohesive and homogenous.

The beginning stage is about discussing the purpose, method and ground rules of group meetings, emphasising openness and confidentiality, with members introducing themselves and saying what they would like from the group.

The stage that follows is more problematic, as unconscious negative feelings towards the facilitator may develop, as well as an ambiguity or resistance to self-disclosure by the group members, even though the indirect means used in developmental therapeutic use of literature occur. There may be problem group members – monopolists who are compulsively trying to deal with their own anxieties, who need to be drawn into the group; silent individuals who need to be encouraged to speak; and the self-rejecting complainer (who is asking for help) who needs encouragement in self-learning (schizoid, borderline, psychotic or bipolar individuals will be in the hands of a therapist rather than joining a developmental therapeutic group using books).

Gradually, a group cohesiveness develops in which a common goal, mutual support, intimacy, trust and self-discipline are established. This developmental therapeutic group is used to augment individual therapy.

All group activities should encourage interaction with the here-and-now, rather than the past. The facilitator has to be aware of being flexible and to know the limits of how honest or free you can be and how much transparency to allow. The key is the relationship with each individual within the group, which needs engagement and empathy, and makes a mutual impact. It should be kept in mind how dependent the young people may be feeling, which can result in a need to take away any strengths of the facilitator who needs to remain impartial to this. There may be a hidden agenda that causes a group to become uncommunicative because trust has been undermined, so an uneasiness or resistance occurs. When this happens, the facilitator should ask why this is taking place.

Group members should have enough ego strengths to receive feedback and to engage with the group (though individuals may drop out if their severe traumas resurface or if they cannot cope with their new society). The facilitator defines what they can expect from the group and establishes that it is confidential.

Yalom writes of group pressure as being 'compelling' and some individuals' struggle for dominance in the group. It is the norm of groups to contain feelings of 'resistance, fear, guardedness and distrust' (Yalom 2005, p.164), which should be allowed expression, though the group also offers solutions to the social needs of being seen as powerful or admired. Each individual's goals in attending the group should be kept in mind: the relief of suffering, the need for better relations with others and the need to learn how to live more productively and to arrive at insights as a result of their own efforts (even though their deep wish may be to avoid change, and they may be struggling with a poor image of themselves).

MAINTAINING A COHESIVE READING/WRITING GROUP

In order to set up a group for hurt young people adjusting to a new culture, extrinsic factors have to be taken into account, such as time limits of each session and the availability of a suitable safe place and time in which to conduct it. It has to be borne in mind that the degree of severity of their life circumstances might make for unstable membership of the group.

When beginning a new group, it helps to give a clear statement of its primary task and, because the relationship of facilitator and group is based on trust, if you feel discouraged by the way it is going, to express this simply – you might ask the group what is true for them.

It is essential that the young people perceive this engagement as constructive and supportive within the group – by 'talking', they share pain, know they are being heard and accepted by others and learn that others suffer as they do.

Feedback from sharing the writing improves their communication with others, lessening their isolation. This can be applied outside the group as well. The young people know they are being useful to others, which increases their self-worth.

Part of the work as facilitator is to find out all you can about them as a way of understanding how to approach each personal need before the group begins. Each of our four representative asylum seekers come to a reading/writing for health session for different reasons: Asoum wanted from the group sessions what he called 'creativity' to help him release his pent-up frustrations in connection not only with his disability and the way it prevented him from being with women, but with the loss of his past life; Amina wanted to understand how her life crises are reflected in great literary text that she respects, and so be comforted by knowing the characters and the writers' thoughts on suffering and how best to deal with them; Nomif wanted to have someone listen to his difficult past life circumstances so he could compare them with his present life of becoming a father and a plumber, and to feel more confident about himself and his use of the English language; Asola wanted to write about the areas of her own culture which gave her self-respect and a sense of selfhood – a young person growing into adolescence with a need to empower herself in relation to invasive mothering.

The intervention of therapeutic reading/writing deals specifically with the issues so critical to this stage of the young people's development – self-identity, independence and self-worth, but not all young people are necessarily good candidates for the intervention. Reading (and talking about what has been read together) requires a certain maturity of language and thought, and this may preclude children with severe emotional or developmental problems.

As a group facilitator, you need an understanding of the subtle and shifting ways in which group interactions using the arts take place. You are involving the young people in creative tasks and purposeful action that gives a sense of accomplishment to themselves and the group, which opposes the damage done to them by their trauma. It involves: knowing when to pause things because they are becoming too intense; switching to asking people to think when emotions are too high or, if events become too distant, to explore their feelings; and challenging the group for new directions or strategies to explore new perspectives or options.

Your task is to motivate group members to challenge issues rather than other people, to move the group towards solutions, integrating and adding further information that can help by confronting the problems raised and learning to probe other group members' solutions by asking questions (Pardeck 1998).

It takes patience to activate the group and interact personally with each group member, to be supportive and help members to gain support from each other and to form relationships within the group. You need to be positive, constructive and empathetic as you are creating a sense of 'home' where the young people feel accepted. Each text you select should help each person focus on and learn valuable skills to help them in their present lives.

Finally, a facilitator needs to find a measure of objectivity around the task of maintaining an effective group. As a group leader, Yalom made candid summaries, which he sent to all group members giving his interpretations of group interchanges, sharing client gains or remarking on those who had remained silent or restive, and summarising what constituted a good session. In this way he promoted understanding and integrated everyone's experiences into the group (Yalom 2005). Richard Riordan, in his overview of the value of therapeutic writing as an adjunct to counselling, notes that Yalom believed that 'anything that demystifies counselling strengthens it – a belief and practice that underscores the insight-enriching goal of scriptotherapy [developmental therapeutic writing]' (Riordan 1996, p.266).

How Jane Eyre encouraged group cohesiveness

In a group of young women at Baobab, on reading *Jane Eyre* by Charlotte Brontë (Brontë 1966), we talked about Jane's resistance and resilience in connection with her traumatic position as an unwanted and abused child, her innate spiritedness and her sense of the nature of a moral act that inspires her to stand up to the injustice done to her.

We open this out to talk about how the young women have their own reactions of feeling 'locked in', as they are mirrored in Jane's situation, and how they and Jane used wit and courage to change a difficult situation. We also discuss how, at first, Jane tries hard to please her tormentors, though they return this behaviour with accusations, condemning her as 'bad'. The young women talked of their similar situations in the past. Amina remarks she always felt, as did Jane, that she was 'a nobody at home'.

We read aloud together the remarkable epiphanic passage in the novel when Jane suddenly realises that she has nothing in common with her tormentors and that she does not have to take on their values: she sees herself as they see her – she is useless to them, opposed to them, adding nothing to their pleasure. For the first time, Jane becomes objective to their idea of her and realises she is different from them. From that moment, she can go forward as a person who is beginning to recognise and know who she is.

This leads Amina to ask a surprising question referring indirectly to the harm done to her by her father. She wants to know if a person returns to such a torturer, whether they will have changed. I reply that I doubt it, as such people often stay locked in their own idea of themselves, so sometimes we have to remove ourselves from them and discover who we really are. We talk about how Amina herself is trying to do this now, as Jane did in the book. The group sympathises with this.

The group considers together a further extract from the novel, learning that Mr Rochester lied to Jane about his wife's existence. She is indomitable in her moral stance: 'I care for myself', is her answer (Brontë 1966). It is this capacity to believe in herself and to stand by it that strikes the group as being relevant to their lives. Like Jane, Amina feels she is slowly learning to trust herself to make the right decisions to achieve her goal, despite the obstacles of her past, and the difficulties of her life in the here-and-now. Jane becomes one of her (and the group's) 'heroines'.

A group that is a safe inner space within a safe outer one

Group work concerns the creation of a safe place in which facilitator and the young person can experience a dyadic relation within a group (Meares 2005; Siegel 2003). Here, the young people learn to establish their boundaries – a place where continuing inner trauma memory becomes associated with being calm, and they also have 'a physical experience of how things can be different' (Van der Kolk in Haen 2008, p.231; Pitruzzella 2004). In a session you may want to mark off a place within which safe 'imagined' interior spaces can come into play, where the individual feels able to grow and expand the self, choosing what to control or let go of, negotiate, change, lose or find. This interior safe space can be returned to if distress is re-experienced (Casson 2004; Meares 2005). It can be 'storied', working through metaphor or role-play so the young person is able to address a problem from a place that is safely removed from reality (Haen 2005).

Encouraging self-expression as a key to group work

Haen (2005) regards aiding the return to self-expression as key to group work. Many traumatised adolescents and children reclaim their lost 'voice' through releasing emotions by using metaphor and characterisation (role-play). Sheila Hayman, who runs writing groups for adult victims of torture, asylum seekers and refugees, regards 'writing as a tool and a gift they can take wherever the UK Border Agency chooses to send them, as a magic castle they can build for themselves, from which no housing agency or hostile landlord can evict them' (Hayman in Bolton 2011, p.164). Haen, using Casson's methods, asks children to bring an imaginary pet to a vet and talk about it, in fact, articulating their own needs. This work depends on the facilitator as group leader to know when to stop action that is too intense, suggesting new directions or different options – creative acts that oppose the destruction the children have known, suggesting possibilities and a sense of accomplishment (Haen 2008).

Group 'playing'

The social roles that group members play serve as clues to their inner emotional landscape. The self is conceived of as a 'role system' or a 'repertoire' that performs in the group (Emunah 1994; Landy 1994). A role 'is the behaviour that the person engages in when taking on a position in relation to others' (Meldrum 1994, p.76). This depends on who is in the group – it is a form of self-expression 'whether it is dramatically portrayed or enacted in daily life, whether it is thought of in a daydream, projected onto an external object or dramatised through improvisation...' (Doyle 1998, p.224). A facilitator should be aware that individuals in the group hold within them a self-traumatising system in which a false outer self alternately protects or persecutes an inner core self (Kalsched in Haen and Brannon 2002). A group of traumatised children are 'characters' who themselves, 'act' in a literary or theatrical sense (Pitzele 1991).

Group drama to encourage 'the return to the body' using words

Craig Haen also uses group work to achieve a return to the body (Haen 2008). Trauma at the stage of adolescence means that its biological effects coincide with a maximum time of biological growth that makes them uncomfortable in their bodies, either trying to hide or war against it, avoiding being touched or refusing to eat or they may self-harm. The group work is aimed at encouraging the young people to be comfortable in their bodies. Engaging with the body in group work involves using movement such as manipulating puppets, role-play or mask work, allowing the young people slowly to get used to the idea of physical interchange with others, which gives them a sense of competency, and 'internalizing the locus of control' (Haen 2008).

Warm-up exercises such as running, 'freezing' and praising arrested movements as interesting or holding beauty are fun to do and aid bodily expression of feelings through sound and movement. Young people can also be asked to make sculptures of their bodies in small groups, reflecting an event in their day using additional words or phrases, or they can form a waxwork display using their bodies to reflect a theme such as loneliness or rage, with group members moving about in role-play.

To achieve a sense of reconnection for traumatised young people, dramatisation in group work that draws on identification, representation and shared experience connects hurt young people.

Learning to 'live in the here-and-now' in a group

It is important for a traumatised young person to live in the present moment – they feel they are experiencing the present when they are re-remembering past trauma, so their ability to be in the present and to connect with it is impaired. To help the young people stay focused in the present moment, a sense of their body as part of selfhood is central, and using metaphor is a crucial skill that serves as the bridge that connects the past, separating it from the present (Stern 2004).

To express how they are feeling in the present moment, group members can be asked to express a sound or movement or a description in words of the kind of food or weather that would express this. 'Freezing' and passing on a movement that expresses what is being felt in the moment is a good way of connecting informally in a group.

ENACTMENTS

Children's group

Connecting with one another

1. Warm-up: ask the children to form a circle. Give a ball to a group member and ask them to throw it to connect with someone in the group they feel they would like to make contact with, while calling out their name.

2. Ask the group members to cross from one side of the room to another if they have something in common. This can range from having nightmares to wearing earrings.

3. Ask a group to form in each corner of the room, connected by themes such as 'I am angry', 'I am sad' or 'I feel helpless'. Use 'feeling thermometers', placing how big the worry/anger is on a scale.

4. Encourage them to talk about their experiences among themselves.

Young adults' group
Telling the world A

1. Warm-up: ask the group to form a circle. Begin a body 'movement' and pass it round the group, asking for something to be added to it each time it is passed on. This can be quite amusing.

2. Ask the group to sing their favourite music and dance uninhibitedly to what they are singing. In this cacophony, suddenly ask them to 'freeze'. Select an unexpected encounter between group members that is funny or beautiful, and describe it back to them as a form of 'worded' delight or praise of what they have made.

3. Talk about the difference between their 'inside' and 'outside' selves.

4. Bring in a variety of art materials and ask the group to make puppets resembling characters or figures that can represent their inside self and feelings and another that shows their outside ones. (This can be brimming with a comic sense.)

5. Ask them to perform to the group a dialogue between these two 'characters', each giving their feelings and reactions to the other.

6. Ask them to create group sculptures of these experiences.

7. Give a 'subject' to a pair in a group, such as 'hate', and ask them to enact a scene spontaneously, during which anyone in the group can tell them to 'freeze', so that something said that is of interest to the group can be verbally explored. The key sentence can be said louder and louder, with the group joining in (Haen 2008).

Telling the world B

1. Ask the group members to write in five sentences 'Who am I?' or 'My arrival'.

2. Ask them to make a list of objects to put in 'the museum of my life'.

3. Ask them to describe a 'moment of change' in their life.

4. Ask them to write a one-line inspirational message telling us what helps them through the worse times.

5. Suggest they invent two characters from their life who would not normally meet and write their dialogue (Bolton 2011).

6. Ask them to write about a magical object and how it can help them.

7. Suggest they list some sayings that are part of their growing up and their feelings about them and then list your own sayings.

8. Ask them to write a letter to a strong feeling they have had and write the answer to the letter (Bolton 2011).

I came to realise that the effects of trauma on brain mechanisms are profound, and that it is of particular importance to know what happens in the brain under conditions of trauma and how language is necessary to release repetitive, damaging memories.

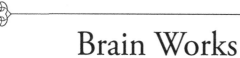

PART 5

Brain Works

Putting the Mind to It

CHAPTER 18

Trauma, Memory, Narrative

The Creative Brain

Writing helps to restore the neurological connections in the brain, and the ability to think through problems, which, in turn, restores confidence. The scientist Pennebaker, specialising in this field, tells us 'If increases in working memory reflect basic ways in which complex emotions are organised, it is important to focus on cognitive processes' (Pennebaker 2000, p.287).

THE BASICS

The brain stem (the first area to mature) regulates basic functions (reflexes, heartbeat, breathing and the arousal of the brain); the cerebellum, connected to the brain stem, co-ordinates smooth movements; the limbic system (the hypothalamus, amygdale and hippocampus) is the 'emotional' brain that controls urges and feelings and is responsible for self-preservation and implicit memory for evaluating the emotional content of experiences; finally, the cortex, particularly the frontal cortex (the 'thinking' brain), is responsible for reasoning, planning and communication (including language), consciousness, thoughts and thinking about thoughts and feelings and behaviour.

In initial trauma reactions, the limbic system fails and the child or young person goes into 'survival mode', and the unused emotional energy is held, rather than released. They experience disruption of normal functioning – psychological numbing, outbursts of uncontrollable feelings or an inability to focus attention, solve problems or use help from others. Much of this behaviour may be about survival, as the child or young person perceives threats in the environment that cause the same terror and helplessness that may lead to post-traumatic stress (Rothchild in Malchiodi 2008).

EFFECTS OF TRAUMA ON THE CHILD'S DEVELOPING BRAIN

Neuroscientists have found that the right-brain hemisphere is deficient in children raised without a secure attachment figure or caregiver. Attention deficit, behavioural problems and cognitive levels were found to be affected in a study of underfed and unloved orphans adopted from infancy to three-and-a-half years old, who were followed up at the ages of four and six years (O'Connor *et al.* 2000). The study found that undernourishment and a small head measurement point to the likelihood of abnormal brain development related to cognitive impairment. The study also looked at how poor social relations in the orphanage affected brain development (Rutter and O'Connor 2004).

Scientists also found that that if a child has little sensori-motor and cognitive experiences in early years because of neglect, the cortex is underdeveloped. Using MRI scans, De Bellis compared brain development in traumatised children of normal weight and height, to a non-traumatised group of similar weight and height, and found that the traumatised children had smaller brain structures (De Bellis 2001).

A group of children adopted at six years of age, who had been in an orphanage for about three years, showed brain abnormalities in areas connected with emotions, and in areas associated with language, memory and executive brain functioning (Davies 2002).

Scientists have also found that in both war veterans and abuse victims memory recall is delayed, distorted and fragmented because of changed brain structures and functions in the hippocampus and medial prefrontal cortex. Problems in talking about trauma are connected with these brain changes (Bremner 2001).

TRAUMA, MEMORY SYSTEMS AND LANGUAGE
Freud and Janet's early research

As a neurologist, Freud's early study of 1888, *Project for a Scientific Psychology* (Freud in Doidge 2007), integrated brain and mind with an early description of synapses which he called 'contact barriers', and how they might change what we learn – two synapses that fire together in time facilitate their ongoing association. This led to his idea of 'free association' in patients – interesting connections emerged in the patients' associations that were normally pushed away. Mental associations are expressions of links in our memory networks. As early as 1896, Freud also realised that events can leave permanent memory traces in our minds and that memories can be changed by subsequent events – he called it a 'retranscription' – the idea that memories are constantly remodelled, but in order to change, memories had to be conscious. Finally, Freud observed that patients were 'reliving' memories instead of 'remembering'. Helping them understand this improved their relationships. 'The underlying neural networks, and the associated memories, could be transcribed and changed' (Freud in Doidge 2007, p.300).

Of equal importance are the lesser-known studies in the early 20th century by Janet, who found that memories of traumatic events – sounds, images and feelings – are as distressing as the original experience, and that by transforming memories into narratives, the effects of the trauma were mitigated (Janet 1919). The latest studies building on Janet's work concern the 'depth of processing'. The degree to which individuals are able to re-experience trauma, emotions, thoughts and sensations is critical for the recovery of these processes; the greater the depth reached, the better the psychological and physiological response (Lepore and Smyth 2002). Lutgendorf and Ullrich built on Janet's idea that a critical task in recovery from stress is the *cognitive* integration of emotions, sensations and thoughts associated with the stress. They show that the degree to which a person can re-experience this is critical for the recovery process and for better psychological functioning (Lutgendorf and Ullrich 2002).

Unconscious memory and verbal memory: unwiring a connection and changing a brain pattern

Neuroscientists now know that there are two memory systems: *implicit unconscious memory*, which comes into play in the early years of a child's development (particularly its interaction with the mother) – it concerns automatic non-verbal actions that concern feelings; and *explicit or verbal memory*, which develops when the child can talk, consciously remember facts, episodes and events that organise memories in time and place. Children traumatised in their first three years have few explicit verbal memories, but implicit memories of trauma are re-triggered in similar traumatic situations. *Therapeutic writing helps young people put their unconscious memories into words and into context so they can understand them – traumatic implicit memory is transcribed into explicit memories so the young people no longer need to relive them.* In the brain they are unwiring a connection and changing a pattern. Threatening ideas or feelings are separated or dissociated from the rest of the psyche. Trauma involves the inability to move the sensory memories of the traumatic experiences from implicit to explicit memory, where the child can reframe them (Rothchild 2000).

When 'memory cannot be linked linguistically in a contextual framework, it remains at the level of images, when there are no words to describe it. It must first be retrieved [for survival] and externalised in its symbolic, perpetual, iconic form' (Steele 2001).

Solomon and Heide found that we process *minor* disturbing memories by thinking, talking and dreaming about them. However, severe traumatic events overwhelm the brain's capacity to process information. Unprocessed traumatic memories can cause cognitive and emotional looping, anxiety, PTSD and depression (Solomon and Heide 2005). Because the traumatic episodic memory is not processed, a relevant semantic memory is not stored. This results in a person avoiding thinking or talking about what happened. Only after the memory is processed and integrated can the normal stasis be established. Terrifying memories may be re-experienced. A participant described it as 'part of me knows it's not really happening now, but it *feels so real* that I get mixed up' (Solomon and Heide 2005, p.54; original emphasis).

Language, a function of explicit memory, is not generally accessible to trauma survivors after a distressing event. In particular, Broca's area, which is one of the centres of language, is affected, making it difficult to relate the trauma narrative. Brain scans show that trauma actually creates changes in Broca's area, which leads to difficulties in identifying and verbalising experiences, a process normally accessible via explicit memory (Van Dalen 2000).

Perhaps this inability to verbalise trauma relates to the human survival response that when experiencing something too painful to recall, the brain literally makes it impossible to talk. The function of a facilitator using books, talking and writing would be to help reconnect and reactivate the ability to use language and imagination expressed in words.

Scientists using brain imaging have shown that when we are reading a story, the brain regions activated are the same as those used if the events were actually happening (Speer in Sautter 2010). The researchers found that obese adolescent girls who read a novel about a teenager who developed more self-sufficiency were more effective in losing weight than a control group who did not read the novel (Sautter 2010).

The role of the prefrontal cortex (thinking) in survival

The prefrontal cortex carries out 'executive functions' or cognitive control functions: these include areas involving attention, self-control, working memory and reasoning, all of which depend on the prefrontal cortex and are critical for mental health and successful functioning, 'whenever going on automatic would be insufficient' (Diamond 2011b).

There are three cognitive control functions from which more complex ones like reasoning, are built: inhibitory control (resisting a strong inclination to do one thing and instead do the one that is most needed); working memory (holding information in mind and working with it); and cognitive flexibility in problem solving.

Professor Diamond's studies show how these brain functions can be modified by the environment, genetics and neurochemistry and become derailed under certain conditions often suffered by young refugees (Diamond 2011b).

Writing helps to restore these neurological connections in the brain and restore the ability to think through problems, which, in turn, restores confidence in what an individual is able to achieve in life (Diamond 2010). What is involved here are the core executive functions mentioned above (working memory and inhibitory control), the building blocks out of which more complex executive functions such as cognitive flexibility, critical thinking, creative problem solving and reasoning, rely on a network of brain structures, the prefrontal cortex being the most important.

THE BRAIN FORMS THOUGHTS IN TWO SYSTEMS TO KEEP US WELL AND HAPPY

Daniel Kahneman, the Nobel prize winner in economics, tells us in his recent book *Thinking Fast and Slow* that 'happiness [well-being] is the experience of spending time with people you love and who love you' (Kahneman 2012, p.401). In examining how we remember this 'well-being', Kahneman tells us the brain forms thoughts in two different systems: System 1, which thinks subconsciously and emotionally quickly, often and automatically, and is highly sensitive to danger; and System 2, which thinks slowly (even sluggishly), infrequently and with effort, logically and consciously planning and making choices and monitoring System 1, allowing it leeway and slowing down emotions.

As part of our evolution towards being fit and well, our thinking process has a bias towards happiness. He calls this 'experienced' well-being, part of System 1 of the brain, which he distinguishes from 'remembered' well-being that is conscious and logical. So we have two selves – the experiencing self and the remembering self: '*The remembering self…composes stories and keeps them for future references… We care intensely for the narrative of our life…[we] very much want it to be a good story, with a decent hero*' (Kahneman 2012, p.351; emphasis added).

System 1 ('intuition') is continually at work and accesses a vast number of memories in order to make judgements fast, because the memories most acceptable to System 1 are those associated with strong feelings such as fear or pain, which enables a person to remember more vividly what you associate with these. The resultant judgements that this level of thinking makes are often wrong – our mental processes are often irrational. System 2's way of thinking is a slow process of forming judgements based on conscious thinking, monitoring and translating into thoughts or responses what flows to it from System 1. It appraises the actions of System 1 and so the chance exists to correct mistakes or revise opinions. *It enables us to create art and culture.* However, it is lazy: to activate it needs mental effort – thinking is hard work. Both systems interact with one another (Kahneman 2012).

The tyranny of the remembering self over the experiencing self

Kahneman writes:

> Memories are all we get to keep from our experience of living, and the only perspective we can adopt as we think about our lives is therefore that of the remembering self... *Confusing experience with the memory of it is a compelling cognitive illusion.* (Kahneman 2012, p.387; emphasis added)

He calls this the 'tyranny of the remembering self' because it makes all the decisions. 'The experiencing self does not have a voice: *The remembering self is sometimes wrong but it is the one that keeps score and governs what we learn from living*' (Kahneman 2012, p.381; emphasis added). So our memory has evolved 'to represent the most intense moment of an episode of pain or pleasure...and the feeling when the episode ends' (Kahneman 2012, p.383). *Associative memory is silent and hidden from our conscious selves,* so we have limited access to the workings of our mind. Our actions and emotions are primed by 'events' or associated ideas of which we are not aware. However, we need to allow the person *to think* in a way that changes their responses to their strong feelings of the past and allows them to understand these in a new light by bringing into play slow-thinking System 2.

Reading/talking/writing brings into play the 'remembering self'

Reading/talking about literature may serve to bring into play 'the remembering self' of a young traumatised person so they can write their painful memories as narrative spontaneously. By examining this written narrative, or the stories written by others that trigger memories, System 2 is pushed out of its laziness into a 'thinking self' that transform the remembering self by re-examining and so coming to see it in a new light, so allowing it to move forward, not only examining the remembered past in a new way, but also allowing a new narrative to be created – one of hope rather than victimhood, a future narrative of self-respect.

Kahneman notes that 'the fact that [a memory] ended badly does not mean it was all bad' (2012, p.385). This is what a facilitator may tell a traumatised young person about their own or another's narrative that begins the process of gaining perspective (System 2).

'WORKING MEMORY' AND CREATIVITY COUNTER THE TRAUMATISED BRAIN

Kitty Klein looked at the relationship between cognitive functions and traumatic life events and found people under high stress are poor problem solvers (Klein and Boals 2001a). Working memory is a core component of reasoning and problem solving. It is 'the capacity for controlled sustained attention [that is goal-orientated] in the face of... distraction, which determines the content of consciousness' (Klein 2002, p.136). It is the site of creativity 'which holds information in mind while mentally working with it and which is critical for making sense of anything that unfolds over time...but it is ephemeral like writing on fogged up glass' (Diamond 2010). It is this part of memory that expressive writing uses and, if brought into play successfully, works to re-contact the part of the brain 'switched off' by trauma that needs to be reactivated by the working memory.

Professor Diamond examined the possible roles of play, the arts, dance, story-telling and physical activity in improving the executive functions. She found that the executive functions depend on the late-maturing prefrontal cortex, yet they can be improved in young children without specialists or equipment. She found that what nourishes the human spirit may also be best for executive functions. Expressive writing (as part of 'story-telling' and 'play') has a role in reconnecting synapses, releasing harmful memories so they may be re-ordered more meaningfully and so allow the individual to survive and to function more effectively in life (Diamond 2010).

Dr William Steele, founder of The National Institute for Trauma and Loss in Children, found over many years of being with traumatised children, that using the imagination is an excellent strategy to reduce the dominance of the deep, primitive limbic system. From a neurological stance, safe experiences develop new memory synapses that lead to synaptic connections that, in time, lessen responses to unsafe sensory memories (Steele 2001).

Cognitions about unresolved stressful events compete for working memory. Klein found that reducing stress by writing narrative as part of expressive writing increases working memory, which makes memory structures more coherent (Klein 2002). Building on Pennebaker and Seagal's study (1999) of the importance of narrative development as necessary to the curative powers of expressive writing, she found that expressive writing, by reducing stress, did lead to improvements in working memory.

Klein also found that expressive writing affected unwanted thoughts about a negative event: these decreased significantly more for those who took part in expressive writing about the trauma, because they had to think about it more. She concludes that, because we remember stressful and non-stressful situations differently, expressive writing helps to transform thoughts about trauma into more coherent memory structures (Klein and Boals 2001a).

She also found that writing about a trauma makes the memory of it smaller and less complex. These memories of negative events may be buried in the story (or recognised in other stories), weakening the accessibility of the bad experiences, so the narrative 'repackages' the memories of trauma so that they are 'retrieved' less often (the effects of the narrative take some time to develop). Klein found that expressive writing or talking reduces the intrusive thoughts about the trauma. Klein's data indicates that the effects of expressive writing about negative events appear to improve working memory linked to linguistic changes in pieces of writing. Emotional disclosure can lead to improvements in working memory capacity. Cognitive functioning seems to be closely tied to writing and the cognitive effects of writing. The improvements in working memory produced by expressive writing might increase the person's ability to focus attention on problem solving, planning and coping, so they can avoid trauma. Reductions in intrusive thinking that follow expressive writing about negative experiences may have independent effects on working memory and health (Klein 2002).

Other researchers found that memories associated with past trauma continue to intrude until they become integrated with schematised knowledge (Horowitz 1975). They discovered that individuals keep unwanted painful thoughts beyond the reach of consciousness, which, though unavailable for controlled thought, are highly accessible and can intrude into consciousness, and so are repressed in an automatic process, which fragments them. This relates to the need for a coherent narrative about trauma to allow the individual to concentrate on attending to other resources. Creating a narrative transforms the content of traumas held in the memory (Wegner 1994).

ALTERING TRAUMA-INDUCED SOCIAL ISOLATION WITH CREATIVITY

Many of our thoughts and perceptions are about our social beings. Our native culture is wired into the brain, and understanding, memory, and recognition of social relationships are held back when the already traumatised brain becomes overloaded by absorbing complex new social structures (Doidge 2007). Professor Diamond's research shows the plasticity of the brain: 'The brain is far more plastic at all ages than previously thought... Neuroscience research shows the powerful role of experience shaping the mind, brain and body' (Diamond 2011c). Because the brain is flexible, we process social experiences that are important for the formation of synaptic connections in the brain (Diamond 2011c). This means that unbalanced installations associated with trauma or stress can be corrected to a certain extent later on in life. However, these 'imbalances', if laid down in the young brain, tend to block further development. If a young person's coping strategies are restricted by stress or trauma, the brain becomes less flexible and they are less able to deal with new psychological conflicts. This often leads to a sense of social isolation. Traumatised individuals may learn to rely solely on themselves, creating their own self-determined world, shutting out external influences, denying themselves new experiences that should become anchored in the brain. Motivation, understanding, memory and recognition of relationships are held back (Hüther 2006).

Professor Diamond found that our brain, and hence our thinking, suffers if we are lonely or socially isolated (Baumeister *et al.* 2005 in Diamond 2010). Her studies show that even mild stress selectively impacts on the prefrontal cortex (Diamond 2011c). Feeling isolated has been shown to impair the executive functions (cognitive flexibility, critical thinking, creative problem solving and reasoning) that rely on a network of brain functions that centre on the prefrontal cortex. Under traumatic conditions, the brain floods the prefrontal cortex with dopamine and norepinephrine, affecting memory learning.

Judith Herman writes that dissociation – the mechanism by which 'intense sensory and emotional experiences are disconnected from the social domain of language and memory' – is an observable clinical response to terror (Herman 1997, p.239). Only when traumatised young people feel safe and accepted and are with genuine caregivers are they able to learn better (Cerqueri *et al.* 2007 in Diamond 2010) 'Translating an emotional experience into coherent prose alters the way it is represented and understood in our minds and brains' (Diamond 2011a). Expressive writing and 'play' that nourish the spirit alter the ways that traumatic emotional experience are represented and understood in the brain (Diamond 2011c).

ENACTMENTS

Young adults' group

Changing memory through thinking and writing –
writing that uses the imagination through 'pictures',
rehearsing experiences of safety and control

1. Warm-up: ask the group to write down a moment when they did something good that was difficult to do, and something not

so 'good' when they could not help themselves. Suggest they write about sights, sounds, sense of place and people.

2. Ask the young people to write five lines on: 'If I could create anything I want, I would…'

3. Read together. Select spontaneous expressive images from these writings.

4. Hand out copies of Doris Lessing's *The Golden Notebook* (2007).

5. Read and discuss the passage dealing with ritual destructive shooting of birds by the trainee war pilot, which becomes deliberate and cruel, like the cruel and senseless killings of war he is about to enter.

6. Talk together about the young man's difficulties and his solutions. Does it say something about the use of violence?

7. Ask the young people to imagine and write another ending to the piece.

I turned to writers who had suffered forms of trauma in their early lives, who thought and wrote about the mind and the imagination in relation to their childhood trauma in original and enlightening ways. I found ways of applying their profound and moving discoveries to new ways of approaching the creativity of shattered young people and their use of language as a way of accessing their inner selves.

CHAPTER 19

The Brain, Literature and Trauma

Scientists may describe our brain in terms of cells and synapses, but that is not how we *experience* the world. Proust's *In Search of Lost Time* describes his realisation that time changes memory and that our memories are unreliable because our intelligence reworks an experience; Virginia Woolf's diary entries and her novel *Mrs Dalloway* reveal how 'the mind' creates fragmented moments of consciousness that need to be brought together in an underlying 'wholeness' or it will disintegrate into madness; Gertrude Stein's creative writing reflects her understanding that the brain 'arranges' language so that there is no strict left-to-right statistical movement of language in the brain (1990).

THE WRITER'S VIEW: EXPERIENCING THE WORLD THROUGH UNRELIABLE MEMORY, THE SPLINTERED MIND AND UNSTRUCTURED LANGUAGE

Scientists describe our brain in terms of cells and synapses, but that is not how we *experience* the world. The neuroscientist Jonah Lehrer was working in the laboratory on the problem of how the mind remembers. He was also reading Proust at that time, and he realised that by artistic intuition, Proust had predicted the results of Lehrer's neuroscientific experiments. Lehrer found that other writers anticipated scientific experiments on the workings of the brain: Virginia Woolf understood the nature of consciousness before scientific experimentation on the subject, and Gertrude Stein rethought how language works in the mind before Chomsky debated the subject (Lehrer 2008).

Proust and the workings of memory as fiction

At the end of *Swann's Way* in *In Search of Lost Time* Proust describes how his narrator tastes the crumbs of a *madeleine* followed by a sip of lime-flower tea, and realises in a single unplanned and intense moment that taste and smell remain 'like souls', allowing him to remember his aunt Leonie, and then to remember his feelings accompanying this memory, finally enabling him to think about the meaning the *madeleines* hold for him – thus being able to find 'lost time' (Proust 1996). In doing so he pre-empted scientists who have established that smell and taste are the only senses that connect directly with the hippocampus, part of the deep limbic system in the brain. Proust also realised that time changes memory and that memories are unreliable, because our intelligence reworks an experience. In terms of science, this is because 'every memory begins as a changed connection between two neurons… Our memories exist as subtle shifts in the strength of synapses' (Lehrer 2008, p.83). Further, memory never ceases – it is not a place to store inert information; it is unconscious. Every time we remember, the neuronal structure is subtly changed, a process Freud called *nachtraglichkeit* or retroactivity. Memory never stops changing, even when the original stimulus is not present, so a memory becomes 'less about what you remember and more about you… Memories are changed to fit what we know now… Our memories are fiction' (Lehrer 2008, p.85). Proust believed in the process of writing memories, using them to tell his narrative on the understanding that they are unreliable.

It is this process of re-remembering that helps traumatised young people towards a cathartic re-telling of their own memories and narrative.

Virginia Woolf's breakdown and the 'splintered mind'

In her diary Virginia Woolf tells us: 'At forty I am beginning to learn the mechanism of my brain' (Woolf 1977). In the diaries she wrote while resting after a mental breakdown, she became more objective to her 'state of mind' and was able to lessen the shame she felt about it. Her mind, she discovered was full of incongruous, ever-changing impressions and the 'self 'she was trying to describe was split into several parts. 'We are splinters and mosaics', she wrote (Woolf 1977). Like Freud, she realised that our minds are not whole but fragmented and made up of disconnected thoughts, yet something at the mind's centre holds it together – 'the whole in one's mind', which she called 'the self' that is the narrative that we tell ourselves (Woolf 1977). Like James Joyce, she wrote her self-narrative in the form of a fragmented and meandering stream of consciousness that reflects inchoate thoughts and feelings in the mind, which she describes as 'consciousness'. Through Septimus Smith – the character in *Mrs Dalloway* who has a nervous breakdown and commits suicide after experiencing the trauma of war – Woolf identifies with the precariousness of the fragile selfhood that lacks a central 'wholeness' and that is always in danger of fragmenting. Woolf's psychiatrist's denial of this 'self' or 'soul', which she experiences, exacerbates her sense of having no 'centre'. It is Mrs Dalloway, at the heart of the novel, who manages to keep the sense of wholeness of self, though this is an illusion and merely 'the ghost controlling the machine', which neuroscientists cannot find – the locus of the 'self', self-awareness or consciousness (Lehrer 2008, pp.183–185).

Virginia Woolf's insights into her troubled mind apply to traumatised young people who need to observe and narrate themselves in order to better understand and come to terms with how their minds work and what is in their minds. By talking and thinking about their 'state of mind' and what caused it, they can better understand the workings of the self.

ENACTMENTS
Children's group
Remembering

1. Ask the children to invent a house in which they are going to tell a story. In it, they should describe their favourite piece of clothing for the group. Where does it come from and how

did it come to them? What does it mean to them when they put it on? How do they feel when they wear it and why? Who or what place does it remind them of? What were the sights, sounds and touch they felt when they were wearing this piece of clothing?

2. Ask them to write a poem/story about when they left their country wearing this clothing – something happens to them that is difficult and they deal with it with the help of others, who think about the problem in another way and find another meaning to their story. They may want to write dialogue (the facilitator may need to encourage this).

3. Suggest the children act it with two others, as they go along. The group may want to bring in their own changes to the story or show different ways of thinking about the problems in the story.

Young adults' group
Remembering for the sake of the self that lacks wholeness

1. Ask the young adults to write a list of 'Things I think are secret'. Ask them to share them with the group so no one feels alone in this.

2. Suggest they write a few lines of dialogue between their 'self' and the person from whom they hid or hide their secrets. What do they think and feel about this now?

3. Ask them to choose symbolic expressions that come up in the writing and discuss how memory connects words and words hold ideas and feelings so we can stand outside and look at ourselves better.

4. Ask them to write a sentence about what they most want now or what they are most good at. Why do they want it and what gets in the way? Share and talk together about these statements.

5. Go round the group circle and ask how each person imagines they will achieve what they want.

Delving into studies of how the brain works in relation to insights from practising writers showed me how the one anticipated and proved the other. My next step concerned the controlled studies and real-world projects that could demonstrate the effectiveness of reading, dialoguing from and writing from fictional accounts of bringing resilience to traumatised young people.

PART 6

Mapping the Research

*The Efficacy of Writing on
Trauma: An Evaluation*

CHAPTER 20

Controlled Laboratory Studies and 'Real-world' Projects

Practitioners and researchers who come from a literary arts or writing background emphasise the healing powers of writing through its ability to provide catharsis and insight. Those from scientific backgrounds, such as medicine or social psychology, prefer to measure, explain, predict and analyse the results of controlled/randomised trials to show how expressive writing improves health.

SCIENCE (SYSTEMATIC RESEARCH FOR MEASURABLE EFFECT) VERSUS THE HUMANITIES

Over the last 30 years there has been an explosion of exploration into the way writing changes people and improves their health. In the practice of the therapeutic use of books as an intervention for health, the literature shows five kinds of investigation: research that recommends the practice; theoretical research; descriptive studies; case studies and experimental research using before-and-after studies; and controlled studies (Rubin 1978, p.49).

Jeannie Wright, in a review of the literature on research on therapeutic writing between 1970 and 2001, found a continuum regarding the underlying debate between the science and humanities paradigms for using writing in a therapeutic setting. Practitioners and researchers who come from a literary arts or writing background emphasise the healing powers of writing through its ability to provide insight; those from scientific backgrounds such as medicine or social psychology prefer to measure, explain, predict and analyse the results of controlled/randomised trials to study the empirical foundations of therapeutic writing and its effect on physical and mental health through the release of emotions (Wright and Chung 2001, p.278).

Meaningful comparisons of theories, methods and findings are fraught because of the great differences between controlled trials and because self-reports differ widely. It is difficult to reduce variables in research trials using a variety of outcome measures for both physiological (immune function) and psychological (cognitive, affective and behavioural) outcomes. Comparisons are also difficult to draw because of variables in follow-ups, diagnosis of initial trauma and number of words written – a kind of reductionism that researchers/practitioners from the humanities avoid, though their research is still considered 'anecdotal'. Wright concludes: 'There seems to be a place for writing therapy across all theoretical orientations' (Wright and Chung 2001, p.286). Even though researchers begin with different perspectives, science can corroborate the humanities' ideas of 'creatively formed hunches' (Rogers 1955 p.275). Riordan found that:

> when writing is used as an adjunct to counselling it may be difficult to assess its unique effects…there is, however, an increase in systematic research pointing to measurable changes when writing is used as a vehicle for processing and conveying significant psychological material. (Riordan 1996, p.263)

One of the earliest experiments on the effectiveness of writing with clients with mental problems was undertaken by Maultsby in 1971. He asked 87 psychiatric patients to write daily about personal problems in an effort to change their damaging self-beliefs. A format of self-analysis was used (event, self-talk, emotional response, rational self-talk). They were assigned to three groups according to how they saw their self-improvement and the amount of written work they had achieved. Maultsby found that the more the clients had written, the better their psychotherapeutic responses. He concludes that the effectiveness of writing helped people to solve daily problems and to improve their ability to think. Maultsby commented *that writing evokes curative factors 'sooner and with equal or even greater intensity than counselling without writing, and the factors may extend beyond the session'*, which is valuable in today's need for therapeutic interventions regarding funding and time (Maultsby 1971; emphasis added).

A SCIENTIFIC EVALUATION OF THERAPEUTIC WRITING FOR REHABILITATION AT THE BAOBAB CENTRE

Leila Sumpton undertook a case study for an MA dissertation (University of London) evaluating the impact on my pilot project using literature and expressive writing to help the process of understanding trauma with the war traumatised child and adolescent asylum seekers and refugees at the Baobab Centre (Sumpton 2012).

Definition of bibliotherapy

In her study, Sumpton provided useful conclusions about an ethical, evidence-based and culturally sensitive approach using literature and expressive writing, which she calls 'bibliotherapy', as providing a unique position to do *effective and rewarding work with traumatised children*. It is an ongoing process of learning and advances the range of therapeutic skills that a facilitator using the intervention can offer the group. Sumpton found there was a lack of empirical research on the impact of writing therapies in the rehabilitation of child survivors of torture in the UK that uses bibliotherapy as an intervention. She aimed to show the positive impacts of the intervention for health *'which shows how human rights principles can be implemented at the service delivery level through a creative therapy'* (Sumpton 2012; emphasis added). She found evidence from many psychosocial researchers who see writing as a natural and necessary response to trauma (Dwivedi and Gardner 1997, p.20).

Limitations of the practice

Sumpton reports on the possible limitations of the effectiveness of bibliotherapy using fiction. Non-fiction books can be more useful in rehabilitation than fiction (Riordan and Wilson 1989 in Detrixhe 2010, p.60). She finds evidence of the effectiveness of CBT as long-term rehabilitation for PTSD sufferers (Day 2009, p.84). Pardeck and Pardeck were concerned that a person could over-intellectualise their situation if using fiction (1984b), and Shechtman was concerned that bibliotherapy in which a facilitator did not take part adequately was open to provoking anxiety and giving unclear advice (1999). The dynamic between client and facilitator has to work, so that neither a language nor a text should be enforced on a recipient (Dwivedi and Gardner 1997).

Positive findings

Sumpton concludes, *that all the major studies cited show that bibliotherapy does use best practice to promote a traumatised young person's empowerment.* She comments that at the Baobab Centre, bibliotherapy is still in its pilot stages, forming part of other holistic services, making it difficult to assess the particular impact alone as rehabilitation, but rather it assesses the impact it brings to other services for those who request it. This included the fact that bibliotherapy was involved at the Baobab Centre in helping the young people with their English language practise as part of building their confidence and coping ability, as many of the young people have had their education interrupted. Therapy was more accessible to some because of a range of factors, including cultural differences.

Methodology

Sumpton used quantitative methods of collecting, analysing and drawing conclusions from data within a qualitative context of a review of the empirical studies relating to the rehabilitation of the child. Bibliotherapy is both an art and a science, as is the way literature is used in the research.

To collect data, she used staff-selected participants under 18 years old who were survivors of torture and who had: completed or near completed bibliotherapeutic intervention at the Baobab Centre; given their consent for the use of information; and had a good level of

English. They took part in an anonymous self-answered questionnaire and written document submission, using the guidelines from the 'Hear by Right' youth participation framework.

Qualitative content analysis of the impact of bibliotherapy, coding changes from pre-therapy to post-therapy, was made using samples of children's initial and final expressive writing pieces at the Baobab Centre. A self-completed questionnaire of closed and open questions on the impact of bibliotherapy was used for 15–20 children in the presence of staff, who had been briefed, and the researcher did not meet the children. Data was coded and imputed into a spreadsheet along with information from the demographic questions. Staff also filled in a self-completed questionnaire. Sumpton used semi-structured interviews to test if the bibliotherapeutic intervention attained Pardeck and Pardeck's six aims (Pehrsson 2005; see Part 2 in this volume).

Sumpton's conclusions

Sumpton's conclusions mention the restrictions of time, space and funds affected bibliotherapy sessions. It has 'best impact when tailored to the young person's story' (Sumpton 2012). Bibliotherapy is suitable for clients with low support needs; there were only a few exceptions. Some young people did not continue with the therapy and this needs to be investigated further. She concludes that:

despite this, aptness of bibliotherapy and expressive writing both for rehabilitation, education, cultural awareness and supporting the confident narratives needed for the asylum process, was seen in the enthusiasm shown by the Baobab Centre staff, and the [sample of] young people who took part in the research. Investigating the potential for this to be extended to other young survivors, supported by other organisations through training and the creation of best practice resources would also be a positive step... The potential of bibliotherapy to be combined with English as a Second Language teaching for refugees is another area that would be interesting to investigate...

Truth-telling supported by story-telling is at the heart of the research on the right to rehabilitation, both to encourage reparations

> *and asylum claims and to support a young person's capacity to*
> *begin the healing process and understand what they have suffered.*
> (Sumpton 2012; emphasis added)

THE SCIENTIFIC WORK OF
JAMES PENNEBAKER

The value of free, expressive writing

In a recent overview of his lifetime's work of over 300 published studies in the laboratory, Dr James Pennebaker, the most eminent researcher in the field of expressive writing in a clinical setting, concluded that 'when people are asked to write about emotional upheavals for 15–20 minutes on at least three separate occasions, their health improves' (Pennebaker 2010, p.23).

At a time when society was still inhibited and dismissive about discussing emotions, the first scientific evidence that people's health improved when they write expressively came in 1983 when Pennebaker and Beall (1986) conducted a pivotal experiment that transformed our understanding of the subject and for the first time found hard evidence that putting disturbing feelings into words – writing them – improves health.

As a social psychologist, Pennebaker had noticed that a high percentage of his University of Texas women students suffered from eating disorders. What struck him was the secretiveness of their behaviour that the usual questionnaires were not addressing. He devised a new questionnaire for 800 women students that probed their eating habits, their parental relationships and their traumatic sexual experiences. He found a significant link between their hidden trauma and their health problems. Experimental participants asked to write for 15 minutes a day for four consecutive days about traumatic life experiences showed significant drops (about half the rate) in physician visits in the six months following study completion compared with control groups (Pennebaker and Beall 1986, pp.274–281).

His conclusion that keeping trauma secret is bad for people was transformational (Hammond 2013, interviewing Pennebaker). Within the next four years, he and colleagues published papers showing that expressive writing could influence immune function, reduce a broad spectrum of health complaints, improve students' adjustment to college and improve their grades (Pennebaker 2010, p.24). Pennebaker writes that 'Clearly writing about the emotional side of traumatic effects was upsetting and physiologically arousing' (Pennebaker and Beall 1986, p.280). Free writing about trauma forced subjects to think about the changes differently (Pennebaker *et al.* 1989).

In Murray's study, students either wrote or talked to a therapist about a trauma or about a superficial subject. Participants expressed greater emotions in describing trauma, but also experienced greater thought changes across the four days. These cognitive changes were measured by objective assessors. In the subsequent writing and talking in groups and self-reports, greater cognitive changes were found (Murray, Lamnin and Carver 1989).

Writing a coherent narrative leads to better socialising

Relevant to trauma and its effects on the cognitive abilities is Pennebaker's study on the relationship of stress to working memory, and the importance of relieving stress by writing a more coherent narrative. His experiments show that if stress is allowed to overload the working memory, the ability to focus and hence to relate meaningfully to others, or to study, is limited. If people write about this trauma, working memory responsible for the capacity to think more clearly is increased, which allows people to become more socially integrated. His study showed that narrative creations could alter the original memory so that it can be 'summarized, stored and forgotten more efficiently' (Pennebaker and Beall 1986, p.1248).

Pennebaker found that constructing stories is a natural human process that helps people to understand their experiences and themselves: 'It allows us to organise and remember events in a coherent fashion while integrating thoughts and feelings... [which] gives individuals a sense of control over their lives' (Pennebaker and Seagal 1999, p.1243). Once experience has structure and meaning, emotional effects (traumatic experiences) of that experience are more manageable, and a sense of resolution (occurs so that there is) less rumination and disturbing situations subside gradually from conscious thought (Pennebaker and Seagal 1999). Painful events that are not structured this way may lead to negative thoughts and feelings. Self-narratives are stories that help us account for 'critical events' in our lives. He concluded that when people put their emotional upheavals into words, their physical and mental health improves a great deal (Pennebaker and Seagal 1999, pp.1243–1254).

The Linguistic Inquiry Word Count (LIWC)

Pennebaker's experiments showed that immediately after writing participants tended to feel unhappy, but two weeks later their mood improved. He found that the longer time the study lasted, the better they felt. The group that used writing improved the most significantly. He concluded that turning emotions and images into words changes the way people organise and think about the trauma. He found the writing was 'self-reflective, emotionally open, and thoughtful' (Pennebaker and Seagal 1999, p.1249).

Because 'text is everywhere' Pennebaker (1993) devised the Linguistic Inquiry Word Count (LIWC) to track how word usage changes when people write expressively with no regard to grammar and only for themselves, and do so consistently. On analysing the material, he found as trauma was progressively expressed, people's word usage changed as they used more cognitive words that changed perspective and ways of thinking about trauma that constructed a story-line. He found the more individuals used positive emotion words, the better their subsequent health, while negative emotions correlated with poorer health, and an increase in causal and insight words was strongly associated with improved health. Over the course of writing, the first group greatly changed the number of insight and causal words they used (Pennebaker 1993).

The benefits of writing work for different populations

Pennebaker also discovered that benefits are found across different populations, social classes and ethnic groups. This is valuable information for the work at the Baobab Centre for, as Pennebaker notes, 'among members of stigmatised groups, writing about being a group member changes the individual's level of collective group esteem' (Pennebaker and Seagal 1999, p.1249), and that focusing on what individuals share with a group can be productive.

Pennebaker's conclusions

Pennebaker's experiments echo Freud's 'talking cure' that stresses the fundamental links between thinking and feeling in the context of a threatening experience. Pennebaker found that:

> Forgotten memories were recalled and linked to the anxiety... To inhibit one's behaviour requires physiological work... Actively inhibiting one's behaviour, thoughts and feelings over time places cumulative stress on the body and increases the probability of stress-related diseases. (Pennebaker in Lepore and Smyth 2002, p.274)

Those most likely to become ill are those who have not confided in others about their troubling experiences, so confronting this may be cathartic. He points out that most of Western culture implicitly believes in a Cartesian split between mind and body, but the writing paradigm affects a wide range of heath and biological markers that crosses mind and body. '*On the broadest level the field has witnessed a striking number of experiments that have demonstrated the remarkable power of translating emotional experiences into language particularly written language*' (Pennebaker in Lepore and Smyth 2002, pp.281–291; emphasis added).

Finally, Pennebaker asks if writing can change behaviour and if people learn to interact differently or see themselves in a new light. His answer is that writing is a useful accompaniment to other therapies and that a client keeping a journal facilitates the process of forming a narrative about their difficult experiences (Pennebaker and Seagal 1999, p.1251). He quotes Jourard's 1971 study that showed that 'tying both the cognitions and affect surrounding traumatic events was optimally effective in maintaining long-term health' (Pennebaker and Beall 1986, p.280). It also allows feelings and thoughts to become more concrete, resulting in greater self-knowledge. Disorders form when the motive towards self-knowledge is blocked. The act of writing about an event and the emotions surrounding it reduces the effect of inhibition (Pennebaker and Beall 1986, p.281). One student involved in his studies of the effects of writing on trauma regarding health commented: 'Although I have not talked with anyone about what I wrote, I was finally able to deal with, it, work through the pain instead of trying to block it out'; another wrote 'It helped me to think about what I felt during those times' (Pennebaker and Beall 1986, p.280).

These reflect the comments made to me by young asylum seekers and refugees working with writing as an intervention. They are of critical importance because the subjects were writing entirely on their own, that is there was no feedback or other means to explain that other therapies were at work in the writing. *The essence of the writing technique is one of the few times that allows people to realise where they have been and where they are going without having to please anyone.* The process includes self-regulation, the search for meaning, creation of coherent stories about one's life, emotional awareness and creative expression (Pennebaker and Beall 1986, p.281; emphasis added).

Applying Pennebaker's findings to young asylum seekers and refugees

'It is difficult to convey the powerful and personal nature' of written responses about traumas (Pennebaker and Beall 1986, p.277). Pennebaker's studies, rather than asking traumatised people only to talk about their experiences, asks them to write about their traumas and to form them into coherent stories. They may write freely about their traumas without any intervention and entirely for themselves, bringing into play, in the long term, coping mechanisms for healing, both physical and psychological. I found this to be true in working indirectly with literature using reading, talking and writing with traumatised young people (as can be seen from the many and varied examples described). In Pennebaker's studies, individuals asked to write about past trauma, commented: 'It helped me to think about what I felt during those times. I never realised how it affected me before', and: 'Although I have not talked with anyone about what I wrote, I was finally able to deal with it, through the pain instead of trying to block it out. Now it doesn't hurt to think about it'

(Pennebaker and Beall 1986, p.279). These comments reflect those of young asylums seekers and refugees – it helped with 'the cognitive work of organising, assimilating, or finding meaning to the events surrounding the trauma' (Pennebaker and Beall 1986, p.280).

Expressive writing can change behaviour: the author and her four 'characters'

Pennebaker asks if writing can change behaviour and allow people to interact differently or see themselves in a new light. Here are the answers given by the four young people we have followed through this book: the effect of Amina's journal writing confirms that for a traumatised young person, keeping a journal facilitates the process of forming a narrative about remembered harsh experiences and manages the emotions around it more objectively, allowing the event no longer to dominate her as she re-writes her story. The disabled young man, Asoum, asked for 'creativity', and wrote several stories about his past life through the books we were reading that allowed him to assimilate better his traumatic past. Nomif's rethinking of his prison experiences through those of the character of a prisoner he read in a fictional account, and then discussed and wrote about, helped him to came to terms with the circumstances of his own flight and imprisonment. The memories of the humiliation and hurt received by the young Asola when kept in detention were alleviated when she told the story, with such pride, about her princely family origins as expressed in the red beads they threaded in their hair.

THE SCIENTIFIC WORK OF PENNEBAKER'S FOLLOWERS

Reconstructive narrative writing helps to control unwanted thoughts

Kitty Klein found that people under stress were poorer problem solvers compared with people who experience less stress (Baradell and Klein 1993). She found that people with high stress performed worse on the OSPAN (Operation Span), a reliable test that requires switching attention between reading and solving equations and retaining words.

Those with more stress performed poorly and had poor inhibitory control on OSPAN. Unwanted thoughts about negative experience correlated with the OSPAN performance. Expressive writing also improved working memory (Klein and Boals 2001b).

She also discovered that unwanted thoughts decreased significantly more for students assigned to write about that event. She set out to show that the benefits of expressive writing are linked to an ability to transform 'poorly organised cognitive representations of stressful experiences into more coherent memory structures' and that 'stressful memories consume attentional resources' (King in Lepore and Smyth 2002, p.140).

Klein found that improvements in working memory a week after writing were small but became relevant after seven weeks. She examined self-reports and found expressive writing or talking reduced intrusive thoughts of trauma in some people (Klein and Boals 2001b). She concluded that working memory improvements produced by expressive writing increase the ability to focus attention on problem solving, planning and proactive coping (Klein in Lepore and Smyth 2002).

Helping self-regulation of thoughts

Laura King's research centres on how expressive writing helps self-regulation (the ability to pursue goals, to give feedback in the form of negative and positive feelings and to adjust) in traumatised individuals. Writing about experiences that allow people to understand the meaning of their emotional reactions helps to pursue goals. As individuals learn more about themselves and the meaning of their feelings, they become more effective in pursuing their goals, whereas traumatised people's emotional disturbances disrupt self-regulation.

King pursues the idea that the presence of positive feelings in the context of traumatic life events has been neglected (Folkman and Moskowitz 2000; King and Miner 2000). Stories we tell are the building blocks of identity. To integrate experiences we construct narratives that fit our storied selves – 'we make them something we are, not something that happened to us' (King in Lepore and Smyth 2002, p.125) and that this is adaptive as the coherent life narrative we construct after trauma contains positive benefits within the negative events.

Personal growth emerges from extreme experiences (Tedeschi and Calhoun 1995). Writing about goals is self-regulatory, as it leads people to write about future aspects of their narrative and relates to outcome measures of well-being (King 2001). In King's study, participants rated writing about trauma and their best selves as important, emotional and challenging, and this group showed significantly lower illness (King in Lepore and Smyth 2002, p.127).

King points out that Pennebaker would like to see how all facilitators: 'specialising in language, cognition, social processes, and psychotherapy can work together in better understanding the mechanisms of this phenomenon' (King in Lepore and Smyth 2002, p.165).

Who is helped most by expressive therapeutic writing?

Jeannie Wright summarises the circumstances in which the people for whom writing therapy has been proved to be beneficial. These include those in therapy when detail can be written outside the therapy room; people who are self-directed to write journals, diaries or letters; those who perceive themselves as powerless; people who need to use their first language; people silenced by shame; people who need to externalise disturbing thoughts and feelings; and those who are facing a time when strong feelings predominate, such as adolescence (Wright and Chung 2001, p.287).

Writing is not always appropriate or beneficial. This happens if a person's experience is not yet put into words, when writing is connected with negative experiences, when people do not want to re-experience their trauma in reading or writing, or a person is dyslexic (Wright and Chung 2001, p.287).

Summing up

Pennebaker summarises his early findings as: 'the real magic of the writing paradigm is that it affects such a wide range of health and biological markers' (Pennebaker 2002b, p.281). Pennebaker's later experiments are about whether 'we can train people to write in healthy ways' (Pennebaker 2002b), in other words learn to change their perspectives through writing and write their stories as part of this process. Pennebaker tells us that 'People need to grow over the course of writing' (Pennebaker 2002b, p.288). Writing about trauma changes the ways people think and therefore interact with others, changing their social lives as they talk more and use more positive emotion words (Pennebaker 2002b, p.291). Pennebaker's conclusions are supported by Brian Esterling whose review on the mental and physical outcomes of the empirical foundations for writing 'supports the therapeutic and preventative use of writing and suggests that writing about upsetting experiences can improve mental and physical health' (Esterling *et al.* 1999, p.92). Esterling tells us that 'The construction of a story rather than having a constructed story may be the desired end of writing, and, by extension, psychotherapy' (Esterling *et al.* 1999, p.94).

The literature also shows that writing can be used as a very helpful cost-effective, mass-orientated medium of expression and communication. Esterling concludes that 'Writing is a powerful therapeutic technique…when writing is coupled with verbal psychotherapy it may reduce the length of the therapy and thus its costs' (Esterling *et al.* 1999, p.94).

SHECHTMAN'S SCIENTIFIC RESEARCH USING LITERATURE WITH DISTURBED CHILDREN

The bibliotherapist Zipora Shechtman defines bibliotherapy as 'the use of literature for therapeutic or educational outcome' (Shechtman and Nachshol 1996, p.537). It is an 'indirect, projective technique by which participants attribute socially undesirable affects which they would normally tend to deny, to literary characters' (Shechtman and Nachshol 1996, p.538). Shechtman comments that the aggressive adolescents with whom she works, who are often victims of violence themselves, find it difficult to express themselves, lack empathy and self-control and misunderstand power and force, and that in her studies, bibliotherapy is aimed at improving these areas of behaviour. Her approach is a considerable influence on the way I approach young refugees and asylum seekers who have known war violence or abuse, who need to be reached in order to change their way of thinking and feeling about themselves. It should be kept in mind that: 'it is hard, perhaps impossible, to separate the unique contribution of the particular bibliotherapy intervention form the effect of therapy in general' (Reynolds, Nabors and Quinlin 2000).

Since 1966, Shechtman has conducted several studies of large samples of aggressive young people in both regular and special education who took part in therapeutic intervention using fiction, measuring their behavioural changes based on self-reports and those of teachers.

Her first study was aimed at finding their motives or beliefs for their aggression. Psychodynamically orientated, Shechtman's intervention was used to reduce adolescent aggressive behaviour and beliefs that endorse it, based on the idea that 'learning is not only a rational process, but incorporates a strong emotionally driven experiential system' (Shechtman and Nachshol 1996, p.535). She notes that maladapted adolescents have problems with self-reflection and 'are unwilling to consider the feelings, thoughts and intentions of others, lacking the skills of interpersonal relationships.' The internalisation of appropriate standards of behaviour was a crucial variable (Shechtman and Nachshol 1996); this is true of traumatised young asylum seekers.

In her study, Shechtman used stories, filmstrips and photographs to enhance the language of feelings. A story is presented, followed by a group discussion in which the feelings of the literary characters are discussed and the motives of their behaviour explored and 'generalised into broad psychological dynamics of human functioning' (Shechtman and Nachshol 1996, p.538). She used a rating scale in which students placed themselves on a 1–10 scale about how often they were victims of aggression. Attitudes towards aggression were measured on techniques similar to the Direct Situation Test that assumes 'attitudes [towards their problems] are the scripts internalized' (Shechtman and Nachshol 1996, p.542). The study took place over two years with 117 maladapted adolescent boys. Results based on self, teacher, parent and peer measures showed that aggressive behaviour was reduced in the experimental group only in the second year of study, after three months had passed, but in the control group increased aggression occurred. The experimental group showed a reduced level of aggression and endorsement of aggression, increased empathy and also went through cognitive change. However, 'the effectiveness of the intervention is highly dependent on the skilful application of the technique with children and adolescents' (Shechtman 2009, p.65).

In a later study, children received either bibliotherapy or other helping sessions. Results showed that overall, less productive responses were shown in the helping sessions, and the children worked more effectively in the bibliotherapy sessions as *they were engaged in cognitive exploration and reported more therapeutic change – the children perceived the change, which is important. Using literature also acted as a buffer for resistance to change* (Shechtman and Effrati 2008).

ASSESSING RESEARCH RESULTS FOR EFFECTIVE CHANGE

It is important to ascertain if research using randomised control trials changes practice, and if they assess the difference between controlled experiments and the effectiveness of their application to reality. They also need to demonstrate the effectiveness of the writing intervention in a clinical setting. Results from these experiments may not be applicable to the actual therapeutic intervention. The experiments should be seen in the perspective of selection of experimental participants and characteristics of the therapist and therapy settings, as well as the feasibility of the intervention to be delivered, which includes patient acceptability and compliance, cost effectiveness in terms of community and public health orientation in the future.

Smyth and Catley conclude that although 'the efficacy of structured writing exercises has been substantial, there remains areas of concern about generalization to treatment effectiveness' (Smyth and Catley 2002, p.32). They maintain that thoughtful examination of existing research through effectiveness studies can remedy this. They acknowledge that evidence exists that structured writing exercises can readily be adapted as effective supplementary treatment, particularly in the realm of community interventions in public health (Glanz, Lewis and Rimer 1997; Smyth and Catley 2002).

Scientific proof that therapeutic writing helps illness

In their book, *The Writing Cure: How Expressive Writing Promotes Health and Emotional Well-Being*, Lepore and Smyth set out to give examples of research that advances basic scientific understanding on why expressive writing influences health, what health outcomes it affects and the conditions under which it is most and least beneficial, as well as exploring new avenues of research, and clinicians are applying their research discoveries (2002, p.7). They conclude that 'Expressive writing interventions are exciting to clinicians and researchers alike because of their relative simplicity and their robust effects on a wide range of mental and physical outcomes' (Lepore and Smyth 2002, p.99).

Smyth shows the mounting evidence that people who have experienced extreme stress gain physical and psychological health improvements when they write expressively (Smyth 1998). Findings give a wide range of benefits, such as lung functioning in asthma sufferers, reduced symptoms in rheumatoid arthritis patients and fewer physical and emotional complaints (Greenberg and Stone 1992; Lepore 1997), as well as improved social relations and role functions (Lepore and Greenberg in press; Spera, Buhrfeind and Pennebaker 1994).

Lepore and Smyth's book includes research on writing and adjustment to stress, and research that shows that writing shapes children's thoughts and influences social identity and ways to deal with conflict positively, as well as showing how narrative writing can influence thoughts and feelings around social development so that health improves (Daiute and Buteau 2002). They also include scientific evidence of the underlying mechanisms that link expressive writing to health outcomes, but show that painful memories need not be explicitly addressed to give health benefits. They show current thought about 'mechanisms of adaptation' involving feeling, thinking and biological systems (Lepore and Smyth 2002, p.9).

The book includes an overview by Stephen Lepore *et al.* of experiments evaluating the evidence that expressive writing regulates feelings, including Pennebaker's research that expressive writing encourages a stressed person to pay attention, that writing desensitises an individual's responses to intrusive stressful emotions and that it also changes thought processes about stress (Pennebaker, Mayne and Francis 1997). Further, paying attention to positive aspects of stress by writing about them acts as a buffer to negative aspect, leading to new social and personal resources (Smyth and Pennebaker 2001). Some research shows writing inhibits intrusive thoughts (Schoutrop 2000), whereas other research found that expressive writing extended the negative effect of intrusive thoughts on psychological and physical responses (Lepore 1997; Smyth, True and Souto 2001).

In studies of clients' self-reports on rating writing, results showed that interventions were felt more positive (Donnelly and Murray 1991). Other self-disclosure studies found a positive change in self-perception after writing and a greater degree of feeling connected to themselves and being able to accept their deep feelings about themselves (Lepore *et al.* 1996). This may be difficult if cultural mores impede this (Lepore *et al.* 1996). Writing about deep feelings without having to present the self in front of others, keeping a personal perspective and telling the story from this viewpoint may help disturbed people to admit rather than deny their deepest feelings as being part of themselves, both in the past and the present, and to accept these feelings (Greenberg and Safran 1987, p.193).

Other studies on how writing changes self-concept show how writing helps people to observe themselves controlling negative emotions, increasing their own ability to control their emotions, lessening negative moods and chronic stress and its physical symptoms (Brashares and Catanzaro 1994).

EMPIRICAL RESEARCH ON EXPRESSIVE WRITING AND TRAUMA

Writing for therapeutic ends to relieve illness associated with traumatic experiences has been a part of the psychotherapeutic tradition that uses identification, exploration and expressions of traumatic thoughts and feelings.

Arleen McCarty Hynes and Mary Hynes-Berry established the first hospital-based training programme in bibliotherapy in 1974 in Washington, and published their *Biblio/poetry Therapy: The Interactive Process: A Handbook* (1994), the first textbook for the training and practice of psychologists and other facilitators for the therapeutic treatment of individuals (including children) who have been abused or emotionally disturbed or who face stressful life circumstances, in order to improve their mental health. They use case studies and training experience in this work of reference in 'a new and significant field' (Hynes and Hynes-Berry 1994). They explore the dynamics of the bibliotherapeutic process and its goals, outlining valid differences in clinical and developmental modes using a humanistic therapeutic outlook, knowledge of groups, how to conduct sessions, co-operate with other staff and write reports and methods of training. It covers the bibliotherapeutic process as applied to mental health (versus 'education' and 'therapy'), the tools (books), the bibliotherapist's responsibilities and knowledge of the participants and group dynamics. Their work is invaluable for its understanding, experience and grasp of the processes involved in the effectiveness of the use of books in healing, and stands as a witness to the importance and value of the intervention.

In 1993 Mazza updated the need for both quantitative and qualitative research at the National Association for Poetry Therapy (USA) where the 'art' and 'psychology' approaches meet (Mazza 1993). He considers the combination of quantitative approaches (replication and verification) and qualitative ones (narrative reports) as complementary methods (Mazza 1993, p.51). He emphasises that research and practice need not be separate, as an inter-disciplinary research paradigm includes social, economic and political factors, concern with language and communication, cultural diversity and gender sensitivity emphasising power and connectedness. He acknowledges the problem of isolating variables 'that effect change in one's belief system and well-being... If the subjective method of writing can restore choice and one's voice, it should be used as a therapeutic technique and assessment device' (Mazza 1993, p.52). His empirical research with a poetry therapy group model found that it advanced 'group cohesion and self-discovery', basing it on the Moos Group Environment Scale (Mazza 1993, p.55).

Celia Hunt, a founder member of the Association for the Literary Arts in Personal Development (Lapidus), used a literary-psychoanalytic approach around autobiographic writing to explore the tension between writing as art and writing as therapy, though she admits the limitations of this research for not including cultural-sociological approaches to class, gender and ethnicity. She also acknowledges this work needs an awareness of the therapeutic relationship (Hunt 2000).

Gillie Bolton, researcher and practitioner working largely in healthcare settings, uses small groups in which therapeutic writing or narrative is used to encourage confidence and self-empowerment. Her pilot study for the Institute of General Practice challenged doctors to work with patients suffering terminal or debilitating diseases using expressive writing, which gives the power to the patient rather than the practitioner (Bolton 1998). The limitations of this approach might be an unawareness of the dangers of allowing ill patients free self-expression without any checks, though severely mentally disturbed or depressed patients would not be included. It is also a difficult area of therapeutic writing to research. She feels that scientific researchers should rely on their experience of working with clients and therapeutic writing rather than finding explanations for effect. She feels that researchers interested more in the science of research in this area of client-centred social psychology should be more aware of the fluid and changeable nature of the human psyche and the singular way the creative arts, such as writing, connect with the creativity of the mind, which provides a form of self-direction for those who choose to write as a possible adjunct to therapy. Bolton found that therapeutic and reflective writing can enable exploration of narratives, values, ethics, feelings, metaphors, 'imaginative, acute observations' and 'dialoguing with the inner selves' (Bolton 1998, p.259). Through expressive writing 'we need to take ourselves close to our boundaries in order for change to happen' (Bolton 2011, pp.258–259). She quotes Thorne on Carl Rogers's idea that 'human beings become increasingly trustworthy once they feel at a deep level that their subjective experience is both respected and progressively understood' (Rogers in Thorne in Bolton 2011, p.265).

John Pardeck and followers: fiction, insight and values

John Pardeck spent a lifetime discovering and applying his understanding of the principles and use of books in clinical social work practice and writing about the value of the approach, giving guidelines for its application to professional practice as a medium through which clients can discuss problems objectively and apply this to their own situations with the help of a therapist or facilitator. He reports studies analysing the effect of fiction and related material as successful in changing self-concepts and the concept that fiction, together with self-help readings, effectively improves emotional adjustment of clients. He advocates that it is critical to continue to conduct empirical research on the efficacy of the discipline (Pardeck 1998, pp.1–5). He describes the usefulness of using fiction in the stages of the development of insight (Pardeck and Pardeck 1984b, p.196). Later, he added further advantages of therapeutic reading such as learning new values and ideas and avoiding isolation by sharing problems with others (Pardeck 1994).

Coleman and Ganong have used books therapeutically with clients for a decade, matching a client's problem to that of a character in an appropriate book that meets moral and aesthetic guidelines so that the client can learn 'facts' about their own position. They raise the question of the possibility of measuring 'insight or deeper understanding', which may be the reason that they did no controlled experiments on their findings (Coleman and Ganong 1990, p.327). Riordan found that writing that is interactive with talking is a valuable adjunct to counselling (Riordan 1996, p.263).

Studies from the 1990s report a number of good outcomes using fiction with those in disturbing social situations. Cohen found that reduced stress levels occurred (Cohen 1993; Gaffney 1993); Coleman and Ganong found using children's books helped as a way of working with children of step-families (Coleman and Ganong 1990); and Farkas and Yorker's research found that using fiction was effective in working with the emotional problems of homeless children (Farkas and Yorker 1993). Lanza found that using fiction can promote emotional catharsis, active problem solving and insight into problems (Lanza 1996).

Writing in relation to other therapies

Studies of the intervention of writing about traumatic events have been compared with psychotherapy as the process of support, as empathy and interpretation are present in both. The studies were set up to discover what mechanisms of change to place, as well as the similarities in both practices. Donnelly and Murray asked undergraduates to write about very traumatic events, and incidental events, and they also talked to a psychotherapist. Both writing therapy and psychotherapy showed positive changes occurring in thoughts, self-esteem and adaptive behaviour. Both writing and psychotherapy were found to be equally effective in dealing with traumatic experience, with both groups feeling more positive than the control groups. They showed greater self-esteem and adaptive behaviour and reduced negative feelings. After each session, the writing group showed more negative mood but felt more positive overall by the end of the sessions. Dramatic differences in mood produced by the two interventions suggested different mechanisms were at play (Donnelly and Murray 1991). Studies still need to be done to address the clinical relevance of these findings.

Brian Esterling defines written expression as: 'specifically referring to that behaviour which includes recalling a stressful event and writing about that event, using both descriptive and emotional words'. He maintains that the fact that writing *during* psychotherapy ameliorates the residual negative mood is important because it keeps the individual dealing with the emotional trauma until this process is complete (Esterling *et al.* 1999, p.83).

Murray and Segal took up the differences in negative mood between those using psychotherapy and those taking part in writing and talking. They asked participants to speak about their emotions into a tape recorder with no one present or to write about them for the same period of 20 minutes, Half the group were asked to describe traumatic experiences and the rest to describe trivial ones. Both writing and talking about traumatic experiences had positive therapeutic effects. This particular study concluded that differences between 'written expression' and psychotherapy are because of the personal interchange present in psychotherapy (Murray and Segal 1994).

L'Abate, an early user of 'distance' writing (writing on the internet) who questioned the client/therapist relationship of traditional family psychotherapy, used programmed writing as assignments, giving commentaries on crucial issues to the client, as an intervention with families to manage anger, shyness, lying, sexuality and relationships. He concluded that whereas writing can augment the therapeutic task involving catharsis and objectification of thought in structured writing, free writing can encourage therapeutic emotional self-searching and celebrate the uniqueness of the writer (L'Abate 1992).

Russ randomly assigned 55 clients with anxiety problems to three groups: those using programmed writing; those using free writing; and a group that did not write. Using a Multiphasic Inventory of Personality Anxiety Content Scale, he found significantly lower anxiety scores for the two therapeutic writing groups. He concluded that writing therapeutically encouraged cognitive and social skills (Russ 1992).

Finally, I needed to assess the future of using literature as a therapeutic intervention in a modern world – to ask if it could be adapted to use online so that everyone with access to a computer could also use the intervention safely and within controlled ethical rules.

CHAPTER 21

Interapy

Therapy Online, Future Research

We are communicating differently today in a more open culture via electronic devices like Twitter, Facebook and YouTube. Expressing ourselves informally and openly means that the need for writing trauma may be lessening. Pennebaker advances the novel idea that perhaps the next generation will cope by telling each other to 'Shut up!' (Pennebaker in Hammond 2013).

RESEARCHING INTERAPY: AN ONLINE THERAPEUTIC RELATIONSHIP

Electronic mental health provision of therapeutic interventions (counselling psychotherapy and therapeutic writing interventions because they use the written word) is challenging and developing fast with new information technology solutions to communication constantly overtaking the field. The possibilities are balanced by the increased risks for clients and pitfalls for facilitators, though, as technology becomes consistently part of our lives, more people seem willing to embrace this new method of assistance (Wright in Bolton *et al.* 2004, p.142).

Even though there is little scientific research debating the effectiveness of the field, there is a great deal of anecdotal evidence around its presence (Anthony 2004). It was first used in 1972, and question-answer sessions advising on mental health began in the early 1990s followed by therapeutic relationships by email and the internet. Kate Anthony, when researching the terrain, discovered that counsellors and psychotherapists largely found this unacceptable as a form of treatment, as they felt that without face-to-face interchanges a relationship could not be nourished and the intervention becames one that merely gave advice, though many of the users' clients thought otherwise. She found online therapy needed more skill and effort (Anthony 2004, p.134). Suler argues that there is huge potential in the use of the internet in therapy that removes physical bias (that is the actual sights and sounds of the interchange) and limited access, and bypasses the defences of both therapist and client (Suler in Anthony 2004, p.134).

The British Association for Counselling and Psychotherapy (BACP) guidelines emphasise that practitioners using this 'innovative and under-researched means of delivery' should do so with caution (Goss *et al.* 1999). The document covers the ethical and practical areas of therapeutic communication via exchange of emails and the use of internet relay chat (IRC, synchronous therapy) using the written (typed) word (Goss and Anthony 2004, p.170).

In terms of competence, there are courses available that cover these procedures, including computer knowledge, communication skills that include 'nettiquette' (norms of using the internet) and coping with the lack of body language. The internet opens up vast world contacts with the implication for the facilitator that wide cultural and psychological differences must be taken into account. There is also the problem of differences in the use of language in various countries – the word 'counsellor', for instance, holds different meanings in different cultures. Issues of jurisdiction may arise and the matter of where the intervention is taking place becomes important. The time taken to respond to emails must be workable, as must the length of emails. Confidentiality and data protection issues should be taken into account.

Jeannie Wright offered email counselling for staff at Sheffield University because 'the connection between "writing therapy" and online text-based counselling is clear' (Wright 2004, p.143). She felt it extended access to the health intervention, allowed people with disabilities or those living at a distance better access and that it reduced inhibition about disclosure of trauma, as email was more private and anonymous. Finally, a client had a permanent record in the emails of the intervention. What is of interest to bibliotherapists is that 'in terms of using confessional and creative writing or keeping a reflective journal (online therapeutic interventions for health) has its roots, like much older and traditional forms of correspondence therapy, in creative writing itself' (Wright 2004, p.143). The convention is cheaper, but it cannot guarantee confidentiality, there are risks of technological breakdown, the 'presence' of the client is missed, there is 'a potential for misunderstanding of meaning' and a possible problem of crisis identity (Wright 2004, p.144).

In Kate Anthony's experience, people using internet communication turn the written experience into one of seeing and hearing (Brice 2000 in Anthony 2004). They rely more on the written word and so there is a need for a client to be able to write more expressively and creatively (Suler 1997). A grasp of writing in shorthand and using symbols as part of the internet language is also important. Anthony feels therapeutic skills need to be developed and extended and that it is necessary to discover what works for each person. Sharing a client's cultural experience is also important.

INTERAPY USING WRITING ASSIGNMENTS WITH TRAUMATISED PEOPLE

Lange *et al.* at the Department of Clinical Psychology, University of Amsterdam, found that some computer-mediated therapies are more effective than having no therapy at all and that they are as effective as face-to-face interventions (Lange *et al.* 2002, p.222; Lange *et al.* 2003). Working on the evidence that overcoming trauma involves habituation through self-confrontation of traumatic memories and cognitive reappraisal of these experiences, and using structured writing assignments as alternatives to confrontations with a therapist, they set up a clinical model of structured writing at the University of Amsterdam. This involved self-confrontation of the most painful images through writing about them, cognitive reappraisal by challenging negative feelings when they find they cannot write and, finally, when taking their leave of the assignment, writing a letter to a designated person, expressing their feelings.

One model showed social workers could be trained to approach clients suffering from severe trauma; a second model used four writing sessions with 32 undergraduates suffering traumas that showed mood and depressive symptoms improved; and a third model using 48 traumatised students showed significant reductions in avoidance and intrusions Their data showed short and simple writing interventions yielded positive results on trauma symptoms, and this holds for long periods and strengthens with time (Lange *et al.* 2003, p.218–223).

Lange *et al.* continued their interest in writing as a creative intervention for trauma by using the internet, as they believe it increases the therapeutic possibilities of computers because many people prefer to reveal their inmost thoughts using this method, though this applies more to well-established treatments with defined disorders. Their study involves treatment through the internet involving people suffering from PTSD and grief. They did so using a model based on self-confrontation, cognitive appraisal and social sharing through structured writing assignments (Lange *et al.* 2002, p.223). They developed an interactive website for computer-mediated communication between participants and facilitators. When a person first contacts the site, they browse the Interapy web pages for their symptoms and the structured writing assignments, as well as information about facilitators and where to go should this prove unsatisfactory. They then complete questionnaires and the system examines and scores these responses. If they do not meet the inclusion criteria they are given information about other institutions. Those that stay describe their traumatic experiences and they are assigned a facilitator and sign an informed consent form. They are screened for signs of any extreme psychoses.

A controlled trial was conducted with 41 traumatised students and showed a strong decrease in trauma symptoms and reduction in intrusion and avoidance symptoms. A second study using a controlled trial allowed participants from all over the world who could speak Dutch, aged between 22 and 55 years. Of the 50 applicants, 28 passed the screening and 15 completed Interapy with similar results. Lange concluded that this method works best for those experienced with the internet who did not want face-to-face treatment. They had not spoken of or written about their trauma before. They did feel the presence of the facilitator, and a positive relationship was established. Facilitators felt they had more time to react to emails, and they felt they were not distracted from the core elements of the intervention. The transparency of the process benefited the client–facilitator relationship. Lange *et al.* emphasised that facilitators give unconditional support even with those who avoid painful subjects. They found the letter writing had long-term positive effects, as clients were creating a meaningful document with symbolic power. Clients who had not spoken of their trauma benefitted more than those who had done so (Lange *et al.* 2002, pp.228-235).

After their information on Interapy was made public, they completed a further experiment. Their measured results showed that 'intrusions and avoidance' decreased strongly in the treatment group, whereas the control group showed no decrease in these symptoms. Lange *et al.* found that written disclosure is a powerful predictor of positive outcome. An evaluation questionnaire of the participants' response administered by email, expressed positive experiences about writing about their feelings and confidence in their internet treatment. The effect sizes were considerably higher than those in face-to-face interventions (Lange *et al.* 2003).

EPILOGUE

It is time to express the pleasure I took in being able to voice the progression of the four young asylum seekers and refugees in search of themselves through language and their encounters with fiction, despite the ups and downs and ins and outs that continue in their lives in the here-and-now as part of coping with their pasts.

Amina is taking her A-levels and wants to become a teacher; Asoum, despite his disability and his sense of isolation, is continuing his studies in international politics; Nomif is completing his training to become a plumber and has become a father; and Asola is a bright young school student gaining in confidence in her own abilities. My heart, and yours I am sure, goes out to them in the years ahead as listeners, readers and writers, each in their own very individual way.

FURTHER INFORMATION

ORGANISATIONS

Arts for Health
Information and advice on the arts as part of healthcare.
Manchester Metropolitan University, Righton Building, Cavendish Street,
Manchester M15 6BG
Tel: 0161 247 1094
artsforhealth@mmu.ac.uk
www.artsforhealth.org

Baobab Centre for Young Survivors in Exile
Clinical Director: Sheila Melzak
6–9 Manor Gardens, London N7 6LA
Tel: 0207 263 1301
www.baobabsurvivors.org

Booktrust
A charity supporting readers and writers: changing lives through books. Book
recommendations, prizes, free book programmes: Bookstart, Bookfinder,
Best Book Guide 2013. Best poetry books for children.
Chief executive: Viv Bird
Book House, 45 East Hill, London SW18 2QZ
Tel: 020 8516 2977
www.booktrust.org.uk

Children's Society, The
For children who are refugees from violence.
Edward Rudolph House, Margery Street, London WC1X 0JL
Tel: 020 7841 4400
www.childrenssociety.org.uk

Confer
An independent organisation (established in 1998) that provides innovative,
recent educational interdisciplinary events in research and theory for
psychotherapists, psychologists and mental health workers to understand the
mind and for best practice, including a seminar on 'stories of resiliance'.

Director: Jane Ryan
4 Snape Road, Tunstall, Woodbridge, Suffolk IP12 2JL
ryan@confer.uk.com
Tel: 01728 689090
www.confer.uk.com

English PEN and English PEN Magazine

Readers' and writers' programme that sends writers into closed communities of all ages to open up the power of reading and writing.
Editor: Heather Norman Soderlind
Free Word Centre, 60 Farringdon Road, London EC1R 3GA
Tel: 020 7324 2535
www.englishpen.org

Freedom from Torture: Write to Life

A charity that provides for asylum seekers and refugees (referred by a clinician) a bridge between their freedom and a new life, using writing. Centres in Birmingham, Glasgow, London, Manchester, Newcastle, Yorkshire and Humberside.
Convenor: Sheila Hayman
111 Isledon Road, London N7 7JW
Tel: 020 7697 7777
www.freedomfromtorture.org

Kids Company

Camila Batmanghelidjh's organisation that provides support for vulnerable inner-city children.
1 Kenbury Street, London SE5 9BS
Tel: 0845 644 6838
info@kidsco.org.uk
www.kidsco.org.uk

Lapidus (The Writing for Wellbeing Organisation)

Conferences, newsletter, database.
Membership secretary: Natalie Kennedy
BCM Lapidus, London WC1N 3XX
nataliekennedy@yahoo.co.uk
www.lapidus.org.uk

Metanoia Institute

Offering a one-year part-time postgraduate MSc in Creative Writing for Therapeutic Purposes or a two-year part-time postgraduate Diploma in Creative Writing for Therapeutic Purposes (to obtain the MSc students write a research-based dissertation in their third year). A London (Ealing) and Bristol non-clinical course validated by Middlesex University Academic Course.

Coordinator: Mandy Kersey

Metanoia Institute (2014): MSc Cyberculture: Online Therapy and Coaching

13 Gunnersbury Avenue, Ealing, London W5 3XD

Tel: 020 8579 2505

www.metanoia.ac.uk

National Association of Writers in Education, The (NAWE)

Conferences, courses, journal for writers in residencies in education.

PO Box 1, Sheriff Hutton, York YO6 7YU

www.nawe.co.uk

National Association for Poetry Therapy, The (NAPT)

1625 Mid Valley Dr, Unit 1, Suite 126 Steamboat Springs, CO 80487, USA

admin@nfbpt.com

www.poetrytherapy.org

National Literacy Trust

A charity that transforms lives through literacy and provides information, researches and informs and improves public understanding of the importance of literacy. For children, young people and families. It also runs Words for Life for children's speech, writing and reading skill (www.wordsforlife.org.uk).

68 South Lambeth Rd, London SW8 1RL

Tel: 020 7820 6256

www.literacytrust.org.uk

Place2Be, The

The leading UK provider of school-based mental health support.

13/14 Angel Gate, 326 City Road, London EC1V 2PT

Tel: 020 7932 5500

enquires@place2be.org.uk

www.theplace2be.org.uk

Poetry Reach

Poetry therapy in action.

Contact: Dr Niall Hickey

17 Railpark, Maynooth, County Kildare, Republic of Ireland

Tel: 01 6291066

poetryreachireland@gmail.com

Reading Agency, The
Focuses on reader development producing resources and courses for librarians to reach new readers and reader development through *Opening the Book*. Develops new partnerships and research. It has a recent list of 'mood-boosting' books.
60 Farringdon Road, London EC1R 3GA
www.readingagency.org.uk

Refugee Council
A charity founded in 1951 to support and empower refugees and asylum seekers to rebuild their lives, including advice on destitution, therapeutic support, help for unaccompanied children and research and training for advisors.
PO 68614, London, Greater London E15 9DQ
Tel: 020 7346 6700
www.refugeecouncil.org.uk

Victoria Field
Biblio/poetry therapist (NAPT) working in the UK.
www.poetrytherapynews.wordpress.com

RECOMMENDED RESOURCES

IBBY (International Board on Books for Young People)
View their virtual exhibition 'Books for Africa, Books from Africa'.
Contact: Mr John Dunne
Goodison Close, Fair Oak, Hampshire SO50 7LE
Tel: 023 8069 3000
j.f.dunne@btinternet.com
www.ibby.org.uk

Women Writing Africa
An up-to-date and extensive compilation of books by women from Africa, writing about Africa, including South Africa. Available from The Feminist Press, City University of New York.
www.feministpress.org/books/fp-series/women-writing-africa

Major novels from African writers
For a list of major novels from African writers, such as Chinua Achebe and Bessie Head, refer to: *http://en.wikipedia.org/wiki/African_literature#Major_nocels_from_African _writers*

Famous refugees who have written great literature

For a list of famous people who are or were refugees, refer to: *http:// en.wikipedia.org/wiki/List_of_refugees*

For a list of Commonwealth Writers' Prizes, refer to: *http://en.wikipedia.org/ wiki/List_of_Commonwealth_Writers_Prizes*

See also the following titles:

Benson, G., Cherniak, J. and Herbert, C. (eds) (1996) *Poems on the Underground*. London: Cassell.
> The poetry and short story anthologies are listed in Chavis, G.G. (2011) *Poetry and Story Therapy: The Healing Power of Creative Expression*. London: Jessica Kingsley Publishers, pp.237–240.

Childhood Education Winter 2002/03, pp.78–79
> This gives a good selection of bibliographic titles for children and young people dealing with perceiving and managing emotions and social relationships, and a list of professional resources on bibliotherapy, emotional intelligence and social skills.

Eccleshare, J. (ed.) (2009) *1001 Children's Books You Must Read Before You Grow Up*. London: Cassell Illustrated.
> For children up to the age of 12 years. Preface by Quentin Blake.

Heath, M.A., Sheen, D., Leavy, D. *et al.* (2005) 'Bibliotherapy: a resource to facilitate emotional healing and growth.' *School Psychology International 26*, 5, 563–580.
> This has a useful appendix of books on emotions and feelings, death and loss, family instability, divorce, community and national disasters, bullying and social skills.

Malchiodi, C. and Ginns-Gruenberg, D. (2008) 'Trauma, Loss and Bibliotherapy: The Healing Power of Stories.' In C. Malchiodi and D. Ginns-Gruenberg (eds) *Creative Interventions with Traumatized Children*. New York: The Guilford Press, pp.173–183.
> See the booklist on trauma, loss and bibliotherapy.

Pardeck, J.A. (1998) 'Useful Books for Clinical Intervention.' In J.A. Pardeck (ed.) *Using Books in Clinical Social Work Practice*. New York: Psychology Press, pp.58–124.
> Books for involving changing role models, blended families, separation and divorce, child abuse, foster care, adoption and childhood fears:

Pardeck, J.T. and Pardeck, J.A. (eds) (1993) *Bibliotherapy: A Clinical Approach for Helping Children*. Langhorne, PA: Harwood Academic.

School Psychology International (2005) 26, 5.
> This provides a useful list of internet resources for bibliotherapy.

Schechtman, Z. (2009) 'Appendix A: Translated Stories and Poems.' In Z. Shechtman (ed.) *Treating Child and Adolescent Aggression Through Bibliotherapy*. New York: Springer, pp.209–219.

REFERENCES

Abse, D. (1998) 'More than a green placebo.' *The Lancet 351*, 9099, 362–364.

Achebe, C. (2001) *Things Fall Apart*. London: Penguin. (First published in 1958 by Heinemann.)

Aleichem, S (1953) 'On Account of a Hat.' In I. Howe and E. Greenberg (eds) *A Treasury of Yiddish Stories*. New York: Viking Press.

Aleichem, S. (1987) 'Today's Children.' In S. Aleichem, *Tevye the Dairyman and the Railroad Stories*. New York: Schocken Books, pp.35–52.

Almedon, A.M. and Glandon, D. (2007) 'Resilience is not the absence of PTSD any more than health is the absence of disease.' *Journal of Loss and Trauma 12*, 2, 127–143.

Andersen, H.C. (2004) *Fairy Tales*. London: Allen Lane.

Anonymous (no date) *The Cracked Pot Story*. Available at www.thecrackedpot.co.uk/CMS/TheCrackedPotstory.aspx

Anthony, K. (2004) 'Therapy Online: The Therapeutic Relationship in Typed Text.' In G. Bolton *et al.* (eds) *Writing Cures: An Introductory Handbook of Writing in Counselling and Therapy*. London and New York: Routledge.

Badiou, A. (2005) *Being and Event*. London: Continuum.

Bakhtin, M.M. (1981a) *The Dialogic Imagination*. Austin, TX: University of Texas Press.

Bakhtin, M.M. (1981b) 'Discourse in the Novel.' In M. Holquist (ed.) *The Dialogic Imagination: Four Essays by M.M. Bakhtin*. Austin, TX: University of Texas Press.

Bandele, B. (2001) 'Introduction.' In C. Achebe, *Things Fall Apart*. London: Penguin.

Baradell, J.G. and Klein, K. (1993) 'The relationship of life stress and body consciousness to hypervigilant decision-making.' *Journal of Personality and Social Psychology 64*, 267–273.

Baraitser, M. (ed.) (1999) *Theatre of Animation: Contemporary Adult Puppet Plays in Context. Contemporary Theatre Review 9*, 4.

Baraitser, M. (2000) *The Story of an African Farm*. London: Oberon Books.

Baraitser, M. (2009) Introduction to a talk at the opening exhibition for Baobab of 'We're Not Here, We're Not There.' London.

Baraitser, M. (2010) 'Tiekiedraai.' In J. Langer and E. Lipton (eds) *Exiled Ink*. London: Exiled Writers Ink.

Baraitser, M. and Evans A. (2006) *Home Number One*. London: Loki Books Ltd.

Bateman, A.W. and Fonagy, P. (2004) *Psychotherapy for Borderline Personality Disorder: Mentalisation Based Treatment*. Oxford: Oxford University Press.

Batmanghelidjh, C. (2006) *Shattered Lives*. London and Philadelphia, PA: Jessica Kingsley Publishers.

Beah, I. (2008) *A Long Way Gone*. New York: Harper Perennial.

Berry, I. (1978) 'Contemporary Bibliotherapy: Systematizing the Field.' In E. Rubin (ed.) *Bibliotherapy Sourcebook*. Phoenix, AZ: Oryx Press, pp.185–190.

Best, D. (1996) 'On the experience of keeping a therapeutic journal while training.' *Therapeutic Communities 17*, 4, 293–301.

Bettleheim, B. (1977) *The Use of Enchantment: The Meaning of Fairy Tales*. New York: Random House.

Bettleheim, B. (1986) 'Foreword.' In H. Dieckmann, *Twice-told Tales: the Psychological Use of Fairy Tales.* Wilmette, IL: Chiron Publications.

Billig, M. (1999) *Freudian Repression: Conversation Creating the Unconscious.* New York: Cambridge University Press.

Bion, W. (1961) *Experiences in Groups and Other Papers.* London: Tavistock Publications.

Blackwell, D. (2005) *Counselling and Psychotherapy with Refugees.* London and Philadelphia, PA: Jessica Kingsley Publishers.

Blackwell, D. (2011) Baobab community meeting leaflet.

Blackwell, D. and Melzak, S. (2000) 'Understanding Childhood.' In Freedom from Torture: Medical Foundation for the Care of Victims of Torture (ed.) *Far from the Battle but Still at War: Troubled Refugee Children at School. London: Freedom from Torture.*

Bollas, C. (1987) *The Shadow of the Object: Psychoanalysis of the Unthought Known.* London: Free Association Books.

Bolton, G. (1998) 'Writing or Pills: Therapeutic Writing in Primary Care.' In C. Hunt and F. Sampson (eds) *The Self on the Page: Theory and Practice in Creative Writing in Personal Development.* London: Jessica Kingsley Publishers.

Bolton, G. (1999) *The Therapeutic Potential of Creative Writing: Writing Myself.* London and Philadelphia, PA: Jessica Kingsley Publishers.

Bolton, G. (2011) *Write Yourself: Creative Writing and Personal Development.* London and Philadelphia, PA: Jessica Kingsley Publishers.

Bolton, G. and Latham, J. (2004) 'Every Poem Breaks a Silence.' In G. Bolton *et al.* (eds) *Writing Cures: An Introductory Handbook of Writing in Counselling and Therapy.* London and New York: Routledge, pp.106–122.

Bolton, G., Field, V. and Thompson, K. (eds) (2006) *Writing Works: A Resource Handbook for Therapeutic Writing Workshops and Activities.* London and Philadelphia, PA: Jessica Kingsley Publishers.

Bolton, G., Howlett, S., Lago, C. and Wright, J.K. (2004) *Writing Cures: An Introductory Handbook of Writing in Counselling and Therapy.* Hove and New York: Routledge.

Brashares, H.J. and Catanzaro, S.J. (1994) 'Mood regulation expectancies, coping responses, depression, and sense of burden in female caregivers of Alzheimer's patients.' *Journal of Nervous and Mental Disease 182,* 437–442.

Bremner J.D. (2001) 'A biological model for delayed recall of childhood abuse.' *Journal of Aggression, Maltreatment and Trauma 4,* 2, 165–183.

Brice, A. (2000) 'Therapeutic support using email: a case study.' *Counselling 12,* 2, 100–101.

Brontë, C. (1966) *Jane Eyre.* London: Penguin Books. (First published in 1847.)

Camus, A. (1994) *The First Man.* London: Penguin Books.

Caspary, A. (1993) 'Aspects of therapeutic action in child analytic treatment.' *Psychoanalytic Psychology 10,* 207–220.

Casson, J. (2004) *Drama, Psychotherapy and Psychosis: Dramatherapy and Psychodrama with People who Hear Voices.* New York: Brunner-Routledge.

Cattanach, A. (2008) 'Working Creatively with Children and their Families after Trauma: the Storied Life.' In C. Malchiodi (ed.) *Creative Interventions with Traumatized Children.* New York: Guilford Press.

Chavis, G. (2011*) Poetry and Story Therapy: The Healing Power of Creative Expression.* London and Philadelphia, PA: Jessica Kingsley Publishers.

Chomsky, N. (1956) *Three Models for the Description of Language.* Available at www.noam-chomsky.org/articles/195609--pdf

Cohen, L.J. (1993) 'The therapeutic use of reading: a qualitative study.' *Journal of Poetry Therapy 7,* 78–83.

Coleman, M. and Ganong, L.H. (1990) 'The uses of juvenile fiction and self-help with step-families.' *Journal of Counseling and Development 68*, 327–331.

Coram Children's Legal Centre (2013) The Migrant Children's Project Factsheet. Colchester: Coram Children's Legal Centre.

Crothers, S. (1816) 'A literary clinic.' *The Atlantic Monthly 118*, 3, 291–301.

Daiute, C. (1998) 'Points of view in children's writing.' *Language Arts 75*, 138–149.

Daiute, C. and Buteau, E. (2002) 'Writing for their Lives: Children's Narratives as Supports for Physical and Psychological Well-Being.' In S.J. Lepore and J.M. Smyth (eds) *The Writing Cure: How Expressive Writing Promotes Health and Emotional Well-Being*, Washington, DC: American Psychological Association, pp.53–74.

Daiute, C., Buteau, E. and Rawlins, C. (2001) 'Social relational wisdom: developmental diversity in children's written narratives about social conflict.' *Narrative Enquiry 11*, 2, 1–30.

Davies, M. (2002) 'A few thoughts about the mind, the brain, and a child with early deprivation.' *Journal of Analytic Psychology 47*, 3 421–435.

Davies, M. and Webb, E. (2000) 'Promoting the psychological well-being of refugee children.' *Clinical Child Psychology and Psychiatry 5*, 4, 541–554.

Davis, J. (2011) 'The Reading Revolution.' In H. Haddon, M. Rosen, Z. Smith, C. Callil *et al.*, *Stop What You Are Doing and Read This*. London: Virago.

Day, K.W. (2009) 'Violence survivors with post-traumatic stress disorder: treatment by integrating existential and narrative therapies.' *Adultspan: Theories, Research and Practice 8*, 84.

De Bellis, M. (2001) 'Developmental traumatology: the psychobiological development of maltreated children and its implications for research, treatment, and policy.' *Development and Psychopathology 13*, 539–564.

De Waal, E. (2011) *The Hare with the Amber Eyes: A Hidden Inheritance*. London: Vintage.

Detrixhe, J. (2010) 'Souls in jeopardy: questions and innovations for bibliotherapy with fiction.' *Journal of Humanistic Counselling, Education and Development 49*, 1, 58–72.

Diamond, A. (2010) 'The evidence base for improving school outcomes by addressing the whole child and by addressing skills and attitudes, not just content.' *Early Education and Development 21*, 780–793.

Diamond, A. (2011a) 'Executive Functions and the Prefrontal Cortex.' Talk at Virginia Tech Carilion Research Institute.

Diamond, A. (2011b) 'Biological and Social Influences on Cognitive Control Processes Dependent on Prefrontal Cortex.' Talk given to the Virginia Tech Carilion Research Institute.

Diamond, A. (2011c) 'Executive Functions and the Prefrontal Cortex: Genetic and Neurochemical Influences, Gender Differences, and Practical Activities and Approaches to Help.' 2 December.

Diamond, A. (2013) 'Executive Functions.' *Annual Review of Psychology 64*, 135–168.

Dickens, C. (1860) *Great Expectations*. (First published 1860–1861; published in Penguin Classics in 1966.)

Dieckmann, H. (1986) *Twice-told Tales: the Psychological use of Fairy Tales*. Wilmette, IL: Chiron Publications.

Doidge, N. (2007) *The Brain that Changes Itself: Stories of Personal Triumph from the Frontiers of Brain Science*. London: Penguin.

Donnelly, D.A. and Murray, E.J. (1991) 'Cognitive and emotional changes in written essays and therapy interviews.' *Journal of Social and Clinical Psychology 10*, 334–350.

Doyle, C. (1998) 'A self psychology theory of role in drama therapy.' *The Arts in Psychotherapy 25*, 223–235.

Dwivedi, K.N. and Gardner, D. (1997) 'Theoretical Perspectives and Approaches.' In K.N. Dwivedi (ed.) *The Therapeutic Use of Stories*. London: Routledge.

Echterling, L.G. and Stewart, A. (2008) 'Creative Crisis Intervention Techniques with Children and Families.' In C. Malchiodi (ed.) *Creative Interventions with Traumatized Children*. New York and London: Guilford Press, pp.189–210.

Eggerman, M. and Panter-Brick, C. (2010) 'Suffering, hope and entrapment: Resilience and cultural values in Afghanistan.' *Social Science and Medicine 7*, 71–83.

Eggers, D. (2000) *A Heartbreaking Work of Staggering Genuis*. New York and London: Simon & Schuster and Picador.

Eggers, D. (2008) *What is the What: The Autobiography of Valentino Achak Deng. A Novel*. London: Penguin.

Eisenbruch, M. (1988) 'The mental health of refugee children and their cultural development.' *International Migration Review 22*, 2, 282–300.

Eliot, T.S. (1925) *The Letters of T.S. Eliot, Volume Two, 1923–1925*. V. Eliot and H. Haughton (eds) London: Faber.

Eliot, T.S. (1951) *Selected Essays*. London: Faber.

Emechata, B. (1974) *Second Class Citizen*. London: Allison & Busby.

Emunah, R. (1994) *Acting for Real: Drama Therapy Process, Technique, and Performance*. New York: Brunner/Mazel.

Engel, S. (1995) *The Stories Children Tell*. New York: Freeman.

Erikson, E. (1950) *Childhood and Society*. New York: Norton.

Esterling, B.A., L'Abate, L., Murray, E.J. and Pennebaker, J.W. (1999) 'Empirical foundations for writing in prevention and psychotherapy: mental and physical health outcomes.' *Clinical Psychology Review 19*, 1, 79–96.

Etherington, K. (2000) *Narrative Approaches to Working with Adult Male Survivors of Child Sexual Abuse, the Client's, the Counsellor's and the Researcher's Story*. London: Jessica Kingsley Publishers.

Fabri, M. R. (2001) 'Reconstructing Safety: Adjustments to the Therapeutic Frame in the Treatment of Survivors of Political Torture.' *Professional Psychology: Research and Practice 32*, 452–457.

Farkas, G.S. and Yorker, B. (1993) 'Case studies of bibliotherapy.' *Issues in Mental Health Nursing 14*, 337–347.

Fazel, M. (2011) 'Trauma, Loss and Uncertainty: the Inner Worlds of Unaccompanied Asylum Seekers.' Talk for Professionals, organised by The Children's Society, Oxford.

Fazel, M. (2012) Findings from questionnaire/interviews for asylum seekers. *Mental Health Therapeutic Service in Schools*.

Figley, C. (1983) 'The Family as Victim: Mental Health Implications.' *Proceedings of the 7th World Congress of Psychiatry*. London: Plenum Press.

Flint, R., Hamilton, F. and Williamson, C. (2004) 'Core competencies for working with the literary arts for personal development, health and well-being.' *Writing in Health Care*. London: Lapidus.

Folkman, S. and Moskowitz J.T. (2000) 'Stress, positive emotion, and coping.' *Current Directions in Psychological Science 9*, 115–118.

Fonagy, P. and Target, M. (2000) 'Mentalisation and the Changing Aims of Child Psychoanalysis.' In K. von Klizing, P. Tyson and D. Bürgin (eds) *Psychoanalysis in Childhood and Adolescence*. Basel: Karger, pp.129–139.

Frank, A. (1954) *The Diary of Anne Frank*. London: Pan Books.

Freud, A. and Burlingham, D. (1943) *War and Children*. New York: Medical War Books.

Freud, S. (1913) *The Interpretation of Dreams* (3rd edition). (Translated by A.A. Brill.) New York: Macmillan.

Freud, S. (1917) 'Mourning and melancholia.' *SE 14*, 243–259.

Freud, S. (1920) *A General Introduction to Psychoanalysis.* New York: Boni and Liveright.

Freud, S. (1953–1974) 'Writings on Art and Literature.' In J. Strachey (ed.) *The Standard Edition of the Complete Psychological Works of Sigmund Freud.* London: Hogarth Press.

Freud, S. (1968) 'Analysis Terminable and Interminable.' In J. Strachey (ed.) *The Standard Edition of the Complete Psychological Works of Sigmund Freud.* London: Hogarth Press, pp.211–253.

Fugard, A. (2006) *Tsotsi.* Edinburgh, New York and Melbourne: Canongate.

Gaffney, D. (1993) 'Bibliotherapy for girls: read two books and see me in the morning.' *Academic Nurse 11*, 6–9.

Garmezy, N. (1982) 'Stress-resistant Children: The Search for Protective Factors.' Invited address to 10th International Congress of the International Association for Child and Adolescent Psychiatry and Allied Professions, Dublin, pp.25–30.

Gersie, A. (1997) *Reflections on Therapeutic Story-making: The Use Of Stories in Groups.* London: Jessica Kingsley Publishers.

Gladding, S. and Gladding, C. (1991) 'The ABC's of bibliotherapy: a clinical approach for school counselors.' *School Counsellor 39*, i, 7–13.

Glanz, K., Lewis, F.M. and Rimer, B.K. (1997) *Health Behaviour and Health Education: Theory, Research and Practice* (2nd edition). San Francisco, CA: Jossey-Bass.

Goldberg, R. (2008) 'Fairy tales and trauma.' *American Journal of Psychoanalysis 68*, 3.

Gordimer, N. (2013) 'The writer who redefined colonialism.' *The Guardian*, 23 March, p.58.

Gorman, W. (2001) 'Refugee survivors of torture: trauma and treatment.' *Professional Psychology, Research and Practice 32*, 5, 443–451.

Goss, S. and Anthony, K. (2004) 'Ethical and Practical Dimensions of Online Writing Cures.' In G. Bolton *et al.* (eds) *Writing Cures: An Introductory Handbook of Writing in Counselling and Therapy.* Hove and New York: Routledge.

Goss, S., Robson, D., Pelling, N.J. and Renard, D.E. (1999) 'The challenge of the Internet.' *Counselling 10*, 37–43.

Green, V. (2013) 'Grief in two disguises: "mourning and melancholia" revisited.' *Journal of Child Psychotherapy 39*, i, 76–89.

Greenberg, L.S. and Safran J.D. (1987) *Emotion in Psychotherapy.* New York: Guilford Press.

Greenberg, M.A. and Stone, A.A. (1992) 'Emotional disclosure about traumas and its relation to health: effects of previous disclosure and trauma severity.' *Journal of Personality and Social Psychology 63*, 75–84.

Grosz, S. (2013) *The Examined Life.* London: Chatto and Windus.

Haen C. (2005) 'Group Drama Therapy in Children's Inpatient Psychiatric Setting.' In A.M. Weber and C. Haen (eds) *Clinical Applications of Drama Therapy in Child and Adolescent Treatment.* New York: Brunner-Routledge, pp.189–204.

Haen, C. (2008) 'Vanquishing Monsters: Drama Therapy for Treating Childhood Trauma in the Group Setting.' In C. Malchiodi (ed.) *Creative Interventions with Traumatized Children.* New York and London: Guilford Press, pp.225–246.

Haen, C. and Brannon, K.H. (2002) 'Superheroes, monsters and babies: roles of strength, destruction and vulnerability for emotionally disturbed boys.' *The Arts in Psychology 29*, 31–40.

Hammond, C. (2013) 'Mind Changers.' *History of Psychology* series for Radio 4.

Harvey, J.H. (1996) *Embracing Their Memory.* Needham Heights, MA: Allyn & Bacon.

Havel, V. (1990) *Disturbing the Peace.* London: Faber & Faber.

REFERENCES

Head, B. (2010) *When Rain Clouds Gather*. London: Virago. (First published by Victor Gollancz in 1969.)

Heath, M.A., Sheen, D., Leavy, D., Young, E. and Money, K. (2005) 'Bibliotherapy: a resource to facilitate emotional healing and growth.' *School Psychology International* 26, 5, 563–580.

Henley, J. (2008) 'Queen of darkness.' Interview with Hannah Segal in *The Guardian*, 8 September.

Henley, J. (2013) 'Quoting Blixen in "Tales from the Couch".' *The Guardian*, 8 January, pp.10–11.

Herman, J. (1997) *Trauma and Recovery: The Aftermath of Violence – From Domestic Abuse To Political Terror*. New York: Basic Books. (First edition published in 1992.)

Herzog, J. (1982) 'World Beyond Metaphor: Thoughts on the Transmission of Trauma.' In M. Bergman and M. Jacovy (eds) *Generations of the Holocaust*. New York: Columbia University Press, pp.103–119.

Hicks, D. (2006) *An Audit of Bibliotherapy/Books on Prescription Activity in England*. London: Arts Council England and the Museums, Libraries and Archives Council.

Hobfall, S., Watson, P., Bell, C.C., Bryant, R.A. *et al.* (2007) 'Five essential elements of immediate and mid-term mass trauma intervention: empirical evidence.' *Psychiatry* 70, 4 283–315.

Hoffman, E. (2000) *Lost in Translation*. London: Vintage.

Honwana, B.L. (1985) 'Papa, Snake and I.' In C. Achebe and C.L. Innes (eds) *African Short Stories*. Oxford: Heinemann, pp.102–114.

Horowitz, M.J. (1975) 'Intrusive and repetitive thoughts after experimental stress: a summary.' *Archives of General Psychiatry 32*, 1457–1463.

Howlett, S. (2004) 'Writing the Link between Body and Mind.' In G. Bolton *et al.* (eds) *Writing Cures: An Introductory Handbook of Writing in Counselling and Therapy*. London and New York: Routledge, pp.85–94.

Hughes, T. (1995) '*Interview*', *The Paris Review*, No. 71.

Hunt, C. (2000) *Therapeutic Dimensions of Autobiography in Creative Writing*. London and Philadelphia, PA: Jessica Kingsley Publishers.

Hunt, C. (2004) 'Reading Ourselves: Imagining the Reader in the Writing Process.' In G. Bolton *et al.* (eds) *Writing Cures: An Introductory Handbook of Writing in Counselling and Therapy*. London and New York: Routledge.

Hüther, G. (2006) *The Compassionate Brain: How Empathy Creates Intelligence*. Boston and London: Trumpeter.

Hüther, G. (2014) *Neurobiological Preconditions for the Development of Curiosity and Creativity*.

Hynes, A. and Hynes-Berry, M. (1994) *Biblio/poetry Therapy: The Interactive Process: A Handbook*. St Cloud, MN: North Star Press.

Jack, S. and Ronan, K. (2008) 'Bibliotherapy: practice and research.' *School Psychology International 29*, 2, 161–182.

Janet, P. (1919) *Les Medications Psychologiques* (volumes 1–3). Paris: Alcan.

Janoff-Bulman, R. (1985) 'The Aftermath of Victimization: Rebuilding Shattered Assumptions.' In C.R. Figley (ed.) *Trauma and Its Wake: The Study and Treatment of Post-traumatic Stress Disorder*. New York: Free Press, pp.15–35.

Jeffries, S. (2012) 'Jacqueline Rose: a life in writing.' Interview by Stuart Jeffries, *Saturday Guardian*, 3 February.

Jennings, S. (1999) *Introduction to Developmental Play Therapy: Playing and Health*. London: Jessica Kingsley Publishers.

Jones, L. (2008) *Mister Pip*. London: John Murray.

Junior, B.A. and Errante, A. (2002) 'Rebuilding Hope on Josina Machel Island: Towards a Culturally Mediated Model of Psychotherapeutic Intervention.' In K. Holm and U. Schultz (eds) *Kindheit in Armut Weltweit.* Opladen: Leske & Budrich, pp.1–21.

Kafka, F. (2008) *Dearest Father.* London: Oneworld Classics Ltd. (First published in 1953.)

Kahneman, D. (2012) *Thinking Fast and Slow.* London: Allen Lane.

Karp, J. (2005) 'Matching Human Dignity with the UN Convention on the Rights of the Child.' In Y. Ronen and C.W. Greenbaum (eds) *The Case for the Child: Towards and New Agenda.* Oxford: Intersentia.

Kay, J. (1994) *Three Has Gone.* London: Blackie Children's Books.

Kay, J. (2010) *Red Dust Road.* London: Picador.

Kenyon, P. (2010) 'Tabloid treatment of asylum seekers under fire.' *The Guardian,* 7 June.

Kerrigan, A. (1998) 'Introduction.' In J.L. Borges. *Collected Fictions.* London: Calder Publications.

King L.A. (2001) 'The health benefits of writing about life goals.' *Personality and Social Psychology Bulletin 27,* 798–807.

King, L. (2002) 'Gain without Pain? Expressive Writing and Self-regulation.' In S. Lepore and J. Smyth (eds) *The Writing Cure: How Expressive Writing Promotes Health and Emotional Well-being.* Washington, DC: American Psychological Association, pp.119–134.

King, L.A. and Miner, K.N. (2000) 'Writing about the perceived benefits of traumatic events: implications for physical health.' *Personality and Psychology Bulletin 26* 220–230.

Kira, I.A., Ahmed, A., Wasim, F., Mahmoud, V., Coltrain, J. and Rai, D. (2012) 'Group therapy for refugees and torture survivors: treatment model innovations.' *International Journal of Group Psychotherapy 62,* 1, 69–88.

Klein, M. (1930) 'On the Importance of Symbol Formation in the Development of the Ego.' In *Contributions of Psychoanalysis (1921–1945).* London: Hogarth Press.

Klein, K. (2002) 'Expressive Writing and Working Memory.' In S.J. Lepore and J.M. Smyth (eds) *The Writing Cure: How Expressive Writing Promotes Health and Emotional Well-Being.* Washington, DC: American Psychological Association, pp.135–155.

Klein, K. and Boals, A. (2001a) 'The relationship of life event stress and working memory capacity.' *Applied Cognitive Psychology 15,* 520–533.

Klein, K. and Boals, A. (2001b) 'Expressive writing can increase working memory capacity.' *Journal of Experimental Psychology, General 130,* 520–533.

Kohli, R. (2001) 'Social work with unaccompanied asylum seeking young people.' *Forced Migration Review 12,* 1–33.

Kohli, R. (2005) 'Sounds of Silence: Listening to What Unaccompanied Asylum Seeking Minors Say and Do Not Say.' *British Journal of Social Work.*

Kohli, R. (2006) 'The Comfort of Strangers: social work practice with unaccompanied asylum-seeking children and young people in the UK.' *Child and Family Social Work 11,* 1, 5.

Kohli, R. and Mather, R. (2003) 'Promoting psychosocial well-being in unaccompanied asylum seeking people in the United Kingdom.' *Child and Family Social Work 8,* 201–212.

Kopp, R. (1995) *Metaphor Therapy: Using Client-centred Metaphors in Psychotherapy.* New York: Brunner/Mazel.

Kundnani, A. (2003) *Official Media Coverage of Asylum is Distorted and Unfair.* London: Institute of Race Relations. Available at www.irr.org.uk/news/its-official-media-coverage-of-asylum-is-distorted-and-unfair, accessed on 6 April 2014.

Kuper, J. (2013) 'Children and Justice: Armed Conflicts and Psychological Conflicts.' *Talk No. 3 for the Baobab Centre.*

L'Abate, L. (1992) *Programme Writing: A Self-administered Approach for Interventions with Individuals, Couples, and Families.* Pacific Grove, CA: Brooks/Cole.

Laird, E. (2004) *The Garbage King.* London: Macmillan's Children's Books.

Landy, R.J. (1993) *Persona and Performance: The Meaning of Role in Drama, Therapy and Everyday Life.* New York: Guilford Press.

Landy, R.J. (1994) *Drama Therapy: Concepts, Theories and Practices* (2nd edition). Springfield, IL: Charles C. Thomas.

Lange, A., Schoutrop, M., Schrieken, B. and van de Ven, J. (2002) 'Interapy: A Model for Therapeutic Writing through the Internet.' In S.J. Lepore and J.M. Smyth (eds) *The Writing Cure: How Expressive Writing Promotes Health and Emotional Well-being.* Washington, DC: American Psychological Association.

Lange, A., Rietdijk, D., Hudcovicova, M., van de Ven, J., Schrieken, B. and Emmelkamp, P.M.G. (2003) 'Interapy: A Controlled Randomised Trial of the Standardised Treatment of Posttraumaticstress Through the Internet.' *Journal of Consulting and Clinical Psychology 71,* 5, 901–909.

Lehrer, J. (2008) *Proust was a Neuroscientist.* Boston and New York: A Mariner Book, Houghton Mifflin Company.

Leichentritt, J. and Schectman, Z. (1998) 'Therapist, trainee and child verbal response models in child group therapy group dynamics.' *Group Dynamics: Theory, Research and Practice 2,* 36–47.

Lemma, A. (2010) 'The power of relationship: a study of key working as an intervention with traumatised young people.' *Journal of Social Work Practice, iFirst article,* 1–19.

Lepore, S.J. (1997) 'Expressive writing moderates the relation between intrusive thoughts and depressive symptoms.' *Journal of Personality and Social Psychology 7,* 1030–1037.

Lepore, S.J. and Greenberg, M.A. (in press) 'Mending broken hearts: effects of expressive writing on mood, cognitive processing, social adjustment, and health following a relationship breakup.' *Psychology and Health.*

Lepore, S.J. and Smyth, J.M (eds) (2002) *The Writing Cure: How Expressive Writing Promotes Health and Well-being.* Washington, DC: American Psychological Association.

Lepore, S.J., Silver, R.C., Wortman, C.B. and Wayment, H.A. (1996) 'Social constraints, intrusive thoughts, and depressive symptoms among bereaved mothers.' *Journal of Personality and Social Psychology 20,* 271–282.

Lessing, D. (2007) *The Golden Notebook.* New York: Harper. (First published in 1962 by Michael Joseph.)

Lido, C. (2006) 'Negative press gives asylum seekers a bad name.' *Medical News Today,* 14 November. Available at http://www.medicalnewstoday.com/releases/56360.php

Linklater, A. (2013) 'The Examined Life by Stephen Groz – Review.' *The Observer,* 27 January 2013.

Lutgendorf, S. and Ullrich, P. (2002) 'Cognitive Processing, Disclosure, and Health: Psychological and Physiological Mechanisms.' In S.J. Lepore and J.M. Smyth (eds) *The Writing Cure: How Expressive Writing Promotes Health and Emotional Well-being.* Washington, DC: American Psychological Association.

Maccoby, E.E. (1990) 'Gender and relationships: a developmental account.' *American Psychologist 45,* 513–520. In C. Haen and K.H. Brannon (2002) 'Superheroes, monsters, and babies: roles of strength, destruction, and vulnerability for emotionally disturbed boys.' *The Arts in Psychotherapy 29,* 31–40.

Malchiodi, C.A. (2005) *Expressive Therapies.* New York: Guilford Press.

Malchiodi, C.A. (ed.) (2008) *Creative Interventions with Traumatized Children.* New York and London: Guilford Press.

Marris, P. (1974) *Loss and Change*. London: Routledge & Kegan Paul.

Masten, A. (2001) 'Ordinary magic: resilience processes in development.' *American Psychologist*, March, 237–235.

Maultsby, M.C. (1971) 'Systematic written homework in psychotherapy.' *Psychotherapy: Theory, Research and Practice 8*, 195–198.

Mazza, N. (1993) 'Poetry therapy: towards a research agenda for the 1990s.' *The Arts in Psychotherapy 20*, 51–59.

McKendree-Smith, N., Floyd, M. and Scogin, F. (2003) 'Self-administered treatment for depression: a review.' *Journal of Clinical Psychology 59*, 275–288.

McLoughlin, D. (2004) 'Accreditation in the Field of Literary Arts in Health and Social Care.' University of Sussex, Lapidus.

Meares, R. (2005) *The Metaphor of Play: Origin and Breakdown of Personal Being* (3rd edition). New York: Routledge.

Meldrum, B. (1994) 'A Role Model of Drama Therapy and its Application with Individuals and Groups.' In S. Jennings, A. Chesner. B. Meldrum and S. Mitchell (eds) *The Handbook of Dramatherapy*. London: Tavistock/Routledge, pp.75–92.

Melzak, S. (1992) 'Secrecy, privacy, survival, repressive regimes and growing up.' *Bulletin of the Anna Freud Centre 15*, 205–224.

Melzak, S. (1995) 'Refugee Children in Exile in Europe.' In J. Trowell and M. Bower (eds) *The Emotional Needs of Young Children and their Families using Psychoanalytic Ideas in the Community*. London: Routledge.

Melzak, S. (2010) Pamphlet for the Baobab Centre.

Melzak, S. (2012) Talk in Bregenz, Austria, October.

Métraux, J.-C. (2004) *Deuils Collectives et Creation Sociale*. Paris: La Dispute.

Milner, M. (1952) 'The Framed Gap.' In *The Suppressed Madness of Sane Men*. London: Tavistock. pp.79–82.

Milner, M. (1987) *Experiment in Leisure*. London: Virago Press.

Modell, A. (1997) 'Reflections on metaphor and affects.' *Annals of Psychoanalysis 25*, 219–233.

Mohr, C., Nixon, D. and Vickers, S. (1991) *Books that Heal: A Whole Language Approach*. Englewood, NJ: Teachers Ideas Press.

Mollica, R.F. (2006) *Healing Invisible Wounds: Paths to Hope and Recovery in a Violent World*. New York: Harcourt.

Morrison, T. (2005) *Sula*. London: Vintage.

Murray, E.J. and Segal, D.L. (1994) 'Emotional processing in vocal and written expression of feelings about traumatic experiences.' *Journal of Traumatic Stress 7*, 391–405.

Murray, E.J., Lamnin, D. and Carver, C.S. (1989) 'Emotional expression in written essays and psychotherapy.' *Journal of Social and Clinical Psychology 8*, 414–429.

Nader, K. (2001) 'Children's Traumatic Dreams.' In D. Barrett (ed.) *Trauma and Dreams*. Cambridge, MA: Harvard University Press.

Naidoo, B. (2000) *The Other Side of Truth*, New York: Amistad.

Naidoo, B. (2004) 'Out of Bounds: "Witness Literature" and the Challenge of Crossing Racialised Boundaries.' 29th IBBY Congress, Cape Town.

Neimeyer, R. (2004) Fostering posttraumatic growth: a narrative elaboration.' *Psychological Enquiry 15*, 1, 53–59.

Neimeyer, R., Herrero O. and Botella, L. (2006) 'Chaos to coherence: psychotherapeutic integration of traumatic loss.' *Journal of Constructivist Psychology 19*, 1–9.

Neimeyer, R., Prigerson, H. and Davies, B. (2002) 'Mourning and meaning.' *American Behavioural Scientist 46*, 235–249.

Nelson, G.M. (1992) 'Growing Up with Fairy Tales.' In K. van der Vort, J.H. Timmerman and E. Lincoln (eds) *Walking in Two Worlds: Women's Spiritual Paths.* St Cloud, MN: North Star Press.

O'Connor, T., Rutter, M. and English and Romanian Adoptees Study Team (2000) 'Attachment disorder behaviour following early severe deprivation: extensional and longitudinal follow-up.' *Child and Adolescent Psychiatry 39*, 6, 703–712.

Okri, B. and Emeagwali, P. (1992) 'Talking with Ben Okri.' *Newsday*, 19 July. Available at http://emeagwali.com/nigeria/ben-okri-19jul92.html, accessed 6 April 2014.

Papadopoulos, R.K. (2002) *Therapeutic Care for Refugees: No Place like Home.* London: Karnac.

Pardeck, J.T. (1990) 'Children's literature and child abuse.' *Child Welfare LXIX*, 1, Jan–Feb, 83–88.

Pardeck, J.T. (1993) *Using Bibliotherapy in Clinical Practice: A Guide to Self-help Books.* Westport, CT: Greenwood Press.

Pardeck, J.T. (1994) 'Using literature to help adolescents cope with problems.' *Adolescence 29*, 114, 421–427.

Pardeck, J.T. (1998) *Using Books in Clinical Social Work Practice: A Guide to Bibliotherapy*, New York: The Haworth Press.

Pardeck, J.T. and Pardeck, J.A. (1984a) 'Treating abused children through bibliotherapy.' *Early Child Development and Care 16*, 195–204.

Pardeck, J.T. and Pardeck, J.A. (1984b) 'Using literature to help adolescents cope with problems.' *Family Therapy 11*, 2, 97–104.

Pardeck, J.T. and Pardeck, J.A. (eds) (1993) *Bibliotherapy: A Clinical Approach for Helping Children.* Langhorne, PA: Gordon and Breach.

Parks, T. (2011) 'Mindful Reading.' In H. Haddon, M. Rosen, Z. Smith, C. Callil *et al.*, *Stop What You Are Doing and Read This.* London: Virago.

Pehrsson, D. (2005) 'Fictive bibliotherapy and therapeutic storytelling with children who hurt.' *Journal of Creativity in Mental Health 1*, 3/4, 273–286.

Pennebaker, J.W. (1990) *Opening Up: The Healing Power of Expressing Emotion.* New York and London: Guilford Press.

Pennebaker, J.W. (1993) 'Putting stress into words: health, linguistic, and therapeutic implications.' *Behavioural Research and Therapy 31*, 6, 531–548.

Pennebaker, J.W. (1997) 'Writing about emotional experiences.' *Psychological Science 8*, 3, 162–166.

Pennebaker, J.W. (2000) 'Telling stories: the health benefits of narrative.' *Literature and Medicine 19*, 1, 3–18.

Pennebaker, J.W. (2002a) 'How Expressive Writing Promotes Health and Emotional Well-being.' In S.J. Lepore and J.M. Smyth (eds) *The Writing Cure: How Expressive Writing Promotes Health and Emotional Well-being*, Washington, DC: American Psychological Association.

Pennebaker, J.W. (2002b) 'Writing, Social Processes, and Psychotherapy: From Past to Future.' In S.J. Lepore and J.M. Smyth (eds) *The Writing Cure: How Expressive Writing Promotes Health and Emotional Well-being*, Washington, DC: American Psychological Association, pp.281–291.

Pennebaker, J.W. (2010) 'Expressive writing in a clinical Setting.' *Independent Practitioner*, Winter, 23–25.

Pennebaker, J.W. and Beall, S. (1986) 'Confronting a traumatic event: toward an understanding of inhibition and disease.' *Journal of Abnormal Psychology 95*, 3, 274–281.

Pennebaker, J. and Seagal, J. (1999) 'Forming a story: the health benefits of narrative.' *Journal of Clinical Psychology 55*, 10, 1243–1254.

Pennebaker, J.W., Barger, S.D. and Tiebout, J. (1989) 'Disclosure of traumas and health among Holocaust survivors.' *Psychosomatic Medicine 51*, 577–589.

Pennebaker, J.W., Mayne T.J. and Francis N.E. (1997) 'Linguistic predictors of adaptive bereavement.' *Journal of Personality and Social Psychology 72*, 863–871.

Peseschkian, N. (1986) *Oriental Stories as Tools in Psychotherapy*. Berlin: Springer-Verlag.

Petocz, A. (1999) *Freud, Psychoanalysis, and Symbolism*. Cambridge: Cambridge University Press.

Philipp, R. (2004) 'Personal Integrity, Professional Recognition and Equivalence with Other Art Practitioners Working in Health Settings.' *Lapidus (UK) Seminar on Accreditation.*

Phillips, A. (2007) *Winnicott*. London: Penguin.

Pitruzzella, S. (2004) *Introduction to Dramatherapy: Person and Threshold*. New York: Brunner-Routledge.

Pitzele, P. (1991) 'Adolescents Inside Out: Intrapsychic Psychodrama.' In P. Holes and M. Karp *Psychodrama: Inspiration and Technique*. London: Routledge, pp.15–31.

Plato (2005) *Phaedrus* (370 BC). London: Penguin.

Poole, O. (2013) 'I want to tell them they have a second chance.' *Evening Standard*, 4 January.

Prochaska, J. (1999) 'How Do People Change, and How Can We Change to help Many More People?' In M. Hubble (ed.) *The Heart and Soul of Change*. Washington, DC: American Psychological Association.

Progoff, I. (1975) *At a Journal Workshop*, New York: Dialogue House Library.

Proust, M. (1996) *Swann's Way, Volume 1, In Search of Lost Time*. London: Vintage Classics. (First translated by C.K. Scott Moncrieff and Terence Kilmartin, revised by D.J. Enright.)

Reader Organisation, The (2009) *The Reader Organisation Annual Report 2008–2009*. Liverpool: The Reader Organisation.

REDRESS (2001) *Torture Survivors' Perceptions of Reparation*. London: REDRESS.

Reynolds, M.W., Nabors, L. and Quinlan, A. (2000) 'The effectiveness of art therapy: does it work?' *Art Therapy: Journal of American Art Therapy Association 17*, 207–213.

Rich, A. (2002) 'Arts of the Possible: Essays and Conversations.' New York: W.W Norton and Co.

Richman, N. (1998) *In the Midst of the Whirlwind: A Manual for Helping Refugee Children*. London: Save the Children.

Riordan, R.J. (1996) 'Scriptotherapy: therapeutic writing as a counseling adjunct.' *Journal of Counseling and Development 74*, 3, 263–269.

Rogers, C.R. (1951) *Client-centred Therapy: Its Current Practice, Implications and Theory*. Boston, MA: Houghton Mifflin.

Rogers, C.R. (1955) 'Persons or science? A philosophical question.' *American Psychologist 10*, 267–278.

Rose, J. (2002) *Albertine*. London: Vintage.

Rosen, M. (2009) *Michael Rosen's A–Z: The Best Children's Poetry from Agard to Zephrenia*. London: Puffin.

Rosen, M. (2011) 'Memories and Expectations.' In H. Haddon, M. Rosen, Z. Smith, C. Callil *et al.*, *Stop What You Are Doing and Read This*. London: Virago, pp.91–113.

Rothchild, B. (2000) *The Body Remembers: The Psychophysiology of Trauma and Trauma Treatment*. New York: Norton.

Rubin, R.J. (1978) *Using Bibliotherapy: A Guide to Theory and Practice*. London: Oryx Press.

Russ, D.A. (1992) 'The use of programmed writing as a treatment for anxiety.' Unpublished doctoral dissertation. Atlanta, GA: Georgia State University.

Rutter, M. and O'Connor, T. (2004) 'Are there biological programming effects for psychological development? Findings from a study of Romanian orphans.' *Developmental Psychology 40*, 1, 81–94.

Sacks, O. (2013) 'Speak, memory.' *The New York Review of Books LX*, 21 February–6 March, 3, 19–21.

Salih, T. (1985) 'A Handful of Dates.' In C. Achebe and C.L. Innes (eds) *African Short Stories*. Oxford: Heinemann, pp.90–94.

Sautter, U. (2010) 'Reading, writing and revelation.' *Ode*, October, 30–40.

Schoutrop, M. (2000) 'Structured writing and processing traumatic events.' Unpublished doctoral dissertation. Amsterdam: University of Amsterdam.

Schrank, F. and Engels, D. (1981) 'Bibliotherapy as a counseling adjunct: research findings.' *The Personal and Guidance Journal 60*, 143–147.

Segal, H. (1957) 'Notes on symbol formation.' *International Journal of Psychoanalysis 38*, 391–397.

Sen, A. (1993) 'Capability and Well-being.' In C. Nussbaum and A. Sen (eds) *The Quality of Life*. Oxford: Clarendon Press.

Sendak, M. (2000) *Where the Wild Things Are*. London: Red Fox.

Shakespeare, W. (1988) 'Hamlet.' In S. Wells and G. Taylor (eds) *William Shakespeare: The Complete Works*. Oxford: Oxford University Press.

Shange, N. (1977) *For Colored Girls who have Considered Suicide when the Rainbow is Enuf.* New York: Scribner Poetry. (First published in 1975.)

Shechtman, Z. (2009) *Treating Child and Adolescent Aggression through Bibliotherapy*. New York: Springer.

Shechtman, Z. and Effrati, R. (2008) 'A comparison of bibliotherapy and individual therapy sessions in the treatment of aggressive boys.' Unpublished manuscript.

Shechtman, Z. and Nachshol, R. (1996) 'A school-based intervention to reduce aggressive behaviour in maladjusted adolescents.' *Journal of Applied Developmental Psychology 17*, 535–553.

Shechtman, Z. and Or, A. (1996) 'Applying counseling methods to challenge teacher beliefs with regard to classroom diversity and mainstreaming: an empirical study.' *Teaching and Teacher Education 12*, 2.

Shishkin, M. (2013) *The Light and the Dark*. London: Quercus.

Shrodes, C. (1949) 'Bibliotherapy: a theoretical and clinical-experimental study.' Doctoral Dissertation. Berkeley, CA: University of California.

Siegel, D.J. (2003) 'An Interpersonal Neurobiology of Psychotherapy: The Developing Mind and the Resolution of Trauma.' In M.F. Solomon and D.J. Siegel (eds) *Healing Trauma: Attachment, Mind, Body and Brain*. New York: Norton, pp.1–56.

Smyth, J.M. (1998) 'Written emotional expression: effect sizes, outcome types, and moderating variables.' *Journal of Consulting and Clinical Psychology 66*, 174–178.

Smyth, J.M. and Catley, D. (2002) 'Translating Research Into Practice: Potential in Expressive Writing in the Field.' In S.J. Lepore and J.M. Smyth (eds) *The Writing Cure: How Expressive Writing Promotes Health and Emotional Well-being*, Washington, DC: American Psychological Association, pp.199–214.

Smyth, J.M. and Pennebaker, J.W. (2001) 'What are the Health Effects of Disclosure?' In A. Baum, T.A. Revenson and J.E. Singer (eds) *Handbook of Health Psychology*. Hillsdale, NJ: Erlbaum, pp.339–348.

Smyth, J.M., True, N. and Souto, J. (2001) 'Effects of writing about traumatic experiences: the necessity of narrative structuring.' *Journal of Social and Clinical Psychology 20*, 161–172.

Snunit, M. (2004) *The Soul Bird*. London: Constable & Robinson. (First published by Robinson in 1998.)

Solomon, E.P. and Heide K.M. (2005) 'The biology of trauma: implications for treatment.' *Journal of Interpersonal Violence 20*, 1, 51–60.

Speedy, J. (2004) 'The Contribution of Narrative Ideas and Practices in Therapy.' In G. Bolton *et al.* (eds) *Writing Cures: An Introductory Handbook of Writing in Counselling and Therapy.* London and New York: Routledge.

Spera, S., Buhrfeind, E. and Pennebaker, J.W. (1994) 'Expressive writing and job loss.' *Academy of Management Journal 37*, 722–733.

Starbuck, E. (1928) *A Guide to Literature for Character Training.* Vol. 1. New York: Macmillan.

Steele, W. (2001) 'Structured Sensory Interventions for Traumatised Children, Adolescents and Parents, TLC (SITCAP).' *Journal of Trauma and Loss, Research and Interventions 1*, 2.

Stein, G. (1990) *The Selected Writings of Gertrude Stein.* New York: Vintage.

Steinberg, D. (2004) 'From Archetypes to Impressions: The Magic of Words.' In G. Bolton *et al.* (eds) *Writing Cures: An Introductory Handbook of Writing in Counselling and Therapy.* London and New York: Routledge, pp.44–55.

Stern, D. (2004) *The Present Moment in Psychotherapy and Everyday Life.* New York: Norton.

Suler, J. (1997) *Psychological Dynamics of Online Synchronous Conversations in Test-driven Chat Environments.* Lawrenceville, NJ: Rider University.

Sullivan, A. and Strang, H. (2003) 'Bibliotherapy in the classroom: using literature to promote the development of emotional intelligence.' *Childhood Education 79*, 2.

Sumpton, L. (2012) 'The right to rehabilitation for children: what are the challenges and impacts of implementing the right to the rehabilitation for child survivors of torture using writing therapies in the UK?' Unpublished MA dissertation. London: MA in Understanding and Securing Human Rights, Institute of Commonwealth Studies, University of London.

Sutton, A. (2013) 'Dr Adrian Sutton.' Talk No. 3 for the Baobab Centre. May.

Taylor, D. (1996) *The Healing Power of Stories.* New York: Bantam Doubleday.

Tedeschi, R.G. and Calhoun, L.G. (1995) *Trauma and Transformation: Growing in the Aftermath of Suffering.* Thousand Oaks, CA: Sage.

Tedeschi, R.G. and Calhoun, L.G. (2004) 'Posttraumatic growth: conceptual foundations and empirical evidence.' *Psychological Enquiry 15*, 1, 1–18.

Terr, L. (1990) *Too Scared to Cry: Psychic Trauma in Childhood.* New York: Basic Books.

Thompson, K. (2004) 'Journal Writing as a Therapeutic Tool.' In G. Bolton *et al.* (eds) *Writing Cures: An Introductory Handbook of Writing in Counselling and Therapy.* London and New York: Routledge.

Thorne, B. (1992) *Carl Rogers.* London: Sage.

Tizon, O. (2001) 'Dreams and other sketches from a torture survivor's notes.' *Professional Psychology: Research and Practice 32*, 5, 465–468.

Tolkien, J.R.R. (1938) 'On Fairy Stories.' In *Tree and Leaf.* London: HarperCollins.

Tribe, R. and Patel, N. (2011) *Refugees and Asylum Seekers.* London: Freedom from Torture, pp.149–151.

UNICEF (2005) 'General Comment No. 6: Treatment of Unaccompanied and Separated Children Outside their Country of Origin.' CRC/GC/2005/6, 2005. Available at www.unicef.org/protection/files/CRCGC6_EN.pdf, accessed 6 April 2014.

Van Dalen, A. (2000) 'Juvenile violence and addiction: tangled roots in childhood trauma.' *Journal of Social Work Practice in the Addictions 1*, 25–40.

Van der Kolk, B.A. (1994) 'The body keeps the score: memory and the emerging psychobiology of posttraumatic stress.' *Harvard Review of Psychiatry 1*, 253–265.

Van der Kolk, B.A. (2003) 'The neurobiology of childhood trauma and abuse.' *Child and Adolescent Psychiatric Clinics of North America 12*, 2, 293–317.

Van der Kolk, B., McFarlane, A. and Van der Hart, O. (1996) 'A general approach to treatment of posttraumatic stress disorder.' In A. Mc-Farlane, B.A. Van der Kolk and L. Wisaeth (eds) *Traumatic Stress: The Effect of Overwhelming Experience on Mind, Body, and Society*. New York: Guildford Press.

Walker, A. (2005) *The Complete Stories*. London: Phoenix Fiction. (First published in 1994 by The Women's Press.)

Walsh, W. and Keenan, R. (1997) 'Narrative family therapy.' *The Family Journal 5*,4.

Wegner, D. (1994) 'Ironic processes of mental control.' *Psychological Review 101*, 34–52.

Wenz, K. and McWhirter, J.J. (1990) 'Enhancing the group experience: creative writing exercises,' *Journal for Specialists in Group Work 15*, 1, 37–42.

Wester, I. (2009) 'Beverley Naidoo's "The Other Side of Truth": a modern fairy tale of loss.' *African Literature Association JALA 3*, 2, Summer.

Winnicott, D. (1960) 'The Theory of the Parent–Infant Relationship.' In (1990) *The Maturational Processes and the Facilitating Environment*. London: Karnac Books, pp.37–55.

Winnicott, D. (1991) *Playing and Reality*, London: Routledge.

Winterson, J. (2011) 'A Bed. A Book. A Mountain.' In H. Haddon, M. Rosen, Z. Smith, C. Callil *et al.*, *Stop What You Are Doing and Read This*. London: Virago.

Winterson, J. (2012) *Why Be Happy When You Could Be Normal?* London: Vintage.

Woolf, V. (1937) 'Craftmanship.' In BBC Radio series *Words Fail Me*. Re-broadcast in 2007.

Woolf, V. (1938) *Three Guineas*. New York: Harcourt, Brace, Jovanovich.

Woolf, V. (1977) *The Diary of Virginia Woolf (volume 1) (1920–1924)*. (*Edited by* Anne Oliver Bell.) London: Penguin.

Woolf, V. (1977) *The Diary of Virginia Woolf (volume 2)*. London: Hogarth.

Woolf, V. (1978) *Moments of Being*. (Edited by J. Schulkind.) Gainsville: Tirad Books.

Wright, J. (2004) 'The Passion of Science, the Precision of Poetry: Therapeutic Writing – A Review of the Literature.' In G. Bolton *et al.* (eds) *Writing Cures: An Introductory Handbook of Writing in Counselling and Therapy*. London and New York: Routledge.

Wright, J. and Chung, M. (2001) 'Mastery of mystery? Therapeutic writing: a review of the literature.' *British Journal of Guidance and Counselling 29*, 3, 277–291.

Wright, J. (2004) 'Developing Online, Text-based Counselling in the Workplace.' In G. Bolton *et al.* (eds) (2004) *Writing Cures: An Introductory Handbook of Writing in Counselling and Therapy*. London and New York: Routledge.

Wroe, N. (2013) 'Rupert Thomas: a life in writing.' *The Guardian*, 8 March.

Yalom, B. (ed.) (1998) *The Yalom Reader*. New York: Basic Books.

Yalom I.D. (2005) *The Theory and Practice of Group Therapy* (5th edition). New York: Basic Books.

Yesilyurt, E. (2011) 'Reflections from a refugee psychologist.' In *Refugees and Asylum Seekers*. London: Freedom from Torture.

Young-Bruehl, E. (2012) *Childism: Confronting Prejudice Against Children*. New Haven, CT: Yale University Press.

Zipes, J. (2008) *Are Fairy Tales Still Useful to Children?* Yellow Springs, OH: The Art of Storytelling Show. Available at www.artofstorytellingshow.com/2008/06/29/jack-zipes-fairy-tales/, accessed 6 April 2014.

Zipes, J. (2012) 'Fairy Tales, Child Abuse and Childism.' Audio given in the Nolte Centre for Continuing Education, Institute for Advanced Studies, University of Minnesota.

SUBJECT INDEX

AUTHOR INDEX